Global Plastics Outlook

ECONOMIC DRIVERS, ENVIRONMENTAL IMPACTS AND POLICY OPTIONS

OECD
BETTER POLICIES FOR BETTER LIVES

Please cite this publication as:
OECD (2022), *Global Plastics Outlook: Economic Drivers, Environmental Impacts and Policy Options*, OECD Publishing, Paris, https://doi.org/10.1787/de747aef-en.

ISBN 978-92-64-65494-5 (print)
ISBN 978-92-64-58406-8 (pdf)
ISBN 978-92-64-59279-7 (HTML)
ISBN 978-92-64-80423-4 (epub)

Revised version, April 2022
Details of revisions available at: https://www.oecd.org/about/publishing/Corrigendum_Global-Plastics-Outlook.pdf

Photo credits: Cover © design by Chantal Rivière/grafiklab.fr based on images © JasminkaM, Liubovart/Shutterstock.com.

Corrigenda to publications may be found on line at: www.oecd.org/about/publishing/corrigenda.htm.

Preface

Global plastics production has grown significantly in recent decades. Highly versatile, light and affordable, plastic materials are employed in countless industrial applications and have become extremely useful for modern society. They help us preserve food, insulate buildings, make electronics work and increase the fuel efficiency of our vehicles, among other things. Yet, the sheer magnitude of our societies' consumption of plastics bears important drawbacks. Plastics use results in a high production-related carbon footprint, high volumes of waste, persistent pollution and harm to wildlife and ecosystems when leakage to the environment occurs, and considerable socio-economic costs due to the negative impacts of plastic litter on tourism and fisheries.

In recent years, the growing awareness of plastic pollution has alerted public opinion and paved the way for stronger policy intervention on this front. Many OECD countries and emerging economies have been implementing policies that specifically aim to reduce the negative environmental impacts associated with different stages of the plastics lifecycle. In addition, global fora like the G7 and the G20 as well as the United Nations Environment Assembly are increasingly focusing on marine litter and plastic pollution. The *Global Plastics Outlook: Economic Drivers, Environmental Impacts and Policy Options* seeks to inform and support these efforts.

This is the first report to comprehensively take stock of current plastics production, use and waste generation, uncover the underlying economic drivers and map the related environmental impacts on a global level. The report also presents four key levers that are essential to bend the plastic curve: markets for recycled (secondary) plastics, technological innovation in plastics, domestic policy measures and international co-operation, including international financing. Our findings point to the need for a whole of life-cycle approach requiring policy interventions both downstream of the value chain, such as end-of-life management, and upstream, like product design, for an effective policy mix.

The Outlook can help decision-makers understand the direction in which we are heading and help to assess which policies can support a more sustainable and circular management of plastic materials. The OECD stands ready to assist governments in making this transition by designing, developing and delivering better policies to eliminate the negative environmental impacts of plastics production and ultimately achieve plastics-free oceans and rivers for future generations. As the challenges associated with plastics production, namely growing leakage and greenhouse gas emissions, are transboundary in nature, it will also be crucial that countries respond to the challenge with co-ordinated and global solutions.

Mathias Cormann
Secretary-General, OECD

Foreword

The *Global Plastics Outlook: Economic Drivers, Environmental Impacts and Policy Options* provides policymakers with a comprehensive overview of the challenges ahead and potential solutions. The report is structured as shown below. Using state-of-the-art environment-economy modelling, the Outlook uncovers the economic drivers that give rise to unprecedented volumes of plastics use and waste. The Outlook also maps and quantifies key environmental impacts such as plastic leakage to the environment and greenhouse gas emissions. The Outlook then presents four levers critical to reduce the environmental impacts of plastics: markets for recycled (secondary) plastics, technological innovation in plastics, domestic policy measures and international co-operation.

Report roadmap

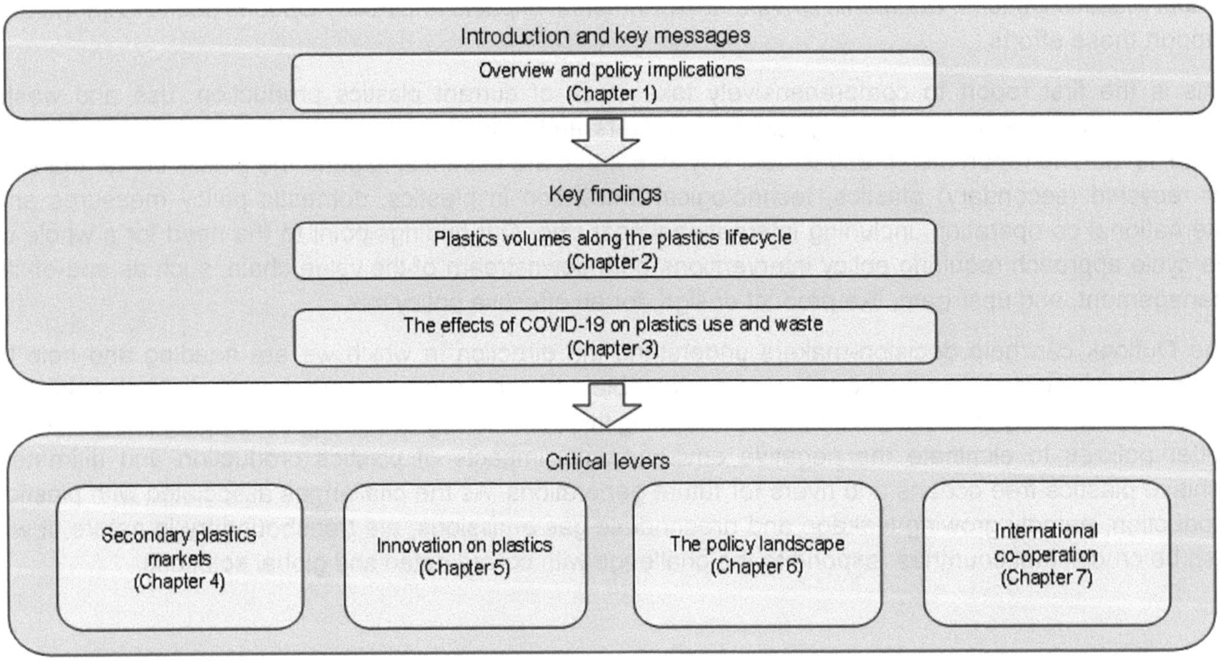

Acknowledgements

This report was conceptualised and directed by Shardul Agrawala, Head of Division of the Environment and Economy Integration Division (EEI) in the Environment Directorate of the OECD. Maarten Dubois led the cross-cutting co-ordination of the report, the modelling team was led by Elisa Lanzi, and the circular economy team was led by Peter Börkey (all OECD Environment Directorate). This report was edited by Shardul Agrawala, Maarten Dubois, Peter Börkey and Elisa Lanzi.

The authorship of the chapters is as follows: Shardul Agrawala and Norbert Monti (Chapter 1); Maarten Dubois, Elisa Lanzi, Ruben Bibas, Eleonora Mavroeidi, Jean Fouré, Rob Dellink, Daniel Ostalé Valriberas, Elena Buzzi and Linda Livingstone (Chapter 2); Rob Dellink and Linda Livingstone (Chapter 3); Andrew Brown, Frithjof Laubinger and Peter Börkey (Chapter 4), Damien Dussaux and Shardul Agrawala (Chapter 5); Maarten Dubois, Peter Börkey, Andrew Brown and Frithjof Laubinger (Chapter 6); Frithjof Laubinger, Peter Börkey, Maarten Dubois and Shunta Yamaguchi (Chapter 7) (all OECD Environment Directorate). Additional contributions on Chapter 7 were provided by Ivan Haščič from the Environment Directorate and Pierra Tortora and Daniel Prosi of the Development Co-operation Directorate. The plastics use and waste estimates presented in the report and reported in the Global Plastic Outlook Database were prepared by Ruben Bibas, Eleonora Mavroeidi, Rob Dellink, Daniel Ostalé Valriberas, Elisa Lanzi, and Maarten Dubois.

The following external experts: Morten Ryberg, Teddy Serrano and Alexis Laurent (Technical University of Denmark), Costas A. Velis, Ed Cook and Josh Cottom (University of Leeds), Laurent Lebreton (The Ocean Cleanup) and Nikolaos Evangeliou (Norwegian Institute for Air Research) contributed to the modelling of global plastic leakage. Roland Geyer (University of California, Santa Barbara) advised on the OECD modelling strategy and provided valuable feedback on the report. Trinomics B.V., the Institute for Global Environmental Studies and Prasad Modak, Louis Tronel, Flavio Ribeiro and Darina Petrova (all independent experts) provided various country-briefs which were used to enrich the policy analysis.

The report received insightful feedback from Rodolfo Lacy (Director), Ingrid Barnsley (Deputy Director), Bob Diderich and Eeva Leinala (all Environment Directorate) and Jens Sedemund (Development Co-operation Directorate). The report also received expert feedback from Stephanie B. Borrelle (University of Toronto), Johan Eyckmans (KU Leuven), Costas A. Velis (University of Leeds) and the Ellen MacArthur Foundation. Earlier drafts also benefited from discussions during the Technical Expert Workshop on Modelling Approaches for Plastics Use Projections, organised by the OECD on the 22 and 23 June 2020.

Aziza Perrière and Illias Mousse Iye (OECD Environment Directorate) provided administrative support. Elizabeth Del Bourgo, William Foster, Stéphanie Simonin-Edwards and Norbert Monti (OECD Environment Directorate), as well as Catherine Bremer (OECD Public Affairs and Communications Directorate) provided assistance with communication and outreach aspects of the report. Linda Livingstone and Elena Buzzi (OECD Environment Directorate) and Chantal Rivière (independent graphic designer) as well as the WeDoData team assisted with the design of the Policy Highlights, the cover and figures throughout the report. The report received copy-editing support from Janine Treves (OECD Public Affairs and Communications Directorate), Fiona Hinchcliffe and Annette Hardcastle (both independent editors).

The OECD Environment Policy Committee (EPOC) was responsible for the oversight of the development of the report. In addition, the Working Party on Resource Productivity and Waste (WPRPW) and the Working Party on Integrating Environmental and Economic Policies (WPIEEP) reviewed earlier drafts.

Table of contents

Tables

Figures

Boxes

Follow OECD Publications on:

http://twitter.com/OECD_Pubs

http://www.facebook.com/OECDPublications

http://www.linkedin.com/groups/OECD-Publications-4645871

http://www.youtube.com/oecdilibrary

http://www.oecd.org/oecddirect/

This book has...

StatLinks

A service that delivers Excel® files from the printed page!

Look for the *StatLinks* at the bottom of the tables or graphs in this book. To download the matching Excel® spreadsheet, just type the link into your Internet browser, starting with the ***https://doi.org*** prefix, or click on the link from the e-book edition.

Abbreviations and acronyms

ABS	Acrylonitrile butadiene styrene
ASA	Acrylonitrile styrene acrylate
BPA	Bisphenol A
BWP(s)	Brake Wear Particle(s)
CO_2	Carbon dioxide
CO_2e	Carbon dioxide equivalent
DDE	Dichlorodiphenyldichloroethylene
DDT	Dichlorodiphenyltrichloroethane
DTU	Technical University of Denmark
EC	European Commission
ECHA	European Chemical Agency
EEA	European Environment Agency
EoL	End of life
EPA	(United States) Environmental Protection Agency
EPR	Extended producer responsibility
EU	European Union
EUR	Euro
FLEXPART	FLEXible PARTicle
GAINS	Greenhouse gas – air pollution Interactions and synergies
GDP	Gross domestic product
GHG	Greenhouse gas
Gt	Gigatonnes (billion tonnes)
GTAP	Global Trade Analysis Project
Ha	Hectare
HDPE	High-density polyethylene
ISO	International Organization for Standardization
kt	Kilotonnes

LCA	Life cycle analysis
LDPE	Low-density polyethylene
MSW	Municipal solid waste
Mt	Million tonnes
NOx	Nitrous oxide
ODA	Official development assistance
PAH	Polycyclic aromatic hydrocarbon
PBT	Polybutylene terephthalate
PC	Polycarbonate
PCB	Polychlorinated biphenyl
PET	Polyethylene terephthalate
PM	Particulate matter
$PM_{2.5}$	Fine particulate matter
PP	Polypropylene
PPE	Personal protective equipment
PPP	Purchasing power parity
PS	Polystyrene
PUR	Polyurethane
PVC	Polyvinyl chloride
SDG	Sustainable development goal
SOx	Sulphur oxide
TWP(s)	Tyre wear particle(s)
UN	United Nations
UNCLOS	United Nations Convention on the Law of the Seas
UNEA	United Nations Environment Assembly
UNEP	United Nations Environment Programme
USD	United States Dollar
UV	Ultraviolet
WEEE	Waste from electrical and electronic equipment
WtE	Waste to energy
WWTP	Waste water treatment plant

Executive Summary

The *Global Plastics Outlook: Economic Drivers, Environmental Impacts and Policy Options* offers a unique quantified picture of the full lifecycle of plastics globally, including production, consumption, waste, recycling, disposal, leakage and greenhouse gas emissions. Five key findings summarize the current challenges while four critical levers are put forward to make the plastics lifecycle more circular.

Key findings

- ***The current plastics lifecycle is far from circular.*** Globally, the annual production of plastics has doubled, soaring from 234 million tonnes (Mt) in 2000 to 460 Mt in 2019. Plastic waste has more than doubled, from 156 Mt in 2000 to 353 Mt in 2019. After taking into account losses during recycling, only 9% of plastic waste was ultimately recycled, while 19% was incinerated and almost 50% went to sanitary landfills. The remaining 22% was disposed of in uncontrolled dumpsites, burned in open pits or leaked into the environment.
- ***COVID-19 increased single-use plastic waste, though plastics use fell overall.*** The lockdowns and decline in economic activity during 2020 reduced plastics use by 2.2% from 2019 levels. However, the increase in the use of protective personal equipment and single-use plastics has exacerbated plastic littering. As the economy rebounds, plastics use is projected to pick up again, leading to a renewed growth of plastic waste and related environmental pressures.
- ***Mismanaged plastic waste is the main source of macroplastic leakage.*** In 2019 alone, 22 Mt of plastic materials leaked into the environment. Macroplastics account for 88% of plastic leakage, mainly resulting from inadequate collection and disposal. Microplastics, polymers with a diameter smaller than 5 mm, account for the remaining 12%, coming from a range of sources such as tyre abrasion, brake wear or textile washing. The documented presence of these small particles in freshwater and terrestrial environments, as well as in several food and beverage streams, suggests that microplastics contribute substantially to the exposure of ecosystems and humans to leaked plastics and their related risks.
- ***Significant stocks of plastics have already accumulated in aquatic environments, with 109 Mt of plastics accumulated in rivers, and 30 Mt in the ocean***. In 2019 alone, 6.1 Mt of plastic waste leaked into rivers, lakes and the ocean. The build-up of plastics in rivers implies that leakage into the ocean will continue for decades to come even if mismanaged plastic waste was significantly reduced. Furthermore, cleaning up these plastics is becoming more difficult and costly as plastics fragment into ever smaller particles.
- ***The carbon footprint of the plastics lifecycle is significant***. Plastics have a significant carbon footprint, contributing 3.4% of global greenhouse gas emissions throughout their lifecycle. In 2019, plastics generated 1.8 billion tonnes of greenhouse gas emissions, with 90% coming from their production and conversion from fossil fuels. Closing material loops could reduce this footprint substantially.

Critical levers to reduce the environmental impact of plastics

- ***Develop recycled plastics markets by combining push and pull policies.*** While global production of secondary plastics from recycling has more than quadrupled in the last two decades, they are still only 6% of the total feedstock. Since secondary plastics are mainly considered substitutes for primary plastics, rather than a valuable resource in their own right, the secondary plastics market remains small and vulnerable. Some countries have successfully strengthened their markets by "pushing" secondary plastics supply – for example, through extended producer responsibility schemes – as well as "pulling" demand via recycled content targets. The recent decoupling of prices for primary and secondary polyethylene terephthalate (PET) in Europe and increasing innovation in recycling technologies are positive signs that the combination of these policies is working.
- ***Boost innovation for a more circular plastics lifecycle.*** Innovation can deliver significant environmental benefits – by reducing the amount of primary plastics needed, prolonging the useful life of products and facilitating recycling. This report shows that patented environmental plastics technologies increased more than threefold between 1990 and 2017. Yet environmentally relevant innovation makes up only 1.2% of all plastics-related innovation. More ambitious policies are needed including a combination of investments in innovation and interventions aimed at increasing demand for circular solutions while restraining plastics consumption overall.
- ***Strengthen the ambition of domestic public policies***. An inventory of key regulatory and economic instruments in 50 OECD, emerging and developing countries developed for this report suggests that the current plastics policy landscape is fragmented and can be strengthened significantly. Only 13 countries from the inventory have national policy instruments in place that provide direct financial incentives to sort plastic waste at source. Only 25 of the countries in the inventory have effectively implemented well-known instruments that encourage recycling, such as national landfill and incineration taxes. Meanwhile, globally more than 120 countries have bans and taxes on single-use plastic items, but most are limited to plastic bags or other small-volume items. This means that these instruments are mainly effective in reducing littering, rather than restraining overall consumption of plastics. A policy roadmap is proposed for countries to reduce the leakage of macroplastics. It involves three increasingly ambitious phases:
    - *Close leakage pathways*. Build sanitary waste management infrastructure, organise waste collection and structurally reduce plastics littering by enlarging the scope of anti-littering policies (bans or taxes of frequently littered items) and enhancing implementation of legislation.
    - *Create incentives for recycling and enhance sorting at source*. The required measures include extended producer responsibility (EPR) schemes, landfill taxes and incineration taxes, as well as deposit-refund and pay-as-you-throw schemes.
    - *Restrain demand and optimise design to make plastic value chains more circular and recycled plastics more price competitive*. Instruments such as plastics taxes and recycled content targets can create financial incentives to reduce use and foster circularity. Their impact could be improved considerably by extending them to more product types and more countries.
- ***Strengthen international co-operation to make plastics value chains more circular and achieve net zero plastic leakage.*** Considering global value chains and international trade in plastics, aligning design approaches and the regulation of chemical substances across countries will be key to improving the circularity of plastics globally. Moreover, with mismanaged waste a widespread problem, especially in developing countries, major investments in basic waste management infrastructure are needed. To finance the required estimated costs of EUR 25 billion a year in low and middle-income countries, all available sources of funding will need to be mobilised, including official development assistance which currently covers only 2% of the financing needs. Efficient use of such investments will also require effective legal frameworks to enforce disposal obligations.

1. Overview and policy highlights

This overview chapter presents the motivation for and approach taken by the *Global Plastics Outlook*, as well as the key findings and policy implications

1.1. Introduction

The first manufactured plastic, *Parkesine*, was developed from cellulose in the mid-19th century and found applications as a clothing waterproofer and as synthetic ivory. Almost half a century later, *Bakelite* became the first truly synthetic plastic to be developed. However, it was not until 1950 that global plastics production began its unprecedented growth, which has seen it expand 230-fold to the present day.

The rapid growth of plastics is due to their unique properties: high strength-to-weight ratio, high moldability, impermeability to liquids, resistance to physical and chemical degradation, and low cost. They can easily substitute for other materials (such as glass, metal, wood and natural fibres) in a wide range of applications. However, some of the desirable qualities of plastics are also their key limitations. Plastics are highly resistant to physical and chemical degradation, which also means that they can persist as waste in the environment for decades or even centuries.

Concern about the environmental externalities of plastics had already emerged by the 1970s when scientists started observing plastic leakage in the aquatic environment. Numerous beach clean-up and citizen-science initiatives burgeoned to deal with what was seen as a threat to marine wildlife. A 1987 publication, *Plastics in the Ocean: More than a Litter Problem*, observed that "A growing body of evidence indicates that when discharged, lost or abandoned in the marine environment, plastic debris adversely affects the oceans and their inhabitants in a multitude of ways" (Center for Environmental Education, 1987[1]). Growing evidence for the presence of plastics in the food chain, water supply and the air we breathe has since raised concerns that plastics could be harming human health as well.

Despite this long history, global public concern over plastic leakage has only become widespread in the second decade of the 21st century. A confluence of seminal research and high-profile media focus on plastic waste in the ocean and on land, has catapulted plastics to the centre of public consciousness and preoccupation for the environment. In 2018, "single-use" was the Collins Dictionary "word of the year" (Collins Dictionary, 2018[2]), while 90.5% - the percentage of plastic that has never been recycled - was the Royal Statistical Society's "statistic of the year" (Royal Statistics Society, 2018[3]).

This surge in public attention has also coincided with a proliferation of local, national and international policy responses. More than 100 countries have imposed restrictions or outright bans on certain single-use plastics. International initiatives to target marine litter and plastic waste have been established under the UN, the G7 and the G20 over the past decade (UNEP, 2020[4]; G7, 2018[5]; G20, 2019[6]). Notably within the G20 process, the Osaka Blue Ocean Vision aims to reduce additional marine plastic litter to zero by 2050. Public-private partnerships and voluntary schemes have been established, with businesses committing to tackle plastic leakage (see Glossary) to the environment, such as the Global Plastics Alliance, and the Alliance to End Plastic Waste, among others (Global Plastics Alliance, 2020[7]; Alliance to End Plastic Waste, 2020[8]).

1.2. Why a *Global Plastics Outlook* and what does it involve?

A global outlook on plastics can help policy makers understand the need for policy action and the scale of the challenge. Plastics are not a homogenous product – they include different polymer types and applications, ranging from drink bottles to cable insulation, food packaging and automotive parts. These various plastics have different lifetimes, recyclability, and risks to the environment and to human health – all of which call for a more granular perspective. In developing a policy agenda, governments would benefit from a stocktake of these aspects, especially as the world emerges from the COVID-19 pandemic.

While a limited number of global stocktakes and projections of plastics along the value chain already exist in the published literature,[1] most of them rely on engineering models that describe the lifecycle of plastic commodities in detail, but do not embed these details into a consistent global macroeconomic framework.

Existing studies also pre-date the COVID-19 pandemic and do not take into account the disruptions and the potential longer-term implications of the pandemic on plastics use and waste generation. Finally, they generally do not provide a comprehensive overview of the performance of key levers available to decision makers to curb plastics use.

The *OECD Global Plastics Outlook* develops a regional and sectoral perspective through a comprehensive mapping of material flows and economic drivers throughout the plastics lifecycle. It provides an internally consistent and comprehensive view on production, trade, and use of plastics, as well as plastic waste management and leakage to the environment. This analysis is based on the OECD's multi-sectoral, multi-regional dynamic computable general equilibrium (CGE) model, ENV-Linkages (Chateau, Dellink and Lanzi, 2014[9]), which has been extended to include plastics in 14 polymer categories and to calculate plastic waste flows.[2] Furthermore, the modelling framework has been enhanced to include both primary and secondary (recycled – see Glossary) plastics production. The strength of CGE models such as ENV-Linkages is their ability to embed the drivers of structural change – such as changes in demand patterns, production modes (including increases in recycling activities) and trade specialisation – in a consistent framework. This framework also facilitates a more detailed understanding of the consequences of policy action, as it links the use of plastics to production input in each sector. Annex A describes the modelling approach in more detail.

The *Global Plastics Outlook* consists of two volumes. This first volume quantifies current plastics production, use, disposal and key environmental impacts throughout the plastics lifecycle. It also examines the impacts of the COVID-19 pandemic on plastics use and waste generation. Furthermore, this volume provides novel analysis of four key levers to improve sustainability and circularity along the plastics value chain: markets for recycled plastics, technological innovation in plastics, domestic policy measures and international co-operation to curb plastics use and waste generation (Box 1.1).

To complement the transversal analysis in this first volume, detailed environmental-economic modelling will be presented in a separate second volume. This second volume makes projections of plastics use, waste and key related environmental impacts to 2060 under a range of scenarios (OECD, forthcoming[10]). The scenario analysis will quantify the environmental benefits and economic consequences of ambitious policy action on plastics, exploring how environmental impacts vary with the stringency of policy action.

Together, the two volumes of the *Global Plastics Outlook* provide a roadmap towards net-zero plastic leakage and a more circular use of plastics all along the lifecycle.

Box 1.1. What is novel about the *OECD's Global Plastics Outlook*?

It provides a first comprehensive mapping of material flows and economic drivers of plastics and develops a regional and sectoral perspective. It does so while taking an internally consistent and comprehensive view on production, trade and use of plastics, as well as on plastic waste management and leakage to the environment.

- The modelling framework has a high-level of granularity with the inclusion of primary and secondary plastics production, 14 polymer categories and various applications.
- The volumes and processes involved in plastic leakage (for both macroplastics and microplastics) into aquatic and terrestrial environments, as well as greenhouse gas emissions are estimated.
- It is the first report to analyse how plastics use and waste have been affected by the COVID-19 pandemic across sectors and regions, and the potential implications for the years to come.
- It offers a first-of-its-kind empirical analysis of environmentally relevant plastics innovation, presented along the entire value chain. The analysis exploits textual analysis methods on patent and trademark data to derive insights into the trends and dynamics in environmentally relevant plastics innovation, with a special focus on the most prolific innovators.
- It develops an inventory of the global plastics policy landscape, based on an in-depth investigation of economic instruments and regulations in 50 different (OECD and non-OECD) countries. This inventory systematically catalogues and categorises policies to allow important insights into their potential to curb plastic waste.
- It assesses the global financial costs of drastic action in low and middle-income countries, and benchmarks these costs to the available funding from official development assistance to facilitate making the required investments and building up the necessary policy frameworks.

1.3. Key findings

This section presents key findings from the report for the entire plastics lifecycle in 2019, from production and accumulation in the economy, to their end-of-life fate and leakage into the environment. Figure 1.1 helps visualise the complex interactions that plastics are subject to throughout their lifecycle and places the numbers presented below in context.

1.3.1. The current plastics lifecycle is far from circular

Population growth and higher incomes have driven up global plastics production, which has doubled, soaring from 234 million tonnes (Mt) in 2000 to 460 Mt in 2019. In this same period, the growth of plastics volumes outpaced economic growth by almost 40%. While COVID-19 temporarily curtailed this growth, it is likely to rebound once again, though with a slight shift in use and waste trends (Box 1.2).

Global annual plastic waste has more than doubled, from 156 Mt in 2000 to 353 Mt in 2019. Almost two-thirds of all plastic waste comes from applications with lifespans of less than five years: packaging (40%), consumer products (12%) and textiles (11%). Only 55 Mt of this waste was collected for recycling, but 22 Mt ended up as a recycling residue that needed further disposal. Ultimately, 9% of plastic waste was recycled, 19% was incinerated and almost 50% went to sanitary landfills. The remaining 22% was disposed of in uncontrolled dumpsites, burned in open pits or leaked to the environment.

Figure 1.1. Only 33 million tonnes (Mt), or 9% of the 353 Mt of plastic waste, was recycled in 2019

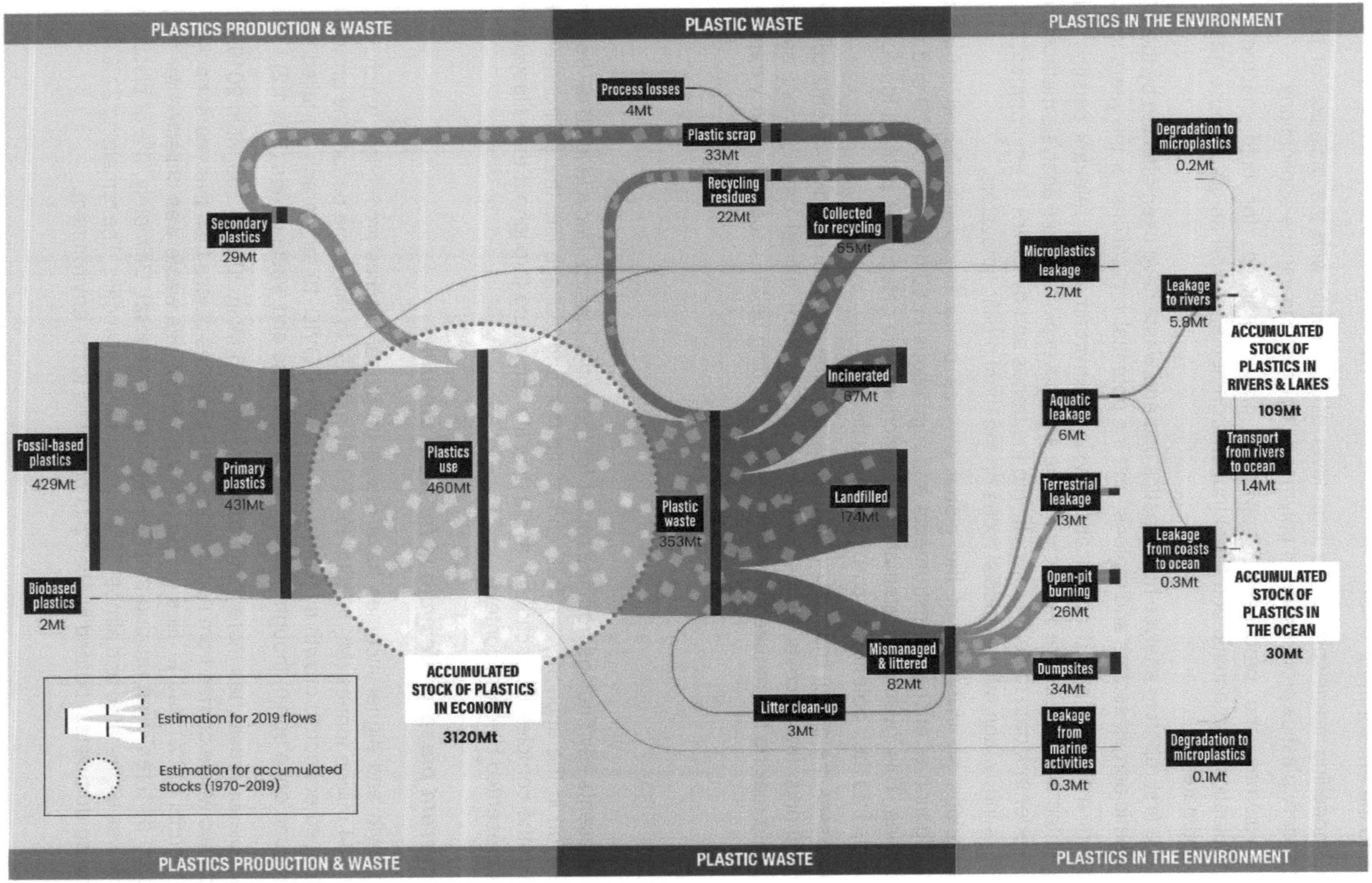

Source: OECD Global Plastics Outlook Database, https://doi.org/10.1787/c0821f81-en.

1.3.2. *Mismanaged plastic waste is the main source of macroplastic leakage*

Widespread plastics use coupled with inadequate end-of-life disposal resulted in 22 Mt of plastic materials leaking into the environment in 2019 (Figure 1.2), contributing to persistent plastic pollution. The vast majority (19.4 Mt) are macroplastics (see Glossary), and most (82%) found their way into the natural environment as a result of inadequate collection and disposal. Other leakage routes include littering or fly-tipping (5%), and marine activities (1%). Microplastics (see Glossary) also make up a sizeable share of total leakage (12%), largely reaching the environment through wear to tyres and road markings, as well as the accidental loss of plastic pellets and washing of synthetic textile fibres.

Leakage occurs in all regions, but there are significant geographical differences in leakage drivers. OECD countries contribute 14% to the global leakage but 36% of microplastic leakage. Non-OECD countries account for 86% of the plastic leakage, driven mainly by the high amount of mismanaged waste ending up in the environment. This problem is becoming worse as leakage from mismanaged waste has more than doubled since 2000. These numbers stress the urgency of addressing waste management practices in rapidly growing economies, while taking into account littering and the steadily increasing microplastic leakage around the world.

Figure 1.2. Global leakage of macro-and microplastics to the environment is estimated at 22 Mt

Share of total plastic leakage into the environment, 2019

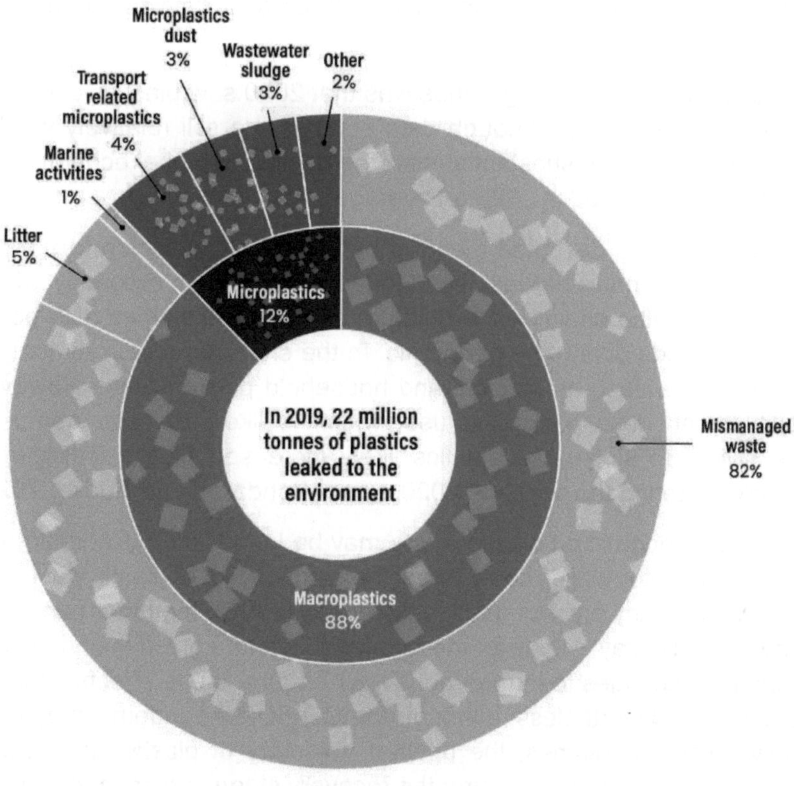

Source: OECD Global Plastics Outlook Database, https://doi.org/10.1787/c0821f81-en.

1.3.3. *The 30 Mt of plastics accumulated in the ocean, and 109 Mt in rivers, will pollute aquatic environments for decades to come*

Plastic leakage is fundamentally altering marine and terrestrial ecosystems, whilst also posing substantial risks to human livelihoods that depend on the integrity of such environments, such as tourism and fishing.

Plastics are also a source of concern for human health through the leaching or adsorption of hazardous chemicals, as well as their bio-accumulation in substances and organisms consumed by humans. In 2019 alone, 6.1 Mt of plastic waste leaked into rivers, lakes and the ocean. As the bulk of plastics reach the ocean through rivers via a slow process that can take years or even decades, 109 Mt of plastics are estimated to have accumulated in rivers globally to date, with 1.7 Mt flowing into the ocean in 2019 (Figure 1.1). Cleaning up these plastics from nature is becoming more difficult and costly as plastics fragment into ever smaller particles.

Box 1.2. How has the COVID-19 pandemic affected plastics use?

The pandemic has altered previous trends in plastics use in myriad ways; however, there were two main, and opposing, trends:

- On the one hand, global demand for certain plastics applications grew significantly. This is particularly true of the healthcare sector, partly driven by the ubiquitous demand for personal protective equipment (PPE). Plastics use for face masks is estimated to be around 300 thousand tonnes in 2020. Similarly, the COVID-19 pandemic also significantly altered economic activity and demand patterns, with a shift in demand towards take-away foods and e-commerce, which use significant amounts of single-use plastics and plastic packaging.
- On the other hand, the substantial decrease in overall economic activity during the pandemic saw use of most plastics fall, with especially large reductions in wholesale and retail trade, motor vehicle manufacture and construction. These three sectors alone reduced plastics use by an estimated 8.2 Mt in 2020.

The overall effect of these countervailing trends was that 2020 saw plastics use decrease overall from 2019 levels by an estimated 2.2%, although data sources are still relatively weak. However, as the decrease in plastics use was less substantial than the decline in global economic activity, the plastics intensity of the economy increased in 2020 on average.

The COVID-19 pandemic also disrupted global progress in the transition to a resource-efficient and circular economy. Many municipalities suspended recycling temporarily due to fears about contamination; recycling value chains were disrupted; and some studies also point to a decrease in waste sorting by households during the pandemic. In the short-run it is likely that certain applications saw waste levels increase, such as medical and household plastic waste. However, the shrinking of commercial activity meant less packaging use, which is likely to have dampened that increase. Nonetheless, the switch to single-use plastics likely increased plastic leakage, with an estimated 1.6 billion face masks entering the ocean in 2020 alone (Bondaroff and Cooke, 2020[11]).

Several impacts of the pandemic on plastic waste may be long lasting. Reduced plastics use in areas such as construction and automobiles could affect the composition of plastic waste for decades to come given the long lifespan of many plastics used in these sectors. On the other hand, littered PPE such as single-use facemasks could stay with us for the foreseeable future given their resistance to degradation. If the pandemic-induced changes to human behaviour endure, these effects could be felt well beyond the end of the pandemic. Nevertheless, although the COVID-19 pandemic may permanently leave its mark on cumulative plastics volumes, the upward trajectory of plastics use, waste generation and leakage will likely resume as economies enter the recovery stage and economic activity picks up again.

1.3.4. The carbon footprint of the plastics lifecycle is significant

Beyond the hazards posed to the marine and terrestrial environment as well as to humans, plastics are also a substantial contributor to global greenhouse gas emissions. In 2019, plastics generated

1.8 gigatonnes (Gt) of greenhouse gas (GHG) emissions – 3.4% of global emissions – with 90% of these emissions coming from their production and conversion from fossil fuels. Closing material loops could lower the carbon footprint of plastics substantially. The use of bioplastics derived from biomass, such as corn, sugarcane, wheat or residues of other processes, could also reduce GHG emissions from plastics production. However, there are important concerns about the indirect environmental effects from the production of the required agricultural feedstock.

1.4. Critical levers to reduce the environmental impact of plastics

As countries seek to rebound from the COVID-19 pandemic and put their economies on a more sustainable path, what levers are available to curb plastics use and reduce the related environmental challenges? The *Global Plastics Outlook* identifies four critical levers for "bending the plastic curve": recycled (secondary) plastics markets, technological innovation for more circular plastics value chains, more coherent and ambitious domestic policy measures and greater international co-operation.

1.4.1. Combine push and pull policies to support recycled plastics markets

Recycling has an important role to play in lowering the environmental footprint of plastics, diverting material from more harmful waste management practices and helping to decrease demand for primary equivalents. Yet secondary plastics, i.e. plastics produced from recycled end-of-life plastic items, currently only account for 6% of the feedstock for new plastics produced globally. This is despite the fact that global production of secondary plastics has more than quadrupled in two decades, from 6.8 Mt in 2000 to 29.1 Mt in 2019 (Figure 1.3).

Figure 1.3. Secondary production is growing, but makes up only six percent of total plastic production

In million tonnes (Mt), 1990-2019

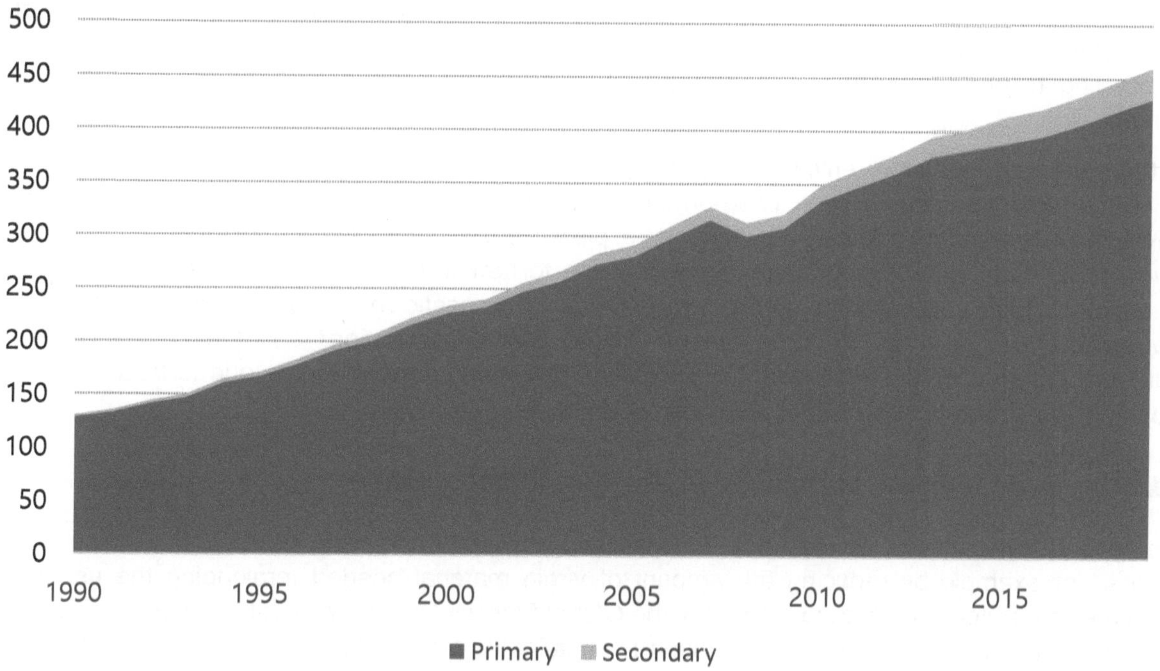

Source: OECD Global Plastics Outlook Database, https://doi.org/10.1787/c0821f81-en.

StatLink https://stat.link/gwun3o

Recycling markets are the fora of exchange for the numerous actors involved at different points in the supply chain, including the public sector, firms, traders (exporters and importers), brokers, and ultimately manufacturers. Markets allocate recycled plastics to the use with the highest value and create a profit motive that incentivises higher recycling rates. The larger the scale and depth of the markets, the better secondary materials are able to compete with primary equivalents, in turn driving the environmental benefits of recycling. However, although global production of secondary (recycled) plastics has more than quadrupled, secondary plastics are still mainly considered substitutes for primary plastics, rather than a valuable resource in their own right. In addition, fluctuations in the price of primary material, which secondary plastics track closely, can greatly affect the economic viability of recycling due to the disconnect between secondary price and the costs of secondary production (e.g. collection, sorting, and processing). Thus, the secondary plastics market is small and vulnerable.

Another barrier inhibiting the growth of secondary plastics is the quality of plastic waste collected. The wide range of polymers and additives (including hazardous chemicals) used in the manufacture of plastics means that polymers in plastic waste are often co-mingled and contaminated. Moreover, if not sorted properly, plastic waste is of little value for secondary material production due to the difficulty of extracting impurities and the limited range of potential applications.

Regulation strongly affects the business case for recycling and the market for secondary plastics. Plastics are only recycled on a large scale if it is profitable to do so. Economic and regulatory policy instruments can ensure a business case for collecting and recycling plastic waste. Moreover, incentivising sorting at source is a critical lever because the quality of sorting determines the purity and value of recycled materials, and therefore the profitability of recycling operations. High landfill and incineration taxes are strong drivers of recycling, as are landfill bans. However, weak environmental standards or enforcement will reduce recycling rates and may result in mismanaged waste (OECD, 2018[12]).

In order to foster secondary plastics markets, several countries have recently strengthened policies to simultaneously "push" supply (for example, through extended producer responsibility schemes) and "pull" demand (e.g. via recycled content targets). The recent decoupling of prices for primary and secondary polyethylene terephthalate (PET) (mainly for food-grade applications) in Europe and increasing innovation in recycling technologies are positive signs that these policies are helping to strengthen secondary markets.

Furthermore, the regulatory environments that govern markets for secondary plastics have undergone important transformations since 2017 when the People's Republic of China (hereafter China) introduced its National Sword policy, banning most imports of plastic waste. These and subsequent import restrictions have shifted trade away from traditional destinations to new markets, while simultaneously decreasing international trade volumes and increasing the need for domestic recycling capacities. Modifications in international law, such as the amendments to the Basel Convention[3] and the OECD Decision on Transboundary Movements of Waste,[4] are expected to reinforce these trends and to lead to further on-shoring of waste plastic recycling in advanced economies.

1.4.2. Do more to boost innovation in environmental plastics

The second lever, innovation, can deliver significant environmental benefits throughout the lifecycle of plastics, for example by reducing the amount of virgin material needed, prolonging the useful life of materials and facilitating recycling. As part of the *Global Plastics Outlook,* a novel approach was developed to unpack the dynamics governing innovation in sustainable plastics technologies. Trends in innovation can help in identifying both the distribution of innovation in the plastics lifecycle, the geographic hotspots of plastics innovation, as well as the possible policy environments that lead to the emergence of intensified innovative activity. Analysis of patent data shows that innovation for more sustainable plastics is increasing, with patented technologies in this area increasing by a factor of 3.4 over 1990-2017. OECD countries and China generated 80% of these innovations; the transfer of these technologies to other countries needs to be accelerated.

There is also a shift occurring in innovation focus from waste prevention to plastics recycling, potentially due to policy emphasis on the latter and higher consumer willingness to pay for products made out of recycled plastics. About half of all environmentally relevant innovations patented in 2017 focused on plastics circularity, i.e. on the prevention and recycling of plastic waste. One-third were related to biobased feedstock, and the remainder were aimed at the conversion or disposal of waste as well as the removal of plastics leaked into the natural environment. Innovation in biodegradable plastics, which grew rapidly during the last decade, has recently slowed down likely due to concerns about poor biodegradation in natural environments. Plastic-to-plastic chemical recycling, which aims to recycle waste that cannot be processed with mechanical recycling, is an emerging technology but faces significant challenges.

Although innovation in environmentally relevant plastics technologies is growing, it still only makes up a minor share of all plastics-related innovation. Indeed, innovation in waste prevention and recycling accounted for only 1.2% of plastics innovation in 2017. Quantitative evidence for plastics recycling suggests that circular economy policies (e.g. EPR schemes) can incentivise innovation effectively; however more ambitious policies are needed to orient technological change towards closing plastics loops and reducing leakage to the environment. These policies should combine investments in innovation with interventions aimed at increasing demand for circular solutions, while restraining plastics consumption overall.

1.4.3. Strengthen the ambition of domestic public policies

Public policies are a key lever for reducing the environmental consequences of plastics production and use. The OECD has recently developed an inventory of policies to analyse economic and regulatory policy instruments that are exclusively focused on plastics, as well as broader instruments that target products and waste streams, such as municipal solid waste (MSW), that contain important fractions of plastics. It covers 50 countries: the 38 OECD member countries, and 12 non-OECD countries selected for the size of their populations and their geographic coverage (Brazil, China, India, Indonesia, Russia and South Africa, as well as several countries with large populations in South-East Asia and Africa).[5] Overall, the inventory covers 69% of the world's population and 84% of global Gross Domestic Product (GDP).

Analysis of this inventory of policies suggests that the current plastics policy landscape is fragmented and can be strengthened significantly. Only 13 countries (representing 4% of the population covered by the inventory) have national policy instruments in place that provide direct financial incentives to sort plastic waste at source. Similarly, only 25 countries (representing 11% of the population covered by the inventory) have implemented well-known instruments to encourage recycling, such as national landfill and incineration taxes. Globally, bans and taxes on single-use plastic items exist in more than 120 countries, but their effectiveness for reducing plastic leakage can be improved. Most regulations are limited to single-use plastic bags or other streams that are small in volume. This means that these instruments are mainly effective in reducing leakage via littering, rather than restraining overall consumption of plastics. Moreover, poor implementation or shifts to alternative materials with larger environmental footprints sometimes reduce the potential benefits of these policies.

Drawing on this assessment a policy roadmap is proposed (Figure 1.4). It involves three increasingly ambitious phases:

1. **Close leakage pathways**: Investing in basic waste management infrastructure and developing legal frameworks that steer economic actors towards environmentally sound management of plastic waste are key first steps within any national context. Organising waste collection, structurally reducing plastics littering by enlarging the scope of anti-littering policies (bans or taxes of frequently littered items) to

cover a broader set of items and enhancing implementation of legislation are also key for closing plastic leakage pathways.

2. **Create incentives for recycling and enhance sorting at source**. Recycling plastics only occurs on a large scale if it is profitable. Policy makers can apply taxes to landfill and incineration to make recycling more cost competitive. By also imposing EPR, policy makers can make producers responsible for recycling packaging and durable products such as cars, batteries, tyres and electronics. As the quality of collected waste streams drives the feasibility and profitability of recycling, countries can achieve much greater circularity by sharpening the financial incentives to sort waste at source. Deposit-refund systems give a strong financial incentive to return beverage bottles, while pay-as-you-throw makes mixed waste disposal by households more costly. If combined with policies to avoid dumping and contaminating other waste streams, making households pay per bag or kilo of mixed waste is an effective way to incentivise sorting at source.
3. **Restrain demand and optimise design to make plastic value chains more circular and recycled plastics more price competitive**. The largest environmental gains can be achieved by reducing the use of virgin materials and by improving product design (Watkins et al., 2019[13]). Removing support schemes for fossil-based plastics, such as shale gas subsidies (OECD, 2016[14]), will make plastic value chains more circular by restraining consumption and by making recycled plastics more price competitive. By removing hazardous substances and recycling inhibitors from plastics at the design stage, chemical hazards can be avoided and recycling rates can be increased. Upstream policy instruments, such as plastics taxes, recycled content targets and EPR with fee modulation can all create financial incentives to reduce use and foster circularity. Their impact could be improved considerably by extending them to more product types and more countries.

Figure 1.4. A policy roadmap for more circular plastics use can involve a stepped approach

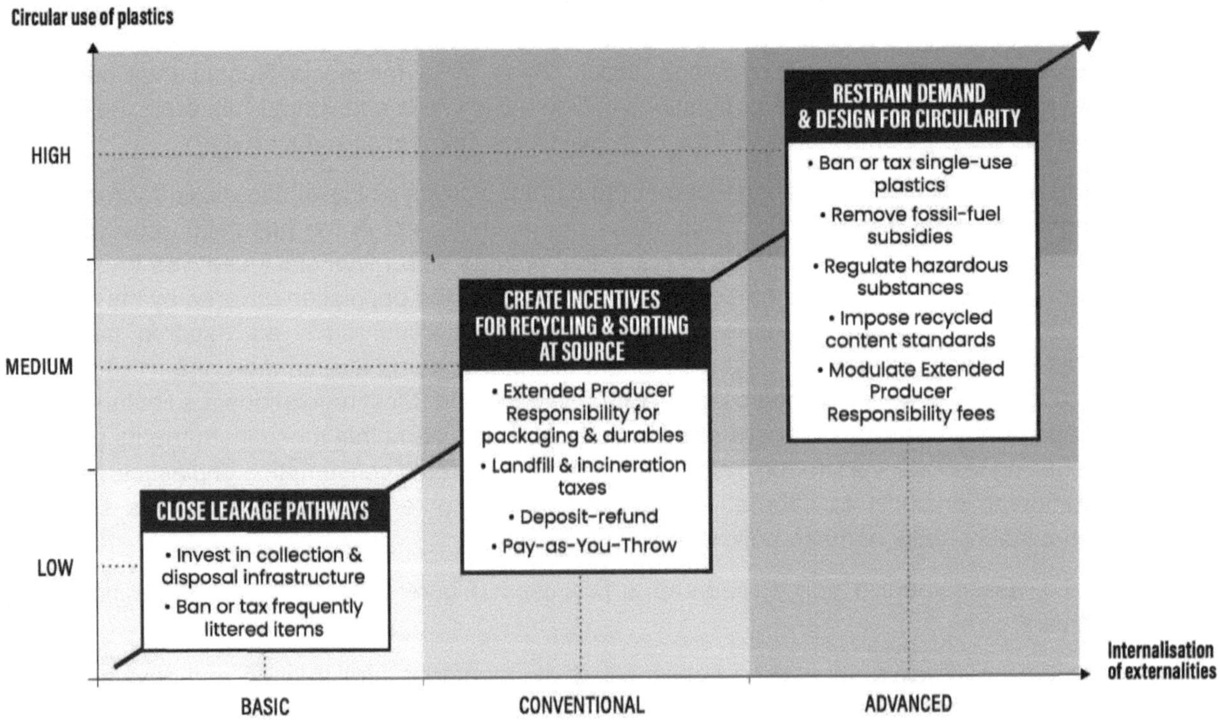

1.4.4. Strengthen international co-operation to make plastics value chains more circular and achieve net zero plastic leakage

National efforts to address the challenges linked to the use of plastics will need to be supplemented with international co-operation for several reasons:

1. The environmental consequences of plastics polluting water bodies are often transboundary and threaten the global commons, such as the ocean.
2. Plastics are shipped across the world as materials, products and waste streams, and supply chains are spread across the globe – policy responses would be more effective if co-ordinated internationally.
3. Tackling both the upstream and downstream environmental challenges posed by plastics requires innovation and investment on a significant scale, all of which can be accelerated through international co-operation.

The international community has voiced strong ambitions to limit the leakage of plastics to the environment and momentum is building to strengthen international co-operation to address environment and health impacts throughout the entire plastics life cycle. Improving waste management to reduce land-based sources of marine plastic is recognised as one of the priorities for action, alongside upstream measures to restrain excessive use of plastics, foster design for circularity and promote reuse. For example, given the global nature of the plastics value chains, aligning regulation of chemical substances and design approaches across countries can reduce health risks and improve circularity.

Mismanaged waste is by far the largest source of plastic leakage. Macroplastics account for almost 90% of total leakage, with land-based leakage coming from improper waste management practices accounting for 93% of all macroplastics. Since the bulk of mismanaged macroplastic waste occurs in low and middle-income countries, the investments needed in these countries are particularly large. Estimates presented in this Outlook suggest that annual costs, of more than EUR 25 billion a year, are needed to drastically reduce plastic leakage in low- and middle-income countries. The annual costs represent 0.3% of low and lower middle-income countries' GDP and would be an important financial burden, especially for the group of least developed countries.

International support will be instrumental in accelerating the investments required in infrastructure and changes to waste management practices, policies and governance. Official development assistance (ODA) could be one avenue for such support. However, the share of plastic-related ODA in total ODA spending remains marginal, accounting for only 0.2% of ODA gross commitments in 2017-19 (Figure 1.5).

Beyond ODA, additional sources of funding will need to be tapped to provide adequate and sustainable levels of funding, including revenue from households and firms benefiting from public waste management services, as well as domestic government subsidies and private sector investment. Enabling policy frameworks and governance mechanisms will need to be put in place to ensure that resources are used effectively. International support and local political leadership will be crucial in facilitating the required investments and governance structures for high-quality infrastructure.

Figure 1.5. Plastic-related gross commitments for ODA have increased steadily but remain small

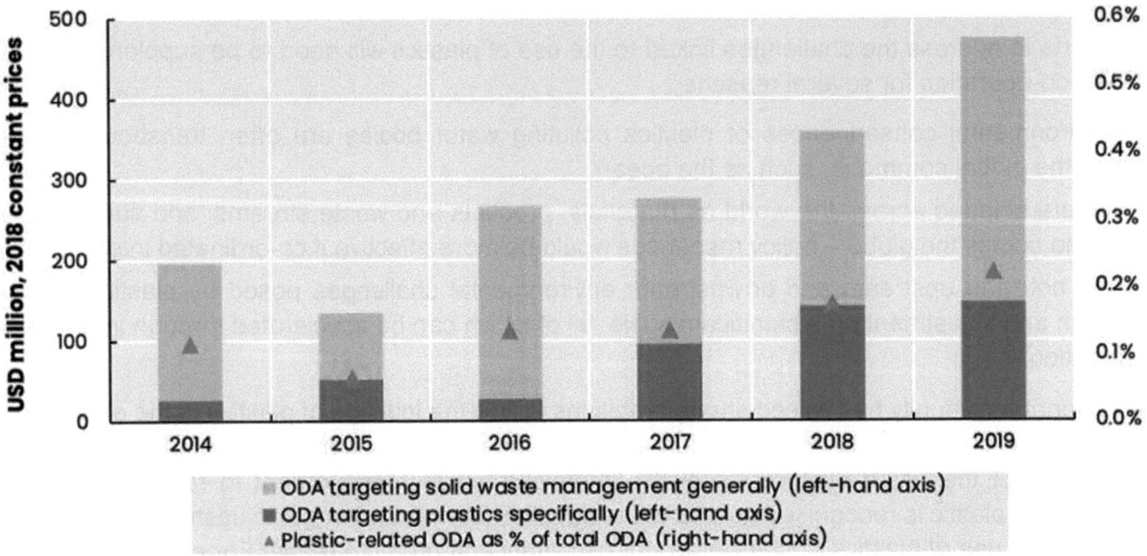

Source: Own calculations based on (OECD, 2021[15]), *OECD Data Platform on Development Finance for the Sustainable Ocean Economy* and the OECD's Creditor Reporting System, https://stats.oecd.org/Index.aspx?DataSetCode=crs1.

StatLink https://stat.link/8iz6x0

References

Aguiar, A. et al. (2019), "The GTAP Data Base: Version 10", *Journal of Global Economic Analysis*, Vol. 4/1, pp. 1-27, http://dx.doi.org/10.21642/jgea.040101af. [18]

Alliance to End Plastic Waste (2020), *Alliance to End Plastic Waste*, https://endplasticwaste.org/about/ (accessed on 1 November 2020). [8]

Benavides, P. et al. (2018), "Exploring Comparative Energy and Environmental Benefits of Virgin, Recycled, and Bio-Derived PET Bottles", *ACS Sustainable Chemistry & Engineering*, Vol. 6/8, pp. 9725-9733, http://dx.doi.org/10.1021/acssuschemeng.8b00750. [17]

Bondaroff, T. and S. Cooke (2020), *Masks on the Beach: The Impact of COVID-19 on Marine Plastic Pollution*, OceansAsia, https://oceansasia.org/wp-content/uploads/2020/12/Marine-Plastic-Pollution-FINAL.pdf. [11]

Borrelle, S. et al. (2020), "Predicted growth in plastic waste exceeds efforts to mitigate plastic pollution", *Science*, Vol. 369/6510, http://dx.doi.org/10.1126/science.aba3656. [22]

Center for Environmental Education (1987), *Plastics in the Ocean: More Than a Litter Problem*, Center for Environmental Education, Washington D.C. [1]

Chateau, J., R. Dellink and E. Lanzi (2014), "An Overview of the OECD ENV-Linkages Model: Version 3", *OECD Environment Working Papers*, No. 65, OECD Publishing, Paris, http://dx.doi.org/10.1787/5jz2qck2b2vd-en. [9]

Collins Dictionary (2018), *Collins 2018 Word of the Year Shortlist*, https://blog.collinsdictionary.com/language-lovers/collins-2018-word-of-the-year-shortlist/ (accessed on 22 October 2021). [2]

Ellen MacArthur Foundation (2017), *The New Plastics Economy: Rethinking the Future of Plastics & Catalysing Action*, https://ellenmacarthurfoundation.org/the-new-plastics-economy-rethinking-the-future-of-plastics-and-catalysing. [25]

G20 (2019), *G20 Implementation Framework for Actions on Marine Plastic Litter*, https://www.mofa.go.jp/policy/economy/g20_summit/osaka19/pdf/documents/en/annex_14.pdf (accessed on 1 November 2021). [6]

G7 (2018), *Ocean Plastics Charter*, https://www.consilium.europa.eu/media/40516/charlevoix_oceans_plastic_charter_en.pdf (accessed on 1 November 2021). [5]

Geyer, R., J. Jambeck and K. Law (2017), "Production, use, and fate of all plastics ever made", *Science Advances*, Vol. 3/7, p. e1700782, http://dx.doi.org/10.1126/sciadv.1700782. [19]

Global Plastics Alliance (2020), *Marine Litter Solutions - 5th Progress Report*, https://www.marinelittersolutions.com/wp-content/uploads/2020/08/ACC_12376_2020-Marine-Litter-Solutions_V5_Pages_NoCropsBleeds.pdf (accessed on 1 November 2020). [7]

Jambeck, J. et al. (2015), "Plastic waste inputs from land into the ocean", *Science*, Vol. 347/6223, pp. 768-771, http://dx.doi.org/10.1126/science.1260352. [20]

Lebreton, L. and A. Andrady (2019), "Future scenarios of global plastic waste generation and disposal", *Palgrave Communications*, Vol. 5/1, p. 6, http://dx.doi.org/10.1057/s41599-018-0212-7. [21]

OECD (2021), *Trends of ODA for a sustainable ocean economy*, OECD, Paris, https://oecd-main.shinyapps.io/ocean/. [15]

OECD (2018), *Improving Markets for Recycled Plastics: Trends, Prospects and Policy Responses*, OECD Publishing, Paris, https://dx.doi.org/10.1787/9789264301016-en. [12]

OECD (2016), *Policy Guidance on Resource Efficiency*, OECD Publishing, Paris, https://dx.doi.org/10.1787/9789264257344-en. [14]

OECD (forthcoming), *Global Plastics Outlook, Volume 2*, OECD. [10]

Royal Statistics Society (2018), *Statistics of the Year 2018: Winners announced*, https://rss.org.uk/news-publication/news-publications/2018/general-news/statistics-of-the-year-2018-winners-announced/ (accessed on 22 October 2021). [3]

Ryberg, M., A. Laurent and H. Michael (2018), "Mapping of global plastics value chain and plastics losses to the environment: with a particular focus on marine environment", *UNEP*. [23]

Stefanini, R. et al. (2020), "Plastic or glass: a new environmental assessment with a marine litter indicator for the comparison of pasteurized milk bottles", *The International Journal of Life Cycle Assessment*, Vol. 26/4, pp. 767-784, http://dx.doi.org/10.1007/s11367-020-01804-x. [16]

The Pew Charitable Trust; SYSTEMIQ (2020), *Breaking The Plastic Wave: A Comprehensive Assessment of Pathways Towards Stopping Ocean Plastic Pollution*, https://www.systemiq.earth/wp-content/uploads/2020/07/BreakingThePlasticWave_MainReport.pdf. [24]

UNEP (2020), *Global Partnership on Marine Litter*, https://www.unenvironment.org/explore-topics/oceans-seas/what-we-do/addressing-land-based-pollution/global-partnership-marine (accessed on 1 November 2020). [4]

Watkins, E. et al. (2019), "Policy approaches to incentivise sustainable plastic design", *OECD Environment Working Papers*, No. 149, OECD Publishing, Paris, https://dx.doi.org/10.1787/233ac351-en. [13]

Notes

[1] Including (Geyer, Jambeck and Law, 2017[19]; Jambeck et al., 2015[20]; Lebreton and Andrady, 2019[21]; Ryberg, Laurent and Michael, 2018[23]; The Pew Charitable Trust; SYSTEMIQ, 2020[24]; Borrelle et al., 2020[22]; Ellen MacArthur Foundation, 2017[25]).

[2] The Annex provides more details on the production structure, as well on the sectoral and regional aggregation of the model.

[3] Amendments to Annexes II, VIII and IX to the Basel Convention on the Control of Transboundary Movements of Hazardous Wastes and their Disposal came into force on the 1 January 2021.

[4] Modifications to Appendices 3 and 4 of the OECD Decision of the Council on the Control of Transboundary Movements of Wastes Destined for Recovery Operations [OECD/LEGAL/0266] came into force on the 1 January 2021.

[5] These additional countries are Egypt, Ghana, Morocco, Nigeria, the Philippines, and Thailand.

2. Plastics flows and their impacts on the environment

From production through to consumption and disposal, plastics interact with the economy and the environment in a multitude of complex ways. Understanding these complexities is critical for identifying challenges and formulating effective policies. This chapter aims to quantify plastic flows in the economy and their impacts on the environment. It begins by discussing the methodology used, before presenting estimates and analysis of the key steps and impacts throughout the plastics lifecycle.

KEY MESSAGES

- Annual global use of plastics, including fibres and additives, has been growing continuously, reaching 460 million tonnes (Mt) in 2019. Plastics in packaging, construction and transportation together account for more than 60% of the weight of plastics use.
- The current use of plastics is far from circular. Of the 353 Mt of global plastic waste generated globally in 2019, only an estimated 55 Mt were collected for recycling, 22 Mt of which were disposed. Secondary plastics accounted for barely 6% of total plastics use in 2019. In total, 67 Mt of plastic waste and residues globally were incinerated in industrial facilities and 174 Mt were disposed of in sanitary landfills. The amount of mismanaged and littered plastic waste is increasing and has reached 82 Mt per year. Of this, only 3 Mt is collected for proper disposal by litter clean-up measures.
- Widespread plastics use and inadequate prevention measures have led to persistent plastic leakage. In 2019 an estimated 22 Mt of plastics leaked into the environment. The largest leakage source (82%) is mismanaged waste, i.e. waste that is inadequately disposed of. Other sources are abrasion and losses of microplastics (12%), littering (5%) and marine activities (1%).
- Rivers are the main route by which plastics enter the ocean, but the process can take years or even decades. In 2019, 6.1 Mt of plastic waste are estimated to have ended up in aquatic environments, of which 1.7 Mt flowed into the ocean. This brings the total accumulated stock of plastics in aquatic environments in 2019 to 139 Mt. While the estimated inflows are lower than earlier studies that do not account for the residence time of leaked plastics in rivers, the amount is still alarming.
- Microplastic emissions from tyre and brake wear particles add to air pollution in highly urbanised regions, but are also transported to remote places, such as the Arctic where they have implications for climate change.
- Greenhouse gas emissions from the plastics lifecycle in 2019 are estimated to be 1.8 billion tonnes, or 3.4% of global emissions, with 90% of these emissions from the production and conversion of plastics from fossil fuel feedstock.
- Overall, these quantified insights, combined with an emerging understanding of the environmental, health and economic impacts, underline the need for an extensive policy package and international co-operation to make plastics more circular throughout the value chain.

2.1. The methodology to compose the OECD Global Plastics Outlook Database

Although the literature offers in-depth research on plastics use and plastic waste, a number of gaps are hindering the analysis of the current situation and decision making by policy makers. The literature on plastics use is limited either to the global level (Geyer, Jambeck and Law, 2017[1]), to plastics production (IEA, 2018[2]), to a specific year across regions for a specific application or sector (Ryberg et al., 2019[3]) or to a specific region (Plastics Europe, 2020[4]). A key gap is the limited information on flows of secondary plastics. Moreover, the scope and volumes covered by the various studies differ. For example, some sources exclude fibres despite being a significant part of overall plastics.

There is also a lack of information on the management of waste across the world, and especially the management of individual waste streams such as plastics. Definitions, available data, measurement methodologies and framework conditions differ widely between countries, even for countries within the

OECD. Recycling rates are often inconsistently reported, for instance national and municipal statistics tend to focus on the weight of household waste collected, and sometimes include commercial waste when it is collected by municipalities. Industrial waste statistics may include pre-consumer waste and typically rely on sampling and extrapolation using methodologies that differ in each country. Recycling can also refer to different concepts: quantities that are collected for recycling, material sent for reprocessing, or material ultimately available for use as a secondary plastic. Furthermore, reported recycling rates may give an overly optimistic view of the current status because they focus on polymers such as PET and applications such as packaging, for which recycling is already established. By contrast, recycling rates of hard-to-recycle plastics such as fibres are rarely reported. Countries with poor waste management infrastructure also have the weakest published data, making it challenging to assess the amount of mismanaged waste. This results in an incomplete view of the current international management of plastic waste.

The Global Plastics Outlook aims at understanding the drivers of plastics use and the impacts on the environment in order to find the best way to reduce the environmental pressures of plastics production, waste generation and management. As a first step, the OECD has developed the Global Plastics Outlook Database[1] to fill the information gaps and provide a comprehensive overview of the entire lifecycle of plastics. The database collects and reconciles data for the full lifecycle of plastics across the world: production, use, waste generation and waste management, including waste that is mismanaged or leaked to the environment (Figure 2.1).

The added value of the database is to gather plastic indicators in a coherent framework. The database was developed through a collection and reconciliation of renowned databases, review of the existing literature and expert input. This information was then integrated in an economic modelling framework, which ensures that all data sources are consistent and allows for analysis of the economic drivers and environmental effects of plastics. To this end, the OECD ENV-Linkages model (Chateau, Dellink and Lanzi, 2014[5]), based on the Global Trade Analysis Project (GTAP) database[2] (Aguiar et al., 2019[6]), has been revised and expanded to link plastics data in volumes to the economic flows in the model. ENV-Linkages splits plastics production into primary plastics and secondary plastics technologies and maps plastics use by polymer and application to the model sectors.

Figure 2.1. The OECD Global Plastics Outlook Database

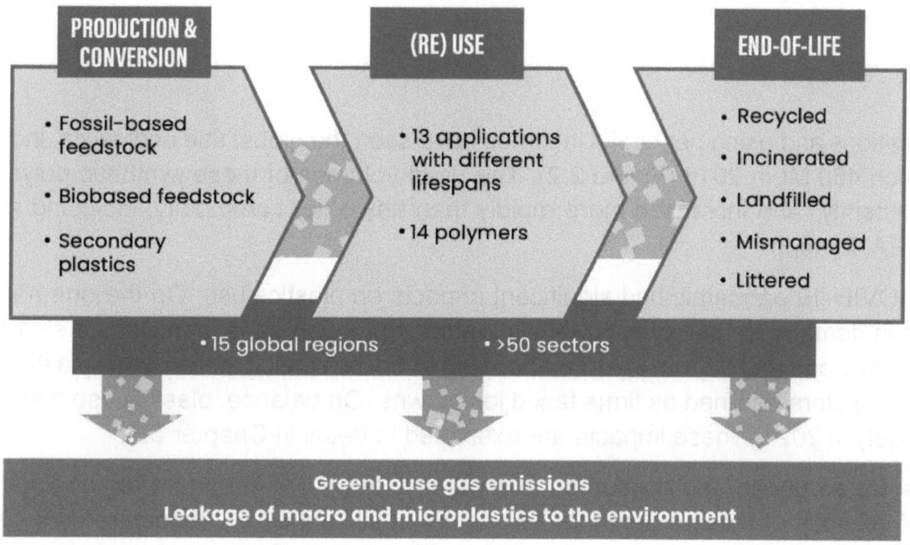

The data and methodology used for each step are summarised in Table 2.1 and more details are provided in Annex A. The database spans the history of the large-scale industrial production of plastics from 1950 to the present day. The database uses 2019 as reference year, since the year 2020 was impacted by COVID-19 and economic indicators as well as materials data are still uncertain for the recently-ended 2021.

Table 2.1. The OECD Global Plastics Outlook Database covers a large range of sources and methodologies

Category	Variable	Sources and assumptions
Production	Primary plastics	OECD ENV-Linkages model, based on GTAP10 (Aguiar et al., 2019[6]).
	Secondary plastics	OECD ENV-Linkages model, using Exiobase (Stadler et al., 2018[7]) and Grand View Research (2020[8]) for the cost structure; recycling shares (see below) and recycling losses from Cottom, Cook and Velis (2020[9]), Chruszcz and Reeve (2018[10]), Roosen et al. (2020[11]) and VinylPlus (2019[12]).
Use	Plastics use by region, application and polymer	Volumes of plastics by polymer and application from (Ryberg et al., 2019[3]) associated with different sectors and regions in OECD ENV-Linkages model.
Waste	Plastic waste by region, application and polymer	OECD ENV-Linkages model, based on historical consumption, and product lifespans from Geyer, Jambeck and Law (2017[1]) .
Waste management end-of-life fates	Recycling share	Country sources (Table A.A.5), Geyer, Jambeck and Law (2017[1]), and Kaza et al. (2018[13]) for Municipal Solid Waste (MSW); rates for non-MSW assumed to match MSW.
	Littering share	Jambeck et al. (2015[14]) for share in MSW; zero for non-MSW.
	Shares for other fates	Cross-country regression based on Kaza et al. (2018[13]) [3]; rates for non-MSW assumed to match MSW.
Environmental impacts	Total leakage of macroplastics and microplastics to the environment by category	Based on plastics consumption, waste and waste management projections from OECD ENV-Linkages model, adapted from Ryberg et al. (2019[3]) methodology.
	Plastic leakage and accumulation in aquatic environments	Based on waste management projections from OECD ENV-Linkages model, adapted from Lebreton and Andrady (2019[15]) methodology.
	GHG emissions for plastic lifecycle	Based on plastic consumption, waste and waste management projections from OECD ENV-Linkages model, based on Zheng and Suh (2019[16]).

2.2. The global use of plastics is growing strongly

Growing populations and rising per capita incomes have seen the global use of plastics, including additives and fibres, reach 460 Mt in 2019 (Figure 2.2). The used volumes of these synthetic polymers have been increasing constantly[4] and increased more rapidly than any other commodity, including steel, aluminium and cement (IEA, 2018[2]).

In 2020, the COVID-19 pandemic had significant impacts on plastics use. On the one hand, there was a rapid increase in demand for personal protective equipment (such as face masks), a shift from restaurant eating to take-away and a shift from in-store shopping to online retail. On the other, plastics use in industry and commercial sectors declined as firms faced lockdowns. On balance, plastics use declined in 2020 but rebounded largely in 2021. These impacts are examined in detail in Chapter 3.

While plastics are produced and consumed everywhere, there are important regional variations when it comes to total volumes of plastics demand. Two-thirds of current use is concentrated in OECD countries and the People's Republic of China (hereafter China) (Figure 2.2). China represents around 20% of global plastics demand, the United States represents approximately 18%, OECD Europe represents about 18% and the rest of the OECD countries represent around 9%. However, the relative importance of each region's plastics use has been changing, mirroring the economic dynamics of regions and countries. For instance, the share of the OECD in global consumption has been declining steadily – from 87% in 1980 to 46% in 2019. As COVID-19 was a worldwide pandemic, this share has been more or less stable since 2019. However, relatively fast economic recovery in the United States and China may have increased their share somewhat in 2021.

Figure 2.2. Global plastics use has quadrupled in 30 years, mainly driven by emerging economies

In million tonnes (Mt), 1950-2021

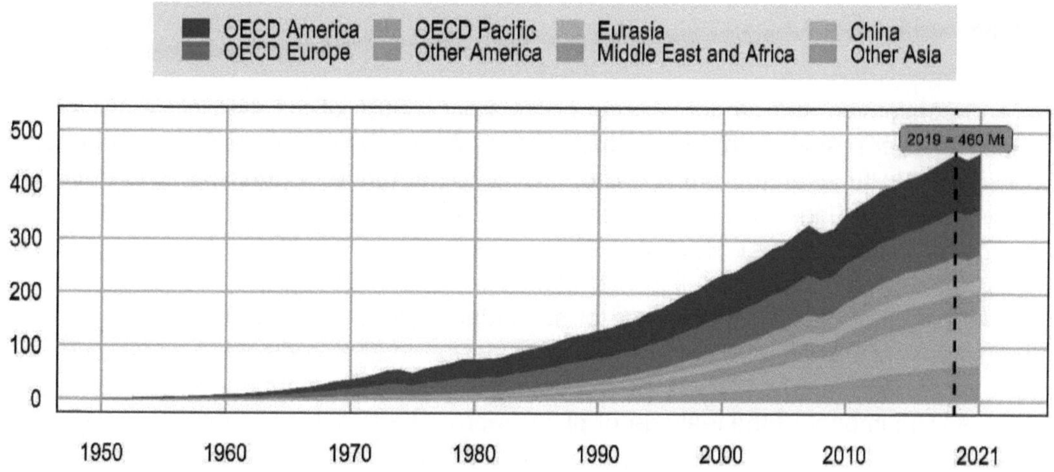

Note: See Annex A for the detailed regional breakdown of the OECD ENV-Linkages regions.
Source: OECD Global Plastics Outlook Database, https://doi.org/10.1787/c0821f81-en.

StatLink https://stat.link/r9vlpe

The majority of plastics in use today are virgin plastics, made from crude oil or gas. Due to the fossil-based feedstock and the high energy consumption during refining, most greenhouse gas (GHG) emissions from plastics can be attributed to the production stage (Box 2.1). Biobased plastics are a rather small group of plastics with similar characteristics to fossil-based plastics, but are derived from biomass (Box 2.2). Together fossil-based and biobased plastics can be referred to as primary plastics. Plastics made from recycled material are called secondary plastics. Secondary plastics contribute less to GHG emissions than primary plastics, but only accounted for 6% of global plastics use in 2019 (Chapter 4).

Box 2.1. Plastics emit a high amount of greenhouse gases throughout their lifecycle

Traditional plastic production uses fossil fuel feedstock which is transformed into monomers in an energy-intensive process. The OECD ENV-Linkages model uses the energy and factor intensity of economic sectors, along with their process emission intensity, to estimate the GHG emissions in the economy. Moreover, to quantify plastic-related emissions, the approach is complemented with plastics lifecycle emissions factors. Based on these calculations, the estimated GHG emissions of fossil-based plastics in 2019 were 1.8 gigatonnes of carbon dioxide equivalent (Gt CO_2eq.), or 3.4% of global emissions that year.[5] If the goals of the Paris Agreement are to be achieved, the growth of emissions related to plastics must cease.

Production and conversion into products account for around 90% of the lifecycle emissions of fossil-based plastics. GHG emissions from the production and conversion of polymers vary depending on the polymer considered (with a range from 2.7 to 6.3 tCO_2eq. per tonne of plastics). End-of-life emissions vary significantly depending on the disposal option, with incineration the most GHG intensive (2.3 tCO_2eq. per tonne of plastics). However, some emissions can be offset when energy is recovered through waste-to-energy processes (Gómez-Sanabria et al., 2018[17]). Recycling directly emits 0.9 tCO_2eq. per tonne of plastic, but the use of secondary plastics can avoid emissions from primary plastics production. Sanitary landfilling is the least emission-intensive disposal alternative in terms of direct emissions, at less than 0.1 tCO_2eq. per tonne of plastic, but does not generate energy that can be used elsewhere. The impact of the leakage of plastics on GHG is not incorporated in the calculations, but recent research by Shen et al. (2020[18]) based on experimental data by Royer et al. (2018[19]) estimates annual methane emissions to be roughly 2 Mt CO_2eq.

So can replacing plastics with other materials reduce the carbon footprint of consumption (Franklin Associates, 2018[20])? The response is ambivalent, partly due to the behavioural components of the use of a product as well as its end-of-life management. For example, as illustrated in Figure 2.3, the carbon footprint of a plastic bottle is not necessarily worse than its glass counterpart.

Figure 2.3. The carbon footprint of a non-returnable glass bottle is higher than a plastic equivalent

Comparison of 1-litre milk bottles, in kg CO_2 eq.

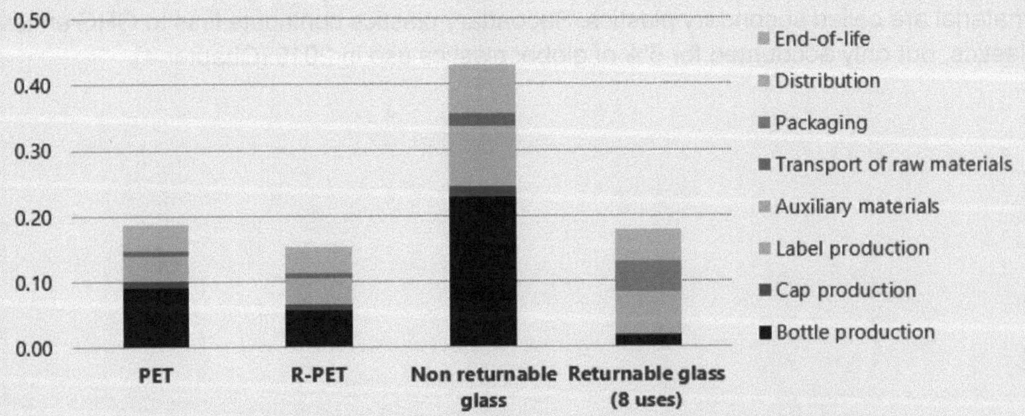

Note: R-PET= 100% recycled polyethylene terephthalate (PET).
Source: Stefanini et al. (2020[21]).

The variety of different polymers that can be produced accounts for the versatility of plastics (Table 2.2). Figure 2.4 provides an overview of the most commonly used polymers and their applications. Different polymers have differing properties. For example, thermoplastics can be remoulded after heating, while thermosets are irreversibly hardened. Elastomers have elastic properties and fibres can be made of various polymers but are defined by their shape. Biobased plastics are made of biomass as feedstock instead of fossil fuels (Box 2.2). In addition, polymers are usually mixed or "compounded" with a wide range of additives to further customise and improve the performance of plastics. Some of the most important functions of additives are to prevent aging, colour the plastic, make rigid material flexible, work as a lubricant, improve the impact resistance, reduce flammability and generate foam as a blowing agent.

Table 2.2. The large range of polymers allows for a multitude of plastics applications

Polymer	Abbreviation	Examples of use
Polypropylene	PP	Food packaging, automotive parts
Low-density polyethylene	LDPE	Reusable bags, food packaging film
High-density polyethylene	HDPE	Toys, shampoo bottles, pipes
Polyvinylchloride	PVC	Window frames, floor covering, pipes, cable insulation
Polystyrene	PS	Food packaging, insulation, electronic equipment
Polyethylene terephthalate	PET	Beverage bottles
Polyurethane	PUR	Insulation, mattresses
ABS, elastomers, biobased plastics, PBT, PC, PMMA, PTFE, …	Other	Tyres, packaging, electronics, automotive, …
Fibres made of different polymers	Fibres	Textile applications but also in many other sectors

Note: ABS stands for Acrylonitrile butadiene styrene, PBT for Polybutylene terephthalate, PC for Polycarbonates, PMMA for Poly (methyl methacrylate) (also known as plexiglas) and PFTE for Polytetrafluoroethylene.

Together, packaging, construction and transportation applications account for more than 60% of total plastics use.[6] The other main applications of plastics use include textiles, household consumer products and non-household or institutional products, electronics, machinery and tyres (Figure 2.4).

Figure 2.4. Global plastics use by application and polymer

Share of plastics by application and polymer, 2019

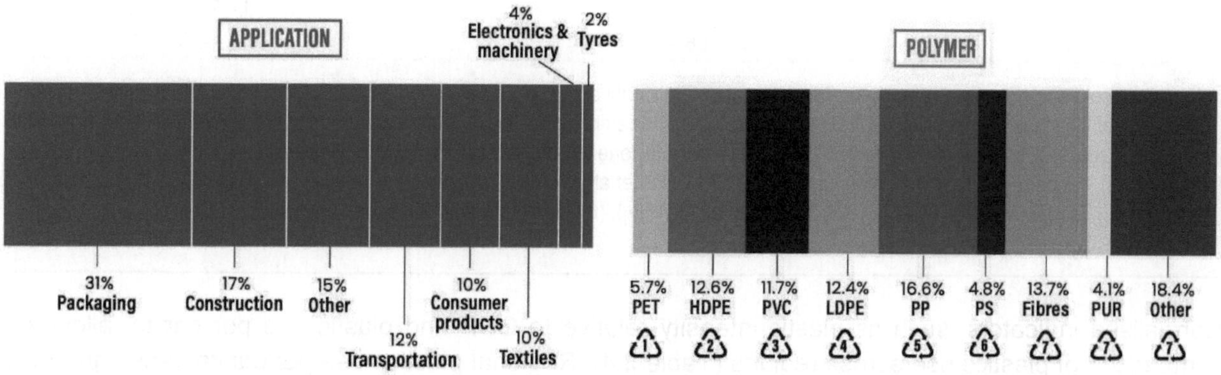

Source: OECD Global Plastics Outlook Database, https://doi.org/10.1787/c0821f81-en.

Box 2.2. Biobased plastics offer potential as long as land-use impacts are managed

Biobased plastics are derived from biomass such as corn, sugarcane, wheat or residues of other processes. Their production generates fewer greenhouse gas emissions than fossil-based plastics They can be produced as drop-in resins (as a substitute together with fossil-based plastics) or as alternative resins with other characteristics. The majority of such plastics are produced for packaging (53%) and textiles (11%). Asia is the region with the largest biobased plastics production capacity (45%), followed by Europe (25%), North America (18%) and South America (12%) (European Bioplastics, 2019[22]). In 2019, biobased plastics represented around 2 Mt or 0.6% of total plastics. The volumes are growing, but not any faster than other plastic types (OECD Global Plastics Outlook Database).

Table 2.3 compares the "cradle-to-gate" (extraction, refining and production) GHG emissions of fossil and biobased feedstock. A negative result indicates that the carbon embodied in the product is greater than the carbon emitted during refining and processing. Despite the positive outlook of biobased plastics in terms of GHG emissions, their environmental impact is controversial due to their potential to drive land-use changes such as deforestation that may lead to significant GHG emissions. If tropical forest or other natural environments are sacrificed to make room for additional agricultural area, this would result in loss of biodiversity and one-off carbon emissions (Brizga, Hubacek and Feng, 2020[23]). Whether the overall carbon balance is positive depends, among others, on assumptions related to the amount of natural area that would be converted (directly for feedstock of biobased plastics or indirectly for agricultural activities that have to compete with feedstock for biobased plastics for arable land) and the method used to compare one-off losses with annual recurring benefits (Liptow and Tillman, 2012[24]; Walker and Rothman, 2020[25]).

Currently only 0.7 million hectares or 0.02% of global agricultural land is used for growing feedstock for biobased plastics (European Bioplastics, 2019[22]). Therefore, the additional pressure on agricultural land is currently negligible and will remain so in the coming years, even if high growth rates are realised.

Table 2.3. Bioplastics could reduce GHG emissions from plastics production as long as negative effects from indirect land use change are avoided

Material	Fossil fuel-based polymer (kg CO_2 eq./kg)	Biobased polymer (kg CO_2 eq./kg)
HDPE	1.9 – 2[a]	-0.55 – -0.88[b]
PET	2.2 – 3[c]	1 – 2.4[d]
PP	1.8 – 2[e]	-0.2 – -0.3[f]

Note: Only cradle-to-gate assessments shown in the table. Thus only extraction, refining and production are taken into account, but not the use or end-of-life stages. A negative result indicates that the carbon embodied in the product is greater than the carbon emitted during refining and processing. HDPE= high-density polyethylene; PET= polyethylene terephthalate; PP= polypropylene.
Sources: (a) Vanderreydt et al. (forthcoming[26]), (b) Tsiropoulos et al. (2015[27]), (c) Akanuma, Selke and Auras (2014[28]), Semba et al. (2018[29]), (d) Tsiropoulos et al. (2015[27]), (e) Broeren et al. (2017[30]), (f) Chen and Patel (2011[31]).

Normalised indicators, such as plastic intensity relative to GDP and plastic use per capita, allow for a comparison of plastics use across regions (Table 2.4). Regional plastics use per capita varies greatly: an inhabitant of the United States uses 255 kg of new plastics every year on average, while the average person in Sub-Saharan Africa uses less than one tenth of that amount. In contrast, the range of plastics intensity relative to GDP across the world is smaller, ranging between 2.5 and 4.5 tonnes per million USD (t/M$). OECD plastic intensity reaches 3.7 tonnes per million USD, while non-OECD countries reach 3.4 tonnes. This correlation is also found in plastics use per capita, whose OECD level is 156 kg per capita, compared to 39 kg per capita for non-OECD countries. The only outlier in this table is Sub-Saharan Africa, which has the lowest plastics use per capita (16 kg/cap), but the highest plastic intensity (4.5 t/USD M). This high intensity reflects the very low level of GDP per capita of Sub-Saharan Africa in 2019 (about five times lower than Middle East and North Africa and twice lower than India).

Table 2.4. GDP is a key driver of global plastics use

2019

			Plastics use per capita (kg/cap)	Plastics intensity relative to GDP (t/M$ in PPP)
World			60.1	3.5
OECD			155.8	3.7
Non-OECD			39.3	3.4
OECD	OECD America	USA	255.2	4.3
		Canada	202.2	4.3
		Other OECD America	65.4	3.6
	OECD Europe	OECD EU countries	152.9	3.6
		OECD non-EU countries	124.3	3.5
	OECD Pacific	OECD Asia	102.4	2.6
		OECD Oceania	143.9	3.1
Non-OECD	Other America	Latin America	50.9	3.5
	Eurasia	Other EU	103.0	4.1
		Other Eurasia	66.7	3.7
	Middle East and Africa	Middle East & North Africa	47.1	2.5
		Other Africa	15.9	4.5
	Other Asia	China	69.0	3.7
		India	22.1	2.7
		Other non-OECD Asia	31.7	3.2

Source: OECD Global Plastics Outlook Database.

2.3. Plastic waste generation depends on plastics use and product lifespans

The generation of plastic waste is strongly related to how plastics are used. The overall average lifespan of a plastic product is almost ten years, though this depends on its use (Figure 2.5). Packaging has an extremely short average lifespan while plastic applications in the construction sector may be in use for several decades. Therefore, packaging waste constitutes a large share (42%) of total plastic waste generated.

Figure 2.5. Average plastic product lifespans range from six months to 35 years

Product lifetime distributions

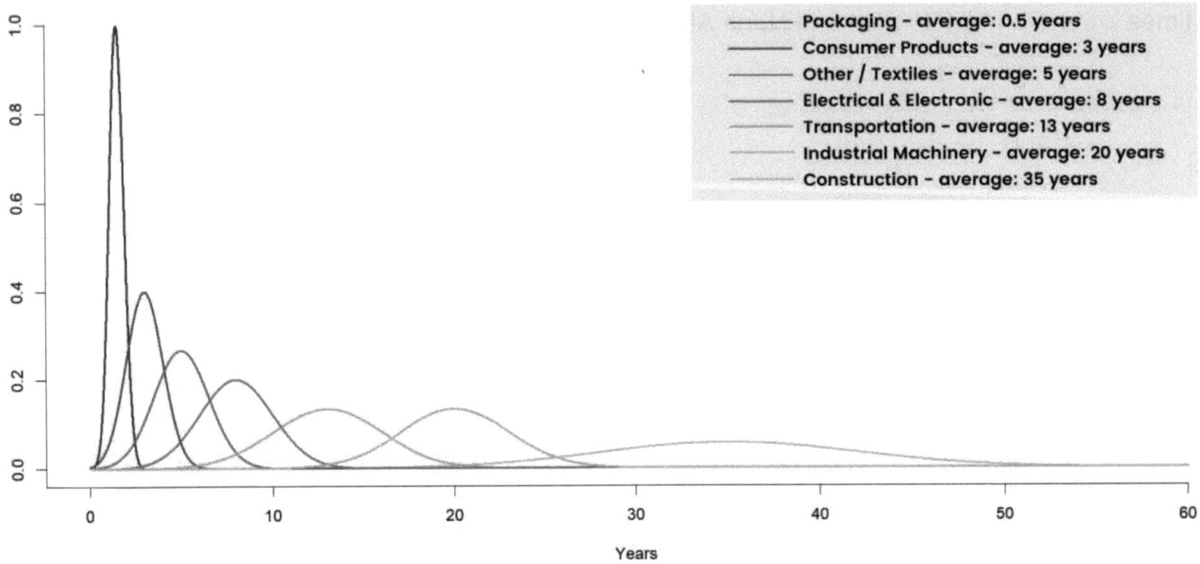

Source: Geyer, Jambeck and Law (2017[1]).

The global generation of plastic waste can be estimated from the amount of plastics used in previous decades, the international trade of plastics and plastic products, as well as the average lifespan of plastics applications (see Annex A for more details on the methodology). According to the OECD Global Plastics Outlook Database, the plastic waste generated in 2019 amounted to 353 Mt.

At the waste stage, the ease of recycling and the potential mobility when lost to the environment are influenced by polymer type, dimensional shape, object size, additive mix, and the items and materials appended in assembly. Figure 2.6 highlights that the applications and polymers present in the waste stage are different than in the consumption stage. The predominance of PP, LDPE and HDPE has become even greater in the waste stage because they are often used for packaging applications with short lifetimes. Similarly, since PET is mainly used for packaging, it will become waste rapidly after its initial use. By contrast, PVC and PUR are mainly used for applications with long lifecycles. They will only enter the waste stage many years later. These long lifecycles, combined with significant growth rates of use, result in a relatively lower presence in plastic waste than in plastics use of those polymers. Conversely, the polymers with long life cycles account for a relatively high share of the stock of plastics that is present in the economy.

The OECD Global Plastics Outlook Database indicates that the OECD generates almost half of all plastic waste: the United States accounts for 21%, OECD Europe 19% and the remaining OECD countries 9%. Outside the OECD, China produces 19% of global plastic waste, India 5% and the rest of the world 27%.

In terms of waste per capita, there are stark differences across the world (Table 2.5). The United States had the largest plastic waste footprint in 2019, at 221 kg per capita, while OECD Europe had 114 kg plastic waste per capita. Japan and Korea's plastic waste generation is relatively low for industrialised countries, averaging 69 kg per capita. Finally, China generated 47 kg of plastic waste per inhabitant in 2019, while India generated only 14 kg per inhabitant.

Figure 2.6. Almost two-thirds of plastic waste comes from relatively short-lived products such as packaging, consumer products and textiles

Plastic waste generated (Mt), 2019

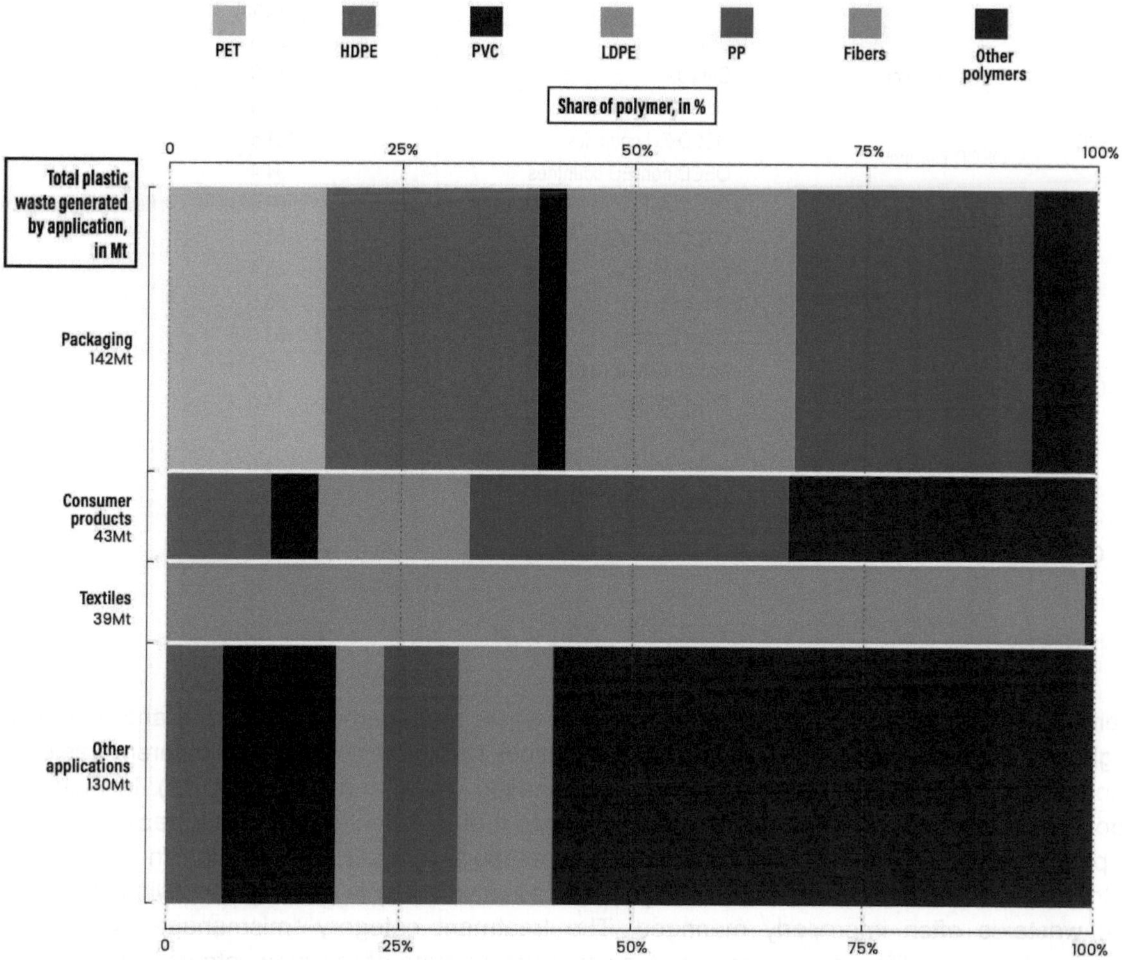

Note: HDPE= High-density polyethylene; PET= Polyethylene terephthalate; High-density polyethylene; PVC= Polyvinylchloride; LDPE= Low-density polyethylene; PP=Polypropylene.
Source: OECD Global Plastics Outlook Database, https://doi.org/10.1787/c0821f81-en.

StatLink https://stat.link/elpign

Table 2.5. Per capita plastic waste generation differs strongly across the world

Kg/cap, 2019

			Plastic waste per capita (kg/cap)
OECD	OECD America	USA	220.5
		Canada	177.9
		Other OECD America	57.9
	OECD Europe	OECD EU countries	121.6
		OECD non-EU countries	94.4
	OECD Pacific	OECD Asia	68.9
		OECD Oceania	62.1
Non-OECD	Other America	Latin America	43.4
	Eurasia	Other EU	75.5
		Other Eurasia	53.0
	Middle East and Africa	Middle East & North Africa	37.6
		Other Africa	14.5
	Other Asia	China	46.6
		India	14.0
		Other non-OECD Asia	21.4

Source: OECD Global Plastics Outlook Database.

2.4. The quality of plastic waste management varies across the world

The end-of-life fate of plastics depends on the local waste management capacities and regulations. As highlighted in Figure 2.1 the OECD Global Plastics Outlook Database contains five different waste handling categories (recycling, incineration, landfilling, mismanaged waste and littered waste). In Figure 2.7, the category "collected for recycling" refers to plastic waste that is collected in order to recycle and that will, after processing, produce secondary plastics. "Incineration" refers to incineration in a state-of-the-art industrial facility. The third approach to manage plastics in a safe way is sanitary "landfilling". Unfortunately, plastic waste is often improperly managed. The treatment category "mismanaged waste" aims at quantifying the end-of-life plastics generated in areas where state-of-the-art waste collection or treatment facilities are not in place. The plastic waste is either not collected, collected but disposed of in dumpsites, or collected for disposing in the environment, for example dumped directly into seas or open waters. Finally, "littered waste" differs from mismanaged waste because littering behaviour is not necessarily correlated to the provision of basic waste collection and disposal infrastructure. The category refers both to littering (i.e. when users discard packaging or other products into the environment), and to fly-tipping (i.e. plastic waste generators who consciously circumvent legislation to discard larger volumes of, for example, construction waste into the environment). Litter can either be collected via street sweepings and other clean-up actions or be left uncollected and leak into the environment. There are also biodegradable plastics that can be composted at the waste stage (European Bioplastics, 2019[22]) (Chapter 5), but due to the small amounts the OECD Plastics Outlook does not track this stream.

In most cases, differences in waste management capacities are related to regulations, geographical and demographic characteristics and other variables. In low-income countries, economic growth can outpace improvements in collection and disposal capacity, leading to increased volumes of mismanaged waste. By contrast, low-income countries typically have low labour costs that make collection and high-quality sorting of recyclables by manual labour economically feasible. Therefore, countries may encounter different waste management challenges depending on the stages of their economic development trajectory (Figure 2.7).

Figure 2.7. More plastic waste is mismanaged than collected for recycling

Share of plastics treated by waste management category, before recycling losses, 2019

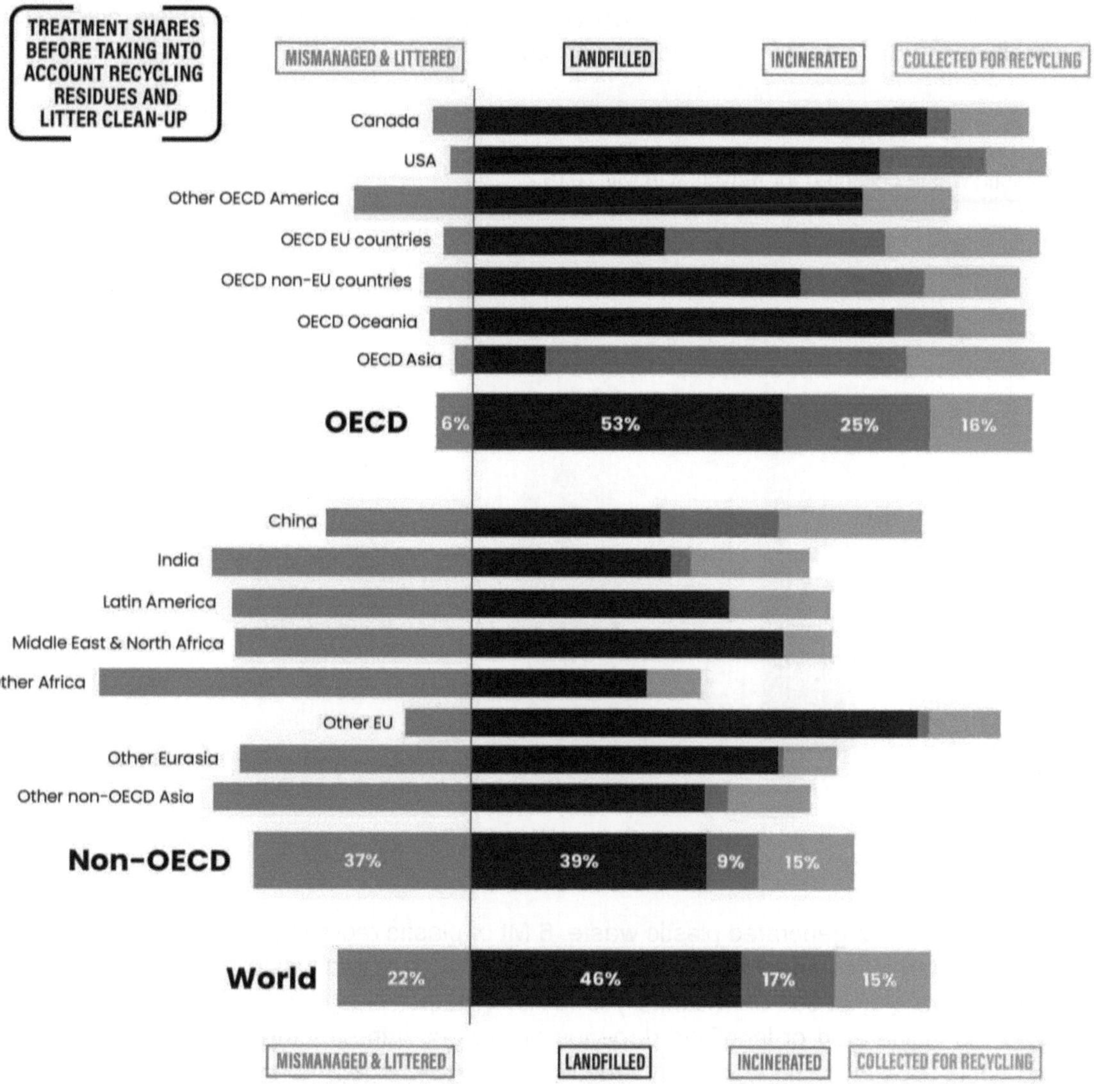

Source: OECD Global Plastics Outlook Database, https://doi.org/10.1787/c0821f81-en.

StatLink https://stat.link/4dumre

Globally, 15% or 55 Mt of plastic waste were collected for recycling in 2019.[7] EU countries, as well as China, India, Japan and Korea have above-average recycling rates. Key drivers of recycling in Europe, Japan and Korea are extensive separate collection facilities and extended producer responsibility (EPR) schemes that put the onus to recycle on producers of plastic products and packaging (Chapter 6). In other parts of the world, the informal economy is the main driver of recycling, incentivised by the value of some of the plastics (Chapter 4).

The underlying regional economic drivers not only determine the volumes of plastic waste collected for recycling – they also affect the process losses from recycling (Figure 2.8). Globally, almost 40% of plastics collected for recycling, or close to 22 Mt, are lost during recycling and end up being incinerated, landfilled or mismanaged. In particular, when formal waste collection is funded by government and free to users, it typically contains large amounts of un-recyclable plastics and non-plastics which need to be removed. These are counted as recycling losses. By contrast, in informal waste systems, waste pickers selectively target high-value plastics at the point of collection, reducing the mass lost when they are cleaned and sorted to get the maximum price. Therefore, there are important regional differences in recycling both in terms of volumes as well as in practices used (see Chapter 4 for a more extensive discussion of the recycling practices and markets for secondary plastics).

Figure 2.8. Formal and informal recycling volumes and losses differ across regions

Volume of plastic waste collected for recycling in Mt, 2019

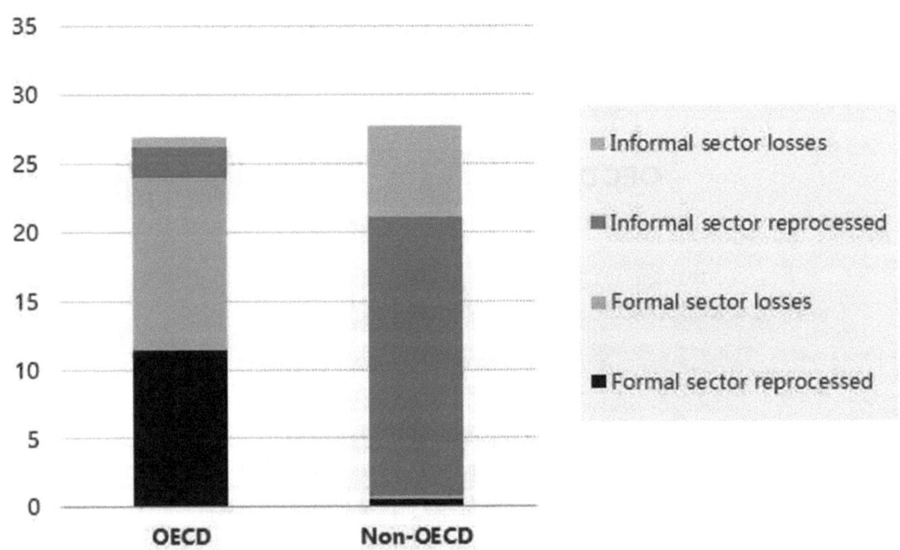

Source: OECD Global Plastics Outlook Database; Cottom, Cook and Velis (2020[9]), "Spatio-temporal quantification of plastic pollution origins and transportation (SPOT)", https://plasticpollution.leeds.ac.uk/toolkits/spot.

Globally in 2019, 60 Mt of generated plastic waste, 6 Mt of plastic recycling residues and 1 Mt of collected litter were incinerated in industrial facilities, while 162 Mt of generated waste, 11 Mt of residues and 1 Mt of collected litter were disposed of in sanitary landfills. Whether plastic waste, especially municipal solid waste (MSW), is incinerated or landfilled depends on historic infrastructure, regulation, local population density and costs (Box 2.3). Since sanitary landfilling requires large amounts of land, densely urbanised countries and regions such as Japan and Western Europe rely heavily on incineration. However, because well-controlled incineration is almost three times more expensive than landfilling, countries and cities with more space have kept sanitary landfilling as their prime disposal method.

Box 2.3. The environmental impacts of incineration are mixed

A waste incineration plant is an industrial facility dedicated to the thermal treatment of waste. In order to minimise potentially hazardous emissions, state-of-the-art plants incorporate extensive air pollution control (APC) equipment. A range of technologies are available, but moving grate incinerators account for more than 93% of global capacity because of their ability to process waste streams with varying characteristics. Waste incineration is expensive and costs almost three times more than landfilling. The main advantage is that incineration reduces the weight and volume of waste. Indeed, the remaining ashes weigh only about 25% of the original waste and the volume can be reduced by up to 90%, which substantially limits the need for landfilling (Neuwahl et al., 2019[32]). Therefore, in megacities and urbanised areas where land is scarce and public opposition to new landfills high, waste incineration can be used to dispose of large volumes of waste.

The energy released during incineration can recovered, often referred to as waste-to-energy (WtE) or energy-from-waste (EfW). State-of-the-art WtE facilities for mixed waste can recover about 25% of the energy contained in waste as electricity, though older facilities recover substantially less (Lombardi, Carnevale and Corti, 2015[33]; Pavlas et al., 2011[34]). In addition, energy efficiency can be increased by recovering heat for use in nearby industrial processes or residential areas. Nonetheless, feedstock and operational priorities can mean that waste incineration plants operate at energy efficiencies that are substantially below coal and gas energy production plants (Pavlas et al., 2011[34]; Colmenar-Santos et al., 2018[35]). European plants recover most energy per tonne of MSW. This can be explained by a combination of regulatory measures and financial incentives, as well as the composition of incinerated waste. Lifestyles and sorting practices mean that mixed waste in Europe has a higher calorific value since it contains less organic (wet) content than elsewhere.

There are around 2 450 active waste incineration plants around the world. Together they processed approximately 400 Mt of MSW and other waste streams in 2019. Waste incinerators are strongly concentrated in OECD countries and China. Japan and Korea have many small incinerators with an average capacity of around 60 000 tonnes, compared to around 200 000 tonnes for OECD Europe, and close to 400 000 tonnes for the United States and China.

Ecoprog (2020[36]) expects that global capacity will increase by more than 3% per year in the coming decade, but with stark differences across regions. The growth will occur almost exclusively in China and non-OECD Asia. Some new capacity will come online in OECD Europe in countries such as the United Kingdom or Poland, but the overall growth is expected to be small. In Japan and Korea, gradual closure of small unprofitable incinerators will see total capacity decline slightly. The market in the US and Canada is expected to remain stable. While there are many plans to build waste incinerators outside of these regions, in the past, these types of projects have been abandoned due to financial concerns, uncertain legal frameworks, public resistance and insufficient local expertise. Therefore, growth in Africa and Latin America is expected to be small in the next decade, but might accelerate later driven by the growth of population and megacities.

Waste incinerators are typically used to treat mixed waste, including plastics. The environmental effects of (plastic) waste incineration are ambiguous. The gains of recovering energy from waste are counterbalanced by the environmental impacts of ash, residual emissions and greenhouse gases (Dijkgraaf and Vollebergh, 2004[37]; Dubois, 2013[38]). Most studies indicate that the overall environmental impact of waste incineration with energy recovery is better than landfilling, but worse than recycling (Lazarevic et al., 2010[39]; Civancik-Uslu et al., 2021[40]). Incineration also destroys the material that could feed the circular economy, which aims to close material loops and maintain the highest value of materials throughout different cycles. Another downside of incineration is that the plants are highly capital intensive, which pushes operators to use them at full capacity. Consequently, large-scale investments in waste incineration can lock-in this infrastructure for many years, leading to competition with recyclers for feedstock (UNEP, 2019[41]). This is especially true when investments are linked to heat recovery and central district heating. To speed up the transition to the circular economy, waste incineration will have to be gradually replaced by recycling and waste prevention.

For many emerging economies, lack of technical capacities, poor governance and insufficient financial resources at the municipal level are major bottlenecks in improving waste management practices. Mismanaged waste is a wide category that includes waste that has not been collected and is therefore "self-managed" by those who generate it – and who usually resort to dumping it on land, in rivers and lakes or burning it in open uncontrolled fires. Mismanaged waste can also include waste that has been collected but which is then subsequently deposited in dumpsites that do not have sufficient controls to prevent its interaction with the natural environment or human receptors. These practices mainly occur in developing countries, but they are also present in more mature economies.

Globally, approximately 79 Mt (73 Mt of waste and 5 Mt of recycling residues and 1 Mt of collected litter) are mismanaged annually. Around 43% of that amount (34 Mt) is estimated to be captured in the inner part of dumpsites where degradation and interaction with the environment is close to zero. One-third (26 Mt) is burned in open, uncontrolled fires. This is mainly done by households who have to manage their waste in the absence of waste collection services, but can also be done at dumpsites where waste is combusted deliberately to reduce volume or to recover valuable metals. It can also be burned due to accidental and spontaneous fires. The remainder is considered to be lost to terrestrial and aquatic environments (Section 2.5 and Annex A). More specifically, the University of Leeds (Box 2.4) estimates that around 10% of mismanaged waste is dumped directly onto land when there is no formal waste collection, while other important leakage pathways are waste directly dumped into aquatic environments, dumped recycling residues, losses from dumpsites and losses during collection and transport.

Littered waste is a specific category of improper waste handling that unfortunately is still a problem throughout the world, even in mature economies. The amount of littered waste was more than 4 Mt globally in 2019. An estimated 3 Mt of this litter was collected via street sweeping and other actions for disposal in an industrial incinerator or a landfill; around 1 Mt was collected but then burned in open pits or sent to dumpsites; and 1 Mt remained uncollected and is likely to have been lost to the environment (Section 2.5 and Annex A). However, as has been pointed out in Boucher et al. (2020[42]), uncollected litter is exceptionally difficult to measure.

2.5. Plastic leakage is substantial

Plastic leakage has now been documented in all the major ocean basins, beaches, rivers, lakes, terrestrial environments and even in remote locations such as the Arctic and Antarctic (OECD, 2021[43]; Eriksen et al., 2014[44]). The research strand that aims to quantify the global magnitude of plastic leakage is relatively recent, but following a seminal paper by Jambeck et al. (2015[14]), several other studies have proposed models and estimates. Some researchers have focused on quantifying global plastic waste (Geyer, Jambeck and Law, 2017[1]), while others have also attempted to understand the geographical and spatial distribution of generated and mismanaged plastic waste (Lebreton and Andrady, 2019[15]). Other studies have focused on leakage into the environment (Ryberg et al., 2019[3]; Borrelle et al., 2020[45]; Lau et al., 2020[46]; Law et al., 2020[47]). Despite these efforts, there remains an urgent need to improve the understanding of the drivers and dynamics of plastics leakage and to align existing assessment methodologies (Box 2.4).

Global leakage to the environment (terrestrial and aquatic) is estimated to be 22 Mt in 2019 (Figure 2.9).[8] However, due to the variety of sources and types of leaked plastics, as well as the unintended nature of these plastic emissions into the environment, there is substantial uncertainty about each of categories of plastic leakage. Moreover, this remains a conservative estimate as only known leakage sources with sufficient data were quantified.

Figure 2.9. Global leakage of macro-and microplastics to the environment is estimated at 22 Mt

Share of total plastic leakage into the environment, 2019

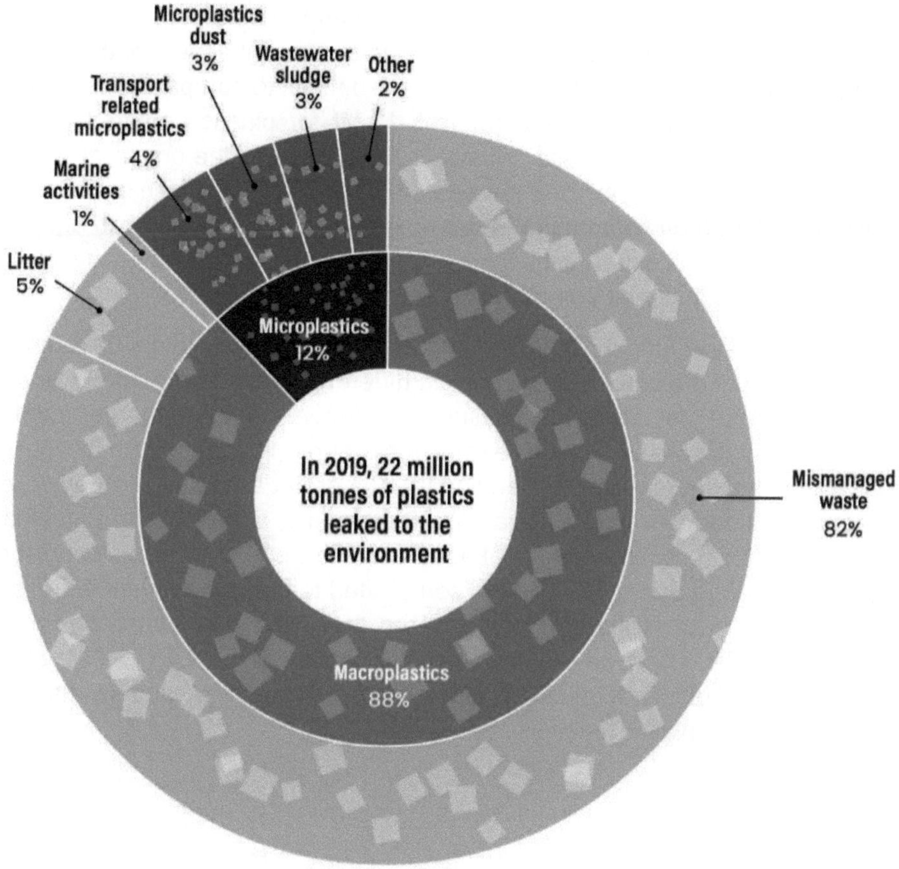

Source: OECD Global Plastics Outlook Database, https://doi.org/10.1787/c0821f81-en.

Since plastic leakage has many types and sources, leakage is often grouped into macroplastics and microplastics. Macroplastics encompass recognisable items such as littered products and packaging, while microplastics are solid synthetic polymers smaller than 5 mm in diameter (OECD, 2021[43]). Microplastics are further split into primary and secondary microplastics. Primary microplastics are plastics that are smaller than 5 mm in diameter by design, such as cosmetic scrubbing agents and biomedical uses as well as plastic pellets accidentally lost during production or handling. By contrast, secondary microplastics refer to microplastics which are formed from the fragmentation of larger plastics and are further differentiated into two categories: 1) those formed during the use phase of products, such as microplastics from tyre abrasion and synthetic microfibres from clothing and other textile products; and 2) those stemming from the degradation and fragmentation of macroplastics that have already been lost in the environment. The size of the plastic items or particles can influence, among other elements, their transport in the environment, where they are deposited and their deposition rates.

Box 2.4. State of the art in estimating the scale of the plastic leakage problem

Given that the quantification of plastic leakage is a relatively new field, studies differ in their scope, methodology and assumptions. This plurality of methods has the benefit of providing a more complete overview of the plastics issue, with each study drawing to a different aspect of the problem. However, it also means that results of earlier studies diverge and are difficult to compare. For example, Jambeck et al. (2015[48]) suggested a range of approximately 5-13 Mt for plastics emitted yearly to the ocean. Lebreton et al. (2017[49]) estimated plastics emissions from rivers to the ocean at 1.2-2.4 Mt. Lau et al. (2020[46]) estimated leakage to the environment at around 22-39 Mt, of which around 38% was released to water. Borrelle et al. (2020[45]) estimated that approximately 19-23 Mt entered aquatic environments. Each of these estimates uses different base years, definitions, estimations for plastics in use and methodologies, all of which limit their comparability.

The OECD Global Plastics Outlook Database complements the existing literature by providing a comprehensive overview of the amount of plastics in different lifecycle stages (Section 2.1). To include leakage estimations in the database and ensure the results of existing methodologies are more comparable, the OECD collaborated with three research groups: 1) a team from the Technical University of Denmark (DTU) that led the research underlying the Ryberg et al. (2019[3]) study; 2) experts from the University of Leeds who contributed to Lau et al. (2020[46]); and 3) Laurent Lebreton, who wrote research papers on plastics waste generation and leakage (Lebreton et al., 2017[49]; Lebreton and Andrady, 2019[15]; Lebreton, Egger and Slat, 2019[50]), and contributed to the leakage estimations in Borrelle et al. (2020[45]). These experts have refined and customised their analytical approaches (see Annex A) to make the most of the information on plastics use and waste in the OECD Global Plastics Outlook Database. Table 2.6 highlights how the complementary approaches used by these three research groups cover key aspects of plastic leakage.

Table 2.6. A complementary approach is needed to improve the understanding of plastic leakage

	Macroplastics			Microplastics	
	Fate of mismanaged waste flows	Leakage to environment (terrestrial and aquatic)	Leakage to aquatic environments (rivers and ocean)	Transport and degradation in aquatic environments	Comprehensive view of various categories
DTU		●			●
Laurent Lebreton			●	●	
University of Leeds	●	●	●		

Reconciling the approaches has allowed key insights to be obtained. However, the lack of empirical data to validate the modelling means that these estimations are still uncertain. Table 2.7 highlights this by showing the leakage from mismanaged waste and litter together with the upper and lower bound estimations prepared for the Global Plastics Outlook. The database has taken the average of the leakage proposed by the University of Leeds (low estimate) and the Danish Technical University (high estimate) (see Annex A for more discussion). The uncertainty ranges highlight that more research is needed to get a better grip on the current challenges.

Table 2.7. Plastic leakage is substantial despite high uncertainty surrounding the estimates

Compartment	Leakage from mismanaged waste and litter	Uncertainty ranges
Lost to environment (terrestrial and aquatic)	19 Mt	13 Mt [a] – 25 Mt [b]
Lost to aquatic environments	6 Mt	4 Mt [a] – 9 Mt [c]

Note: a) estimate made by University of Leeds, b) estimate made by DTU, c) estimate made by Laurent Lebreton.
Source: OECD Global Plastics Outlook Database, https://doi.org/10.1787/c0821f81-en.

Macroplastics account for 19.4 Mt leaked to the environment in 2019, of which 11% comes from OECD countries (Figure 2.10). Mismanaged plastic waste from municipal and non-municipal sources is the main cause of leakage (18.1 Mt – Box 2.4). The second most important source of macroplastic leakage is the littering of end-of-life plastic products (1.1 Mt). Fishing activities and other marine activities also contribute substantially to the leakage of macroplastics due to the loss or discarding of nets at sea, the abrasion of other fishing gear such as dolly ropes and other non-netting waste (0.3 Mt). The potential risks and the regional distribution of these debris emissions stress the urgency to improve waste and litter management all over the world, and especially in emerging economies. Moreover, actions are needed to reduce marine leakage from fisheries.

Figure 2.10. Leakage to the environment is high in emerging economies, especially for macroplastics

2019

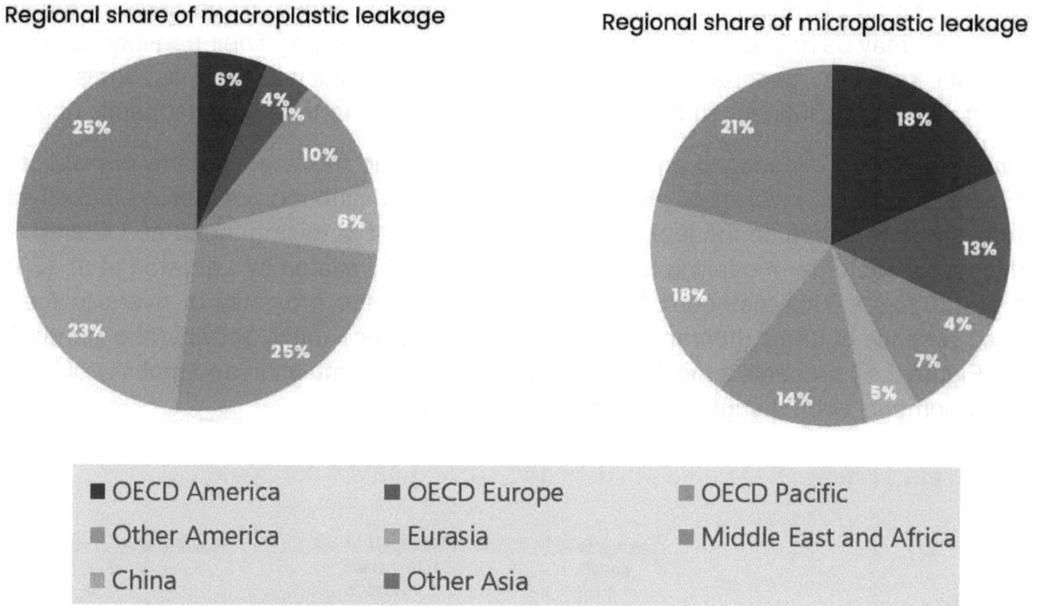

Source: OECD Global Plastics Outlook Database, https://doi.org/10.1787/c0821f81-en.

Total microplastic leakage added up to 2.7 Mt in 2019, 35% of which was generated in OECD countries. The largest source of microplastic leakage is road transport: tyre abrasion (0.7 Mt), brake wear (0.1 Mt) and eroded road markings (0.2 Mt). A second important source of microplastic leakage is the "dust" from the abrasion of shoe soles, paint wear from interior and exterior surfaces, losses from construction and demolition activities and household textile dust (in total 0.8 Mt). Other sources of microplastics are accidental losses of primary pellets, i.e. small blocks of polymers ready for conversion into products, during production, transport or storage (0.28 Mt); abrasion of artificial turf for sports and other activities (0.05 Mt); wear of marine coatings on ships (0.05 Mt); loss of synthetic fibres when washing textiles containing plastics (0.01 Mt); and microbeads intentionally added to rinse-off cosmetic and personal care products such as scrubs, shampoos and detergents (<0.01 Mt).

Additional quantities of microplastics may enter the environment when wastewater sludge is spread on farmland. Wastewater treatment plants (WWTP) filter out plastics from sewage water and concentrate them in the sludge. Since sludge is commonly used as compost on agricultural fields in many countries, some of the microplastics captured during WWT may end up in terrestrial environments (Nizzetto, Futter and Langaas, 2016[51]; OECD, 2017[52]).

This study only included emission sources for which sufficient data were available. However, there could be many others to include (e.g. synthetic fibres lost during other lifecycle phases). Also, the understanding of what influences microplastic losses is still limited, so is the current understanding of the fate of microplastics once leaked into the environment. Whilst more research is needed to develop a thorough accounting of pollution levels and risks, this should not prevent policies from being implemented to reduce microplastics leakage (OECD, 2021[43]).

2.5.1. Plastics enter and accumulate in the aquatic environment through complex pathways

Transport of plastics in the environment is extraordinarily complex and the current understanding of the behaviour of plastics released into the environment is incomplete. Plastics can be transported within and released to three types of environments: terrestrial, aquatic and atmospheric. When plastics are emitted to the environment, the size, weight and characteristics of polymers determine how they are transported. For example, high-density plastics such as PVC tend to remain close to the source of leakage, while a less dense polymer such as LDPE can be transported over large distances. Regardless of density, plastic objects and articles may be hollow, trapping air which allows them to float. Their transport is also governed by local weather patterns, geography and the presence of obstacles such as dams and the built environment. It can also be influenced by extreme events such as earthquakes, tsunamis and hurricanes.

As shown in Figure 2.9, mismanaged and littered waste make up the largest share of plastics leaked to the environment. In order to investigate the amount and spatial distribution of plastics leaked into aquatic environments, the data above on the leakage to the environment of mismanaged and littered waste was used in conjunction with other modelling tools that build on work initiated by Lebreton et al. (2019[50]) and Borrelle et al. (2020[45]). This methodology takes into account the proximity of rivers to the source of emission, the presence of dams, human habitation and coastal economic activity (see Annex A for more information). Figure 2.11 presents a highly stylised view of the accumulation and mobility of macroplastics in aquatic environments even though there are still many unknowns.

Figure 2.11. Rivers accumulate leaked plastics and carry them to the ocean

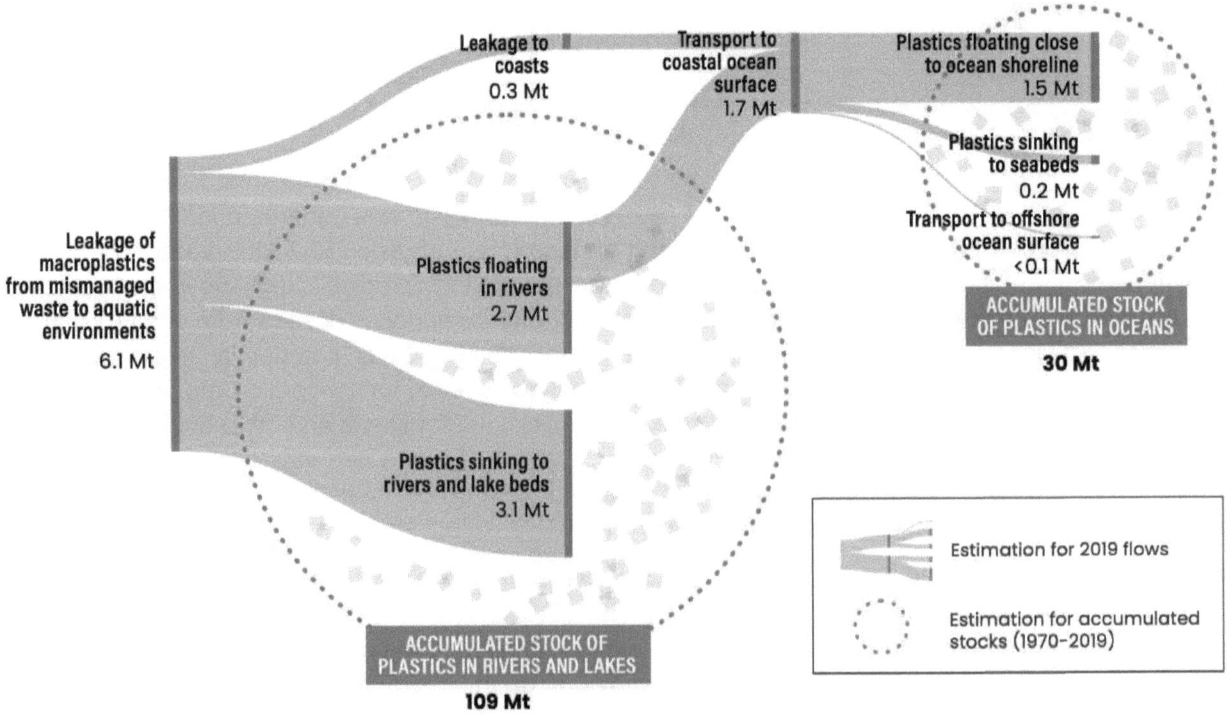

Source: OECD Global Plastics Outlook Database, https://doi.org/10.1787/c0821f81-en.

Once plastics are in aquatic environments, a complex set of factors influences their transportation, including wind, precipitation patterns, river flow and oceanic currents. High-density plastics, e.g. PET or PVC, are likely to sink to lower levels of the water column close to the point of entry into rivers or seas, while low-density polymers (e.g. PE and PP) and air-filled plastic items (e.g. bottles) may stay afloat and be transported for long distances. Other effects may play a role, such as the creation of biofilms on plastics which increases overall density and probability of sinking to the river or sea bed (Schwarz et al., 2019[53]; Tosin et al., 2012[54]). Floating plastics that make it to the ocean tend to accumulate in gyres, such as the Great Pacific Garbage Patch, due to the convergence of the marine currents (GESAMP, 2015[55]).

The estimates for leakage to aquatic environments (6.1 Mt in 2019) and especially inflows into ocean (1.7 Mt in 2019) are lower than most earlier studies that estimated global leakage to water (Jambeck et al., 2015[48]; Lau et al., 2020[46]; Borrelle et al., 2020[45]) (Box 2.4). In addition to using different methodologies, two sets of assumptions drive these differences.

The first set of assumptions relates to the fate of mismanaged waste. The OECD methodology relies on detailed waste management modelling that assumes that one-third of the mismanaged plastic waste and residues is burned in open pits, either locally or in dumpsites – a practice is environmentally harmful and should be discouraged. However, it reduces the amount of plastics that can potentially end up in water (Velis and Cook, 2021[56]). In addition, the waste management modelling assumes that around 44% of all mismanaged waste is buried in the core of dumpsites, where it will remain for decades or even centuries. While this risks leakage of hazardous substances and pollution of groundwater, apart from major incidents, the volumes of plastics leaking to surface waters are small (Cook, 2020[57]). Taken together, these two assumptions imply that less than a quarter of mismanaged plastic waste will end up in terrestrial and aquatic environments, which is lower than the shares put forward by most other studies.

The second set of assumptions concerns the transport of plastics leaked to the environment. The approach used in this report estimates that around 32% of leaked plastics end up in aquatic environments (the rest accumulates in terrestrial environments). Other studies assume higher values. For example, Lau et al. (2020[46]) use a ratio of 38%. Moreover, the OECD estimations for inflow into the ocean build on detailed modelling of the transport and stock of plastics in rivers (Meijer et al., 2021[58]). The projected accumulation in rivers (109 Mt in 2019) slows down the inflow of plastics to the ocean and consequently gives, in the short term, lower estimations for the leakage to seas and ocean. Altogether, the volumes put forward in this chapter can therefore be considered to be conservative estimations.

Once in aquatic environments, plastics are transformed further. They degrade slowly through exposure to UV radiation, temperature differences and physical abrasion. As the material weathers, macroplastics will fragment into microplastics and potentially into nanoplastics. The amount of microplastics produced via the degradation of macroplastics in 2019 is estimated at 0.15 Mt in rivers and lakes, and 0.10 Mt in the ocean. The degradation is highest in rivers and lakes because these contain the largest stocks of accumulated macroplastics. In the ocean, degradation mainly occurs close to the shore where the movement of leaked plastics is intensive due to waves and currents (see Annex A for more information on the methodology).

The buoyancy of plastics also changes when they undergo degradation, fragmentation and fouling. Most fragmented plastics tend to settle below the ocean surface, ultimately reaching sediments, which are considered a final sink for plastic debris. This is supported by the finding that microplastics are much less abundant on the sea surface than larger macroplastics (Eriksen et al., 2014[44]). Some estimates suggest that over 90% of plastics that enter the ocean end up in sediments and in the lower levels of the oceanic water column (GESAMP, 2015[55]). Macroplastics probably stay longer on the surface. Research has found that large shares of plastic debris sampled on the ocean's surface are decades-old (Lebreton, Egger and Slat, 2019[50]). The force of waves and currents around the coast may be circulating plastics above and below the waterline for a long time before plastic debris reaches the open ocean. Further research is needed to better understand the dynamics of plastics in aquatic environments and to design effective ways to prevent or remove risks.

2.5.2. Microplastics from road transport can pollute the air over wide areas

Road transport, and in particular the wear of tyres and brake pads, is one of the main sources of aerial microplastic pollution. Globally in 2019, airborne emissions from tyres were 16 times larger than emissions from brakes, but brakes are responsible for a larger share of fine particulate matter ($PM_{2.5}$, i.e. particles with a diameter below 2.5 µm), which may have more severe health impacts (Evangeliou et al., 2020[59]; OECD, 2020[60]). Road transport-related microplastics are emitted mainly in large urban agglomerations, such as the eastern part of North America, continental Europe and Northeast Asia (Figure 2.12).

While the majority of microplastic emissions tends to remain close to their source, where they increase the concentration levels of PM at ground level, some particles can travel long distances, depending on the location and atmospheric conditions (Figure 2.12). Substantial amounts of deposited microplastics have been found in remote regions (Evangeliou et al., 2020[59]), including mountain regions and the Arctic (Allen et al., 2019[61]; Lusher et al., 2015[62]). In the Arctic, the light-absorbing properties of tyre wear particles may accelerate atmospheric warming, with possible consequences for the balance of the global climate (OECD, 2021[63]).

Figure 2.12. Aerial microplastic pollution from road transport is highest in highly urbanised areas

Total suspended PM depositions from tyres and brakes in 2019, mg/m^3

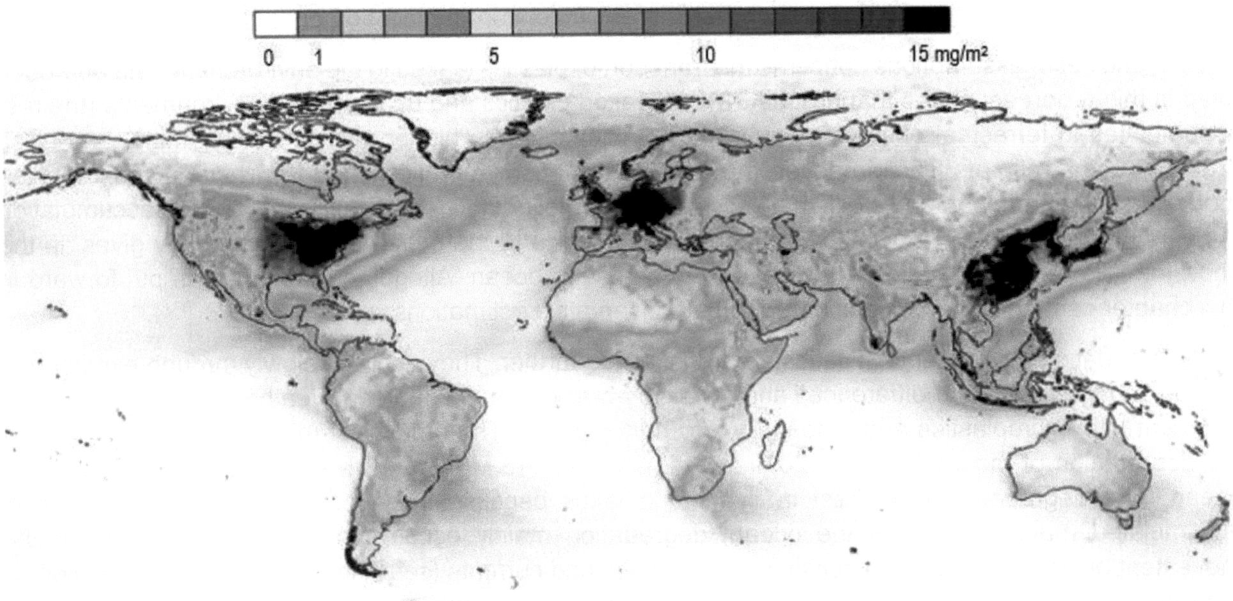

Note: The map displays total suspended PM_{10} (particles of diameter inferior to 10 µm), including particulate matter emissions of smaller sizes (PM_1 and $PM_{2.5}$).
Source: OECD Global Plastics Outlook Database.

Policies can lower transport-related microplastics emissions by reducing the amount of emissions that vehicles generate and the total number of kilometres that vehicles are driven (OECD, 2020[60]). Potential mitigation measures include incentives for producing lighter-weight vehicles, regulating tyre composition and reducing the vehicle-kilometres travelled by regulating urban vehicle access, and promoting public transport, walking and cycling in urban areas. Policy makers should also prioritise research on the magnitude and impacts of non-exhaust particulate emissions from road transport and the effectiveness of mitigation measures to address them. Standardised approaches are needed for measuring non-exhaust particulate matter and developing a better understanding of how various factors (e.g. vehicle characteristics) influence the amount of non-exhaust particulate matter generated.

2.6. Plastic leakage has a variety of environmental, health and economic consequences

The proliferation of plastics combined with poor end-of-life waste management has resulted in widespread, persistent plastic leakage. The longevity of plastics is of particular concern. For example, single-use plastic products like LDPE plastic bags and HDPE milk bottles could have estimated half-lives of 5-250 years on land and 3-58 years in marine environments (Chamas et al., 2020[64]). On the other hand, HDPE pipes need thousands of years to completely degrade, with an estimated half-life of 1 200 years (Chamas et al., 2020[64]).

In aquatic environments, the most visible negative effects on marine wildlife are the entanglement of marine organisms in floating plastic debris and increased mortality following the ingestion of macro and microplastics by marine species such as mussels, turtles, fish and sea birds. At least 690 wildlife species, as well as coral reefs, are known to be affected (Gall and Thompson, 2015[65]). However, the negative consequences of plastics extend beyond these first order impacts. Microplastics have been documented in the digestive tract of several types of mussels and fish destined for human consumption (Lusher, Hollman and Mendoza-Hill, 2017[66]). Thus, the ingestion of seafood contaminated with microplastics has also been identified as a potentially substantial exposure pathway for humans.

Microplastic contamination is not exclusive to marine environments – it has also been documented in freshwater and terrestrial environments, as well as in food and beverages, such as tap water, bottled water and beer (Kosuth, Mason and Wattenberg, 2018[67]; Mintenig et al., 2019[68]). Humans are also exposed to microplastics by inhaling airborne particles and fibres, and microplastics have been reported both in indoor and outdoor environments (Gasperi et al., 2017[69]; Allen et al., 2019[61]). The main studies of human health impacts of airborne microplastics have looked at exposure to non-exhaust road traffic emissions (Figure 2.12).

Plastics may also act as a sink and transportation media for chemicals and persistent organic pollutants (POPs), which accumulate on the surface of plastics while in seawater. Adsorbed chemicals found on sampled plastic debris include PCBs, PAHs, DDE (a breakdown product of DDT) and trace metals (Engler, 2012[70]; Teuten et al., 2007[71]).[9] Plastic fragmentation may enhance leaching of chemical substances to the surrounding environment. Nanoplastics are of particular concern because their small size allows them to potentially be transferred to tissues or cells (SAPEA, 2019[72]).

Furthermore, marine plastic leakage has substantial economic costs for coastal communities due to potential negative impacts on fishing and tourism. Plastics can affect the sustainability of fisheries, while plastic leakage on beaches deters visitors, causing financial distress to local communities reliant on tourism. Beaumont et al. (2019[73]) estimate the economic costs of the loss of marine ecosystem services to be around USD 3 300 per tonne of marine plastic per year.

A major challenge posed by plastics in the environment is the considerable uncertainty about the magnitude of the damage. Firstly, there are still important gaps in the current understanding of the plastic-health-biosphere links. Secondly, there are important uncertainties surrounding the quantities of plastics entering the environment and their accumulation. Ultimately, the estimation of the exact volume of plastic leakage is secondary to the intrinsic message from all these studies: plastic leakage is a major environmental problem and it is getting worse. The longevity of plastics means that the effects of today's plastic leakage could become much larger in the future, causing long-term and potentially irreversible additional damage. The urgency to act for policy makers as well as other societal decision makers is high.

References

Aguiar, A. et al. (2019), "The GTAP Data Base: Version 10", *Journal of Global Economic Analysis*, Vol. 4/1, pp. 1-27, http://dx.doi.org/10.21642/jgea.040101af. [6]

Akanuma, Y., S. Selke and R. Auras (2014), "A preliminary LCA case study: comparison of different pathways to produce purified terephthalic acid suitable for synthesis of 100 % bio-based PET", *The International Journal of Life Cycle Assessment*, Vol. 19/6, pp. 1238-1246, http://dx.doi.org/10.1007/s11367-014-0725-2. [28]

Allen, S. et al. (2019), "Atmospheric transport and deposition of microplastics in a remote mountain catchment", *Nature Geoscience*, Vol. 12/5, pp. 339-344, http://dx.doi.org/10.1038/s41561-019-0335-5. [61]

Beaumont, N. et al. (2019), "Global ecological, social and economic impacts of marine plastic", *Marine Pollution Bulletin*, Vol. 142, pp. 189-195, http://dx.doi.org/10.1016/j.marpolbul.2019.03.022. [73]

Borrelle, S. et al. (2020), "Predicted growth in plastic waste exceeds efforts to mitigate plastic pollution", *Science*, Vol. 369/6510, pp. 1515-1518, http://dx.doi.org/10.1126/science.aba3656. [45]

Boucher, J. et al. (2020), *The marine plastic footprint*, IUCN, International Union for Conservation of Nature, http://dx.doi.org/10.2305/IUCN.CH.2020.01.en. [42]

Brizga, J., K. Hubacek and K. Feng (2020), "The Unintended Side Effects of Bioplastics: Carbon, Land, and Water Footprints", *One Earth*, Vol. 3/1, pp. 45-53, http://dx.doi.org/10.1016/j.oneear.2020.06.016. [23]

Broeren, M. et al. (2017), "Environmental impact assessment of six starch plastics focusing on wastewater-derived starch and additives", *Resources, Conservation and Recycling*, Vol. 127, pp. 246-255, http://dx.doi.org/10.1016/j.resconrec.2017.09.001. [30]

Chamas, A. et al. (2020), "Degradation Rates of Plastics in the Environment", *ACS Sustainable Chemistry & Engineering*, Vol. 8/9, pp. 3494-3511, http://dx.doi.org/10.1021/acssuschemeng.9b06635. [64]

Chateau, J., R. Dellink and E. Lanzi (2014), "An Overview of the OECD ENV-Linkages Model: Version 3", *OECD Environment Working Papers*, No. 65, OECD Publishing, Paris, http://dx.doi.org/10.1787/5jz2qck2b2vd-en. [5]

Chen, G. and M. Patel (2011), "Plastics Derived from Biological Sources: Present and Future: A Technical and Environmental Review", *Chemical Reviews*, Vol. 112/4, pp. 2082-2099, http://dx.doi.org/10.1021/cr200162d. [31]

Chruszcz, A. and S. Reeve (2018), "Composition of plastic waste collected via kerbside. Banbury, UK: W. a. R. A. P. (WRAP)", https://www.wrap.org.uk/sites/files/wrap/Composition%20of%20Plastic%20Waste%20Collected%20via%20Kerbside%20v2.pdf. [10]

Civancik-Uslu, D. et al. (2021), "Moving from linear to circular household plastic packaging in Belgium: Prospective life cycle assessment of mechanical and thermochemical recycling", *Resources Conservation and Recycling*, Vol. 171, p. 105633, http://dx.doi.org/10.1016/j.resconrec.2021.105633. [40]

Colmenar-Santos, A. et al. (2018), "Technological improvements in energetic efficiency and sustainability in existing combined-cycle gas turbine (CCGT) power plants", *Applied Energy*, Vol. 223, pp. 30-51, http://dx.doi.org/10.1016/j.apenergy.2018.03.191. [35]

Cook, E. (2020), *Global review on safer end of engineered life.*. [57]

Cottom, J., E. Cook and C. Velis (2020), "Spatio-temporal quantification of plastic pollution origins and transportation (SPOT)" University of Leeds, UK, https://plasticpollution.leeds.ac.uk/toolkits/spot/. [9]

Dijkgraaf, E. and H. Vollebergh (2004), "Burn or bury? A social cost comparison of final waste disposal methods", *Ecological Economics*, Vol. 50/3-4, pp. 233-247, http://dx.doi.org/10.1016/j.ecolecon.2004.03.029. [37]

Dubois, M. (2013), "Towards a coherent European approach for taxation of combustible waste", *Waste Management*, Vol. 33/8, http://dx.doi.org/10.1016/j.wasman.2013.03.015. [38]

Ecoprog (2020), *Waste to Energy 2020/2021*, https://www.ecoprog.com/fileadmin/user_upload/extract_market_report_WtE_2020-2021_ecoprog.pdf (accessed on 26 May 2021). [36]

Engler, R. (2012), "The Complex Interaction between Marine Debris and Toxic Chemicals in the Ocean", *Environmental Science & Technology*, Vol. 46/22, pp. 12302-12315, http://dx.doi.org/10.1021/es3027105. [70]

Eriksen, M. et al. (2014), "Plastic Pollution in the World's Oceans: More than 5 Trillion Plastic Pieces Weighing over 250,000 Tons Afloat at Sea", *PLOS ONE*, Vol. 9/12, p. e111913, https://doi.org/10.1371/journal.pone.0111913. [44]

European Bioplastics (2019), *Bioplastics market data 2019 - Global production capacities of bioplastics 2019-2024*. [22]

Evangeliou, N. et al. (2020), "Atmospheric transport is a major pathway of microplastics to remote regions", *Nature Communications*, Vol. 11/1, p. 3381, http://dx.doi.org/10.1038/s41467-020-17201-9. [59]

Franklin Associates (2018), *Life cycle impacts of plastic packaging compared to substitutes in the United States and Canada: Theoretical substitution analysis*, https://www.americanchemistry.com/better-policy-regulation/plastics/resources/life-cycle-impacts-of-plastic-packaging-compared-to-substitutes-in-the-united-states-and-canada. [20]

Gall, S. and R. Thompson (2015), "The impact of debris on marine life", *Marine Pollution Bulletin*, Vol. 92/1-2, pp. 170-179, http://dx.doi.org/10.1016/j.marpolbul.2014.12.041. [65]

Gasperi, J. et al. (2017), "Microplastics in air: Are we breathing it in?", *Current Opinion in Environmental Science & Health*, Vol. 1, pp. 1-5, http://dx.doi.org/10.1016/j.coesh.2017.10.002. [69]

GESAMP (2015), *Sources, fate and effects of microplastics in the marine environment: a global assessment*, IMO/FAO/UNESCO-IOC/UNIDO/WMO/IAEA/UN/UNEP/UNDP Joint Group of Experts on the Scientific Aspects of Marine Environmental Protection), http://www.imo.org. [55]

Geyer, R., J. Jambeck and K. Law (2017), "Production, use, and fate of all plastics ever made", *Science Advances*, Vol. 3/7, p. e1700782, http://dx.doi.org/10.1126/sciadv.1700782. [1]

Gómez-Sanabria, A. et al. (2018), "Carbon in global waste and wastewater flows – its potential as energy source under alternative future waste management regimes", *Advances in Geosciences*, Vol. 45, pp. 105-113, http://dx.doi.org/10.5194/adgeo-45-105-2018. [17]

Grand View Research (2020), *Recycled Plastics Market: Market Analysis*. [8]

IEA (2018), *The future of petrochemicals: Towards more sustainable plastics and fertilisers*, International Energy Agency, Paris, https://dx.doi.org/10.1787/9789264307414-en. [2]

IPCC (1995), *Climate Change 1995: A report of the Intergovernmental Panel on Climate Change - IPCC Second Assessment*. [74]

Jambeck, J. et al. (2015), "Plastic waste inputs from land into the ocean", *Science*, Vol. 347/6223, pp. 768-771, http://dx.doi.org/10.1126/science.1260352. [14]

Jambeck, J. et al. (2015), "Plastic waste inputs from land into the ocean", *Science*, Vol. 347/6223, pp. 768-771, http://dx.doi.org/10.1126/science.1260352. [48]

Kaza, S. et al. (2018), *What a Waste 2.0: A Global Snapshot of Solid Waste Management to 2050*, The World Bank, http://dx.doi.org/10.1596/978-1-4648-1329-0. [13]

Kosuth, M., S. Mason and E. Wattenberg (2018), "Anthropogenic contamination of tap water, beer, and sea salt", *PLoS ONE*, Vol. 13/4, http://dx.doi.org/10.1371/journal.pone.0194970. [67]

Lau, W. et al. (2020), "Evaluating scenarios toward zero plastic pollution", *Science*, Vol. 369/6510, pp. 1455-1461, http://dx.doi.org/10.1126/science.aba9475. [46]

Law, K. et al. (2020), "The United States' contribution of plastic waste to land and ocean", *Science Advances*, Vol. 6/44, p. eabd0288, http://dx.doi.org/10.1126/sciadv.abd0288. [47]

Lazarevic, D. et al. (2010), "Plastic waste management in the context of a European recycling society: Comparing results and uncertainties in a life cycle perspective", *Resources, Conservation and Recycling*, Vol. 55/2, pp. 246-259, http://dx.doi.org/10.1016/j.resconrec.2010.09.014. [39]

Lebreton, L. and A. Andrady (2019), "Future scenarios of global plastic waste generation and disposal", *Palgrave Communications*, Vol. 5/1, p. 6, http://dx.doi.org/10.1057/s41599-018-0212-7. [15]

Lebreton, L., M. Egger and B. Slat (2019), "A global mass budget for positively buoyant macroplastic debris in the ocean", *Scientific Reports*, Vol. 9/1, p. 12922, http://dx.doi.org/10.1038/s41598-019-49413-5. [50]

Lebreton, L. et al. (2017), "River plastic emissions to the world's oceans", *Nature Communications*, Vol. 8/1, http://dx.doi.org/10.1038/ncomms15611. [49]

Liptow, C. and A. Tillman (2012), "A Comparative Life Cycle Assessment Study of Polyethylene Based on Sugarcane and Crude Oil", *Journal of Industrial Ecology*, Vol. 16/3, pp. 420-435, http://dx.doi.org/10.1111/j.1530-9290.2011.00405.x. [24]

Lombardi, L., E. Carnevale and A. Corti (2015), "A review of technologies and performances of thermal treatment systems for energy recovery from waste", *Waste Management*, Vol. 37, pp. 26-44, http://dx.doi.org/10.1016/j.wasman.2014.11.010. [33]

Lusher, A., P. Hollman and J. Mendoza-Hill (2017), *Microplastics in fisheries and aquaculture: status of knowledge on their occurrence and implications for aquatic organisms and food safety*, FAO Fisheries and Aquaculture Technical Paper. No. 615, Rome, Italy. [66]

Lusher, A. et al. (2015), "Microplastics in Arctic polar waters: The first reported values of particles in surface and sub-surface samples", *Scientific Reports*, Vol. 5, http://dx.doi.org/10.1038/srep14947. [62]

Meijer, L. et al. (2021), "More than 1000 rivers account for 80% of global riverine plastic emissions into the ocean", *Science Advances*, Vol. 7/18, http://dx.doi.org/10.1126/sciadv.aaz5803. [58]

Mintenig, S. et al. (2019), "Low numbers of microplastics detected in drinking water from ground water sources", *Science of the Total Environment*, Vol. 648, pp. 631-635, http://dx.doi.org/10.1016/j.scitotenv.2018.08.178. [68]

Neuwahl, F. et al. (2019), *Best Available Techniques (BAT) Reference Document for Waste Incineration:Industrial Emissions Directive 2010/75/EU (Integrated Pollution Prevention and Control)*, Publications Office of the European Union, Luxembourg,, http://dx.doi.org/doi:10.2760/761437. [32]

Nizzetto, L., M. Futter and S. Langaas (2016), *Are Agricultural Soils Dumps for Microplastics of Urban Origin?*, American Chemical Society, http://dx.doi.org/10.1021/acs.est.6b04140. [51]

OECD (2021), *Policies to Reduce Microplastics Pollution in Water: Focus on Textiles and Tyres*, OECD Publishing, Paris, https://dx.doi.org/10.1787/7ec7e5ef-en. [43]

OECD (2021), *The Economic Benefits of Air Quality Improvements in Arctic Council Countries*, OECD Publishing, Paris, https://dx.doi.org/10.1787/9c46037d-en. [63]

OECD (2020), *Non-exhaust Particulate Emissions from Road Transport: An Ignored Environmental Policy Challenge*, OECD Publishing, Paris, https://dx.doi.org/10.1787/4a4dc6ca-en. [60]

OECD (2017), "Water: Sewage sludge production and disposal (Edition 2017)", *OECD Environment Statistics* (database), https://dx.doi.org/10.1787/14780a65-en (accessed on 20 February 2020). [52]

Pavlas, M. et al. (2011), "Waste incineration with production of clean and reliable energy", *Clean Technologies and Environmental Policy*, Vol. 13/4, pp. 595-605, http://dx.doi.org/10.1007/s10098-011-0353-5. [34]

Plastics Europe (2020), *Plastics - the Facts: an analysis of European plastics production, demand and waste data*. [4]

Roosen, M. et al. (2020), "Detailed Analysis of the Composition of Selected Plastic Packaging Waste Products and Its Implications for Mechanical and Thermochemical Recycling", *Environmental Science & Technology*, Vol. 54/20, pp. 13282-13293, http://dx.doi.org/10.1021/acs.est.0c03371. [11]

Royer, S. et al. (2018), "Production of methane and ethylene from plastic in the environment", *PLOS ONE*, Vol. 13/8, http://dx.doi.org/10.1371/journal.pone.0200574. [19]

Ryberg, M. et al. (2019), "Global environmental losses of plastics across their value chains", *Resources, Conservation and Recycling*, Vol. 151, p. 104459, http://dx.doi.org/10.1016/j.resconrec.2019.104459. [3]

SAPEA (2019), *A Scientific Perspective on Micro-Plastics in Nature and Society*, Science Advice for Policy by European Academics, http://dx.doi.org/10.26356/microplastics. [72]

Schwarz, A. et al. (2019), "Sources, transport, and accumulation of different types of plastic litter in aquatic environments: A review study", *Marine Pollution Bulletin*, Vol. 143, pp. 92-100, http://dx.doi.org/10.1016/J.MARPOLBUL.2019.04.029. [53]

Semba, T. et al. (2018), "Greenhouse gas emissions of 100% bio-derived polyethylene terephthalate on its life cycle compared with petroleum-derived polyethylene terephthalate", *Journal of Cleaner Production*, Vol. 195, pp. 932-938, http://dx.doi.org/10.1016/j.jclepro.2018.05.069. [29]

Shen, M. et al. (2020), "(Micro)plastic crisis: Un-ignorable contribution to global greenhouse gas emissions and climate change", *Journal of Cleaner Production*, Vol. 254, p. 120138, http://dx.doi.org/10.1016/j.jclepro.2020.120138. [18]

Stadler, K. et al. (2018), "EXIOBASE 3: Developing a Time Series of Detailed Environmentally Extended Multi-Regional Input-Output Tables", *Journal of Industrial Ecology*, Vol. 22/3, pp. 502-515, http://dx.doi.org/10.1111/jiec.12715. [7]

Stefanini, R. et al. (2020), "Plastic or glass: a new environmental assessment with a marine litter indicator for the comparison of pasteurized milk bottles", *The International Journal of Life Cycle Assessment*, Vol. 26/4, pp. 767-784, http://dx.doi.org/10.1007/s11367-020-01804-x. [21]

Teuten, E. et al. (2007), "Potential for plastics to transport hydrophobic contaminants", *Environmental Science and Technology*, Vol. 41/22, pp. 7759-7764, http://dx.doi.org/10.1021/es071737s. [71]

Tosin, M. et al. (2012), "Laboratory Test Methods to Determine the Degradation of Plastics in Marine Environmental Conditions", *Frontiers in Microbiology*, Vol. 3, p. 225, http://dx.doi.org/10.3389/fmicb.2012.00225. [54]

Tsiropoulos, I. et al. (2015), "Life cycle impact assessment of bio-based plastics from sugarcane ethanol", *Journal of Cleaner Production*, Vol. 90, pp. 114-127, http://dx.doi.org/10.1016/j.jclepro.2014.11.071. [27]

UNEP (2019), *Waste to Energy: considerations for informed decision-making*, https://wedocs.unep.org/bitstream/handle/20.500.11822/28413/WTEfull.pdf?sequence=1&isAllowed=y. [41]

Vanderreydt, I. et al. (forthcoming), *European Environment Agency: European Topic Centre on Waste and Materials in a Green Economy.* [26]

Velis, C. and E. Cook (2021), "Mismanagement of Plastic Waste through Open Burning with Emphasis on the Global South: A Systematic Review of Risks to Occupational and Public Health", *Environmental Science & Technology*, Vol. 55/11, pp. 7186-7207, http://dx.doi.org/10.1021/acs.est.0c08536. [56]

VinylPlus (2019), "PVC Recycling in Action", https://vinylplus.eu/uploads/images/Leaflets/Recovinyl_21x21_04-05_web.pdf. [12]

Walker, S. and R. Rothman (2020), "Life cycle assessment of bio-based and fossil-based plastic: A review", *Journal of Cleaner Production*, Vol. 261, p. 121158, http://dx.doi.org/10.1016/j.jclepro.2020.121158. [25]

Zheng, J. and S. Suh (2019), "Strategies to reduce the global carbon footprint of plastics", *Nature Climate Change*, Vol. 9/5, pp. 374-378, http://dx.doi.org/10.1038/s41558-019-0459-z. [16]

Notes

[1] https://doi.org/10.1787/c0821f81-en.

[2] The GTAP 10 database details social accounting matrices for 141 countries and regions, with global coverage. This database describes bilateral trade patterns, production, consumption and intermediate use of commodities and services, including capital, labour and tax revenues and use. This database is at the basis of the OECD ENV-Linkages model's representation of economic flows, which feeds into the Global Plastics Outlook Database.

[3] The cross-country regressions based on the *What a waste 2.0 database* (Kaza et al., 2018[13]) include:
(a) $waste\_pc_i = \alpha + \beta * ln(gdp\_pc_i) + r_i$
(b) $inc_i/(inc_i + dis_i) = \alpha + \beta * ln(gdp\_pc_i) + r_i$
(c) $mis_i/dis_i = \alpha + \beta * ln(gdp\_pc_i) + oecd_i$
where waste_pc = MSW per capita, MIS = mismanaged waste, inc = incinerated waste, dis = mismanaged + landfilled, gdp_pc = GDP per capita, oecd = dummy for OECD economies, r = regional dummies for 15 regions of ENV-Linkages, i = country.

[4] With the exception of a slight dip in demand during the global financial crisis of 2008-09, providing evidence for the correlation between economic growth and plastics use.

[5] Greenhouse gases are aggregated using 100-year global warming potentials of 310 for N_2O, 21 for CH_4, and 1 for CO_2 (IPCC, 1995[74]).

[6] The COVID-19 pandemic has caused some shifts in plastics use by polymer. The size and permanency of these shifts are, however, too uncertain to use as basis for the analysis in this report.

[7] The COVID-19 pandemic caused some disruptions to recycling in 2020, but these tended to be short-lived.

[8] There is anecdotal evidence that since the start of the pandemic, a significant portion of face masks have leaked to the environment (Chapter 3). In terms of volume, this effect is however limited.

[9] PCBs refer to polychlorinated biphenyls, PAHs to polycyclic aromatic hydrocarbon, DDE to dichlorodiphenyldichloroethylene and DDT to dichlorodiphenyltrichloroethane.

3. The effects of the COVID-19 pandemic on plastics use and waste

This chapter investigates the effects of the COVID-19 pandemic and lockdown measures on the production, use and waste of plastics, focusing on the short-term effects in the year 2020, in order to shed light on the complex interactions between the effects of COVD-19 on economic activity and plastics use. It first looks at emerging evidence for the pandemic's impact on specific uses and sectors, followed by an overview of the effects on waste and recycling. It then reports on the results of a detailed OECD modelling framework used to assess the consequences of COVID-induced changes in sectoral and regional economic activity on plastics use more broadly. It ends with a brief discussion of the possible longer-term implications of the pandemic on plastics use.

KEY MESSAGES

- In 2020, the COVID-19 pandemic and lockdown measures had a significant impact on plastics production, use and waste. In most sectors, plastics use declined in line with the reduction in demand and output, especially for large-scale plastics-using sectors such as motor vehicles, trade and construction. Global plastics use in 2020 is estimated to have declined in 2020 by around 10 million tonnes (Mt) or 2.2%, which is 4.5% below the pre-COVID projection for 2020.
- This reduction is substantially smaller than the decline in overall economic activity, with the annual global gross domestic product (GDP) growth rate dropping from around +4% in 2019 to -3.5% in 2020. Consequently, the plastics intensity of the economy increased on average despite the pandemic.
- In some sectors, especially healthcare, plastics use increased significantly – for instance for face masks and other personal protective equipment. Plastics use for face masks and other personal protective equipment is estimated to be around 300 kilotonnes, i.e. less than 0.1% of total plastics use in 2020, or a few percent of the overall impact of the pandemic on plastics use.
- In other sectors, the nature of economic activity changed, for instance from eating in restaurants to take-away, and from in-store shopping to online retail (e-commerce). The net effects of such shifts are unclear at the time of writing of this report, but the boosted activities use significant amounts of single-use plastics. Plastics use declined in industrial sectors, with plastics use in construction and motor vehicles, respectively, estimated to have declined by 4.6 and 2.6 Mt from 2019 levels.
- The pandemic has also resulted in significant disruptions to plastics recycling. This is due to the temporary halting of separate collection in some municipalities, a temporary shift to single-use plastics, disruptions to waste plastic trade, as well as a temporary loss of competitiveness of recycled plastics linked to the low price of oil and resulting low prices for primary plastics.
- Plastics waste has been affected by the pandemic in the short run by a switch to single-use plastics and a switch from industrial and commercial waste to household waste. In 2020, while total plastic waste may have remained roughly stable, municipal plastic waste most likely increased, although robust information is not yet available. However, a significant portion of the effects on plastic waste will be delayed to future years due to the long lifespan of many plastics uses.
- The increase in the use of protective personal equipment and single-use plastics has exacerbated plastic littering on land and in marine environments, with negative environmental consequences. While OECD countries are more likely to spend additional funds to collect litter from cities, non-OECD countries face the risk of plastic litter on land infiltrating the environment.

3.1. The Covid-19 pandemic has disrupted the economy and the use of plastics

The coronavirus that is the cause of an infectious disease known as COVID-19, first discovered in Wuhan in the People's Republic of China in December 2019, spread to other countries and continents in less than a few months and triggered a global health pandemic. Governments responded to the emerging crisis with a range of measures to contain the spread, especially limiting the movement of people and goods and shutting down economic activity.

The COVID-19 pandemic and the associated lockdown measures have led to a significant contraction in the global economy (OECD, 2021[1]; IMF, 2020[2]). Around the world, economic activity shrank as supply, demand and trade were suddenly severely disrupted (Dellink et al., 2021[3]). Recovery will be a long-term process and economic activity will likely be affected even after the health crisis is over.[1]

The COVID-19 pandemic has also highlighted the importance of plastics in our daily lives. Given their properties, plastics are particularly well-suited for personal protective equipment (PPE) such as surgical face masks, single-use medical tools and packaging. Plastics are lightweight; can be resistant to external shocks, contamination and moisture; can be flexible; and offer various degrees of opacity. For instance, polyvinyl chloride (PVC) offers the durability required for surgical gloves (Hamann, Sullivan and Wright, 2014[4]). Another example is polypropylene (PP) which is largely used in food packaging as it is resistant to external influences and has a high melting point, making it suitable for microwavable containers (Marsh and Bugusu, 2007[5]). Plastics are also often less expensive to manufacture than alternatives, such as aluminium, and also cheaper to transport than heavier materials such as glass (Marsh and Bugusu, 2007[5]). Finally, single-use plastic items such as face masks and medical tools can reduce the potential spread of diseases and viruses effectively, as long as they are disposed of in a sanitary manner.

The use of plastics is also ubiquitous in sectors that were negatively affected by the pandemic, such as transport and construction – each accounting for more than 10% of annual plastic use before the COVID-19 pandemic. Meanwhile, sectors such as retail and food services saw a significant shift away from in-store shopping and restaurants towards e-commerce, take-away and food delivery, with mixed effects on plastics use. Thus, because plastics are used in different applications by many sectors, the overall effect of the COVID-19 pandemic on plastics use in 2020 remains unclear. Effects should become clearer when new evidence and data on plastics use in the different applications and sectors becomes available over time. Annex B presents a summary of the main assumptions behind the modelling of the COVID-19 impacts in this report and the associated key economic impacts in 2020.

3.2. The pandemic's impact on plastics production varies by use and sector

3.2.1. Plastics production was temporarily disrupted

Disruptions in supply chains due to lockdowns and border restrictions reduced plastics production overall. Plastics Europe (2021[6]) estimates that worldwide plastics production decreased by 0.3% in 2020 compared to 2019. However, low oil prices at the early stage of the pandemic may have boosted production – especially of primary plastics – by reducing the cost of raw materials (IEA, 2020[7]; US Bureau of Labor Statistics, 2020[8]). By contrast, low oil prices imply that the growth of secondary (recycled) plastics stalled in 2020, as the price of secondary plastics is linked to that of primary.

There are also big regional differences in the economic effects of the pandemic, and lockdown measures varied widely across countries. Thus, the changes in plastics production varied across countries. In the United States, production of plastic and rubber products fell drastically in March and April 2020, but almost returned to pre-COVID levels at the end of the year. The result was a 7.5% annual decline in production in 2020 compared to the previous year (US Board of Governors of the Federal Reserve System, 2021[9]). European plastics production declined the most during the months of April and May, leading to an annual production volume decline of 4.5% in 2020 compared to the previous year (Eurostat, 2021[10]). The Japan Plastics Industry Federation (2021[11]) reports that annual plastics production decreased by 4.1% in 2020 in Japan. By contrast, Plastics Europe (2021[6]) reports that on a yearly basis, China slightly increased its annual plastics production in 2020; this reflected both the active government response and the faster recovery of the Chinese economy in comparison to most other countries in the second half of 2020 (OECD, 2021[1]). Given the contractions in other countries, this implied an increase in China's global market share.

The disruptions to economic activity in 2020 were widespread and covered all economic sectors, either directly or indirectly. Generally, reduced production also implied the reduced use of plastics as an input. In some sectors, plastics are a major share of production inputs, and thus the effects on plastics use were significant, and generally negative. This section briefly presents a few examples of uses and sectors that were significantly affected.

3.2.2. Plastics use for health purposes increased significantly

Plastics use for health purposes increased significantly

The health-related advantages of plastics were put under the spotlight as the COVID-19 pandemic unfolded (Box 3.1). They are used for a variety of sanitary and medical applications and have thus contributed immensely to the healthcare sector and public health safety. In order to limit the spread of the virus, governments across the world mandated the use of face masks in closed spaces, such as in transport, and often in open air spaces too (Patrício Silva et al., 2020[12]).

Box 3.1. Which polymers are used for personal protective equipment, medical devices and COVID-19 tests?

The production of PPE requires a number of polymers as feedstock. Face masks, which include N95 respirators and surgical masks, are commonly made from PP, while the masks' nose wire is made out of polyethylene (PE) (Institute of Medicine, 2006[13]). Surgical gloves are commonly made from rubber or durable plastics such as PVC (Hamann, Sullivan and Wright, 2014[4]); face shields are often made up of polycarbonate (PC), propionate, acetate, PVC or polyethylene terephthalate glycol; and straps holding masks and goggles in place are made out of rubber or polyetherimide (Henneberry, 2021[14]).

Similarly, medical applications need a range of polymers; a number of medical instruments that were traditionally made of steel, ceramic or glass have gradually been replaced with plastics in recent decades (Joseph et al., 2021[15]). PVC is the most commonly used plastic polymer in medical devices, accounting for 25% of medical plastics use (McKeen, 2014[16]) In addition to face masks and surgical gloves, it is used for example, in intravenous bags, drug solutions, and for many medical produces that require tubing (e.g. infusion, injection, respiration) (Oral, Kurtz and Muratoglu, 2017[17]). Another 50% of medical plastics demand is covered by a mix of PE, PP and polystyrene (PS) (Basmage and Hashmi, 2020[18]). PE is typically used in containers, packaging films and joint replacements; PP in syringes, sutures and gowns; while PS is used for diagnostic instruments, disposable laboratory ware and pipettes, for example (Basmage and Hashmi, 2020[18]).

Finally, COVID-19 tests mostly require PP (around 90%), in addition to polyester (8%) and PE (2%) (Celis et al., 2021[19]).

Early on in the pandemic, the spike in demand for face masks was very sudden and caused a dramatic shortage in the supply of masks worldwide (OECD, 2020[20]). Prior to the pandemic, China was responsible for half of global face mask production. It increased its share in global production in the early months of 2020 due to a surge in global demand that could not be met by other countries (Subramanian, 2020[21]). Plastic manufacturers in China were reportedly producing 110 million surgical masks per day at the end of February – 12 times the volume in January (Ren, 2020[22]). By the end of April, 200 million surgical masks were being produced daily (SCIO, 2020[23]). This corresponds to a monthly production of approximately 33 to 42 kilotonnes (kt) of face masks for the first quarter of 2020.

In Thailand, it was reported in April 2020 that 1.5 million face masks were being used every day (National News Bureau of Thailand, 2020[24]). Japan secured the supply of 600 million face masks just for the month of April (METI, 2020[25]). In Bangladesh in March, which marked the first month of their lockdown, 455 million face masks and 1.2 billion gloves were used in total, corresponding to 1.6 and 3 kt of disposable plastics use respectively (ESDO, 2020[26]). To estimate the volume of face masks used in the European Union (EU), the European Environment Agency (EEA) uses data on the net import of PPE into the EU as a proxy for use in the early stage of the pandemic, when European production capacity was severely limited. Based on this, the EEA estimated that 170 kt of additional face masks and 105 kt of additional gloves (not only plastics but also synthetic rubber) were imported between April and September 2020 (compared to business-as-usual projections) (Graulich et al., 2021[27]).

Demand for PPE has been strong throughout the COVID-19 pandemic and although there has been some shift towards cloth masks, demand for plastic face masks remains much higher than before the pandemic. Aside from the regional and anecdotal evidence reported above, robust data on the number of face masks produced and discarded globally in 2020 are not yet available. An often-cited early estimate is presented by Prata et al. (2020[28]), who extrapolate from a local context in heavily hit Italy to a global use of 129 billion face masks per month. This would equate to more than one trillion masks for the year 2020. This reflects the hypothetical demand for face masks that would be needed for optimal protection, but does not consider whether supply could be increased rapidly enough to meet this demand. Using better data and taking into account supply restrictions, more recent estimates suggest more moderate numbers, such as global production of 52 billion face masks in 2020 (Arizton Advisory and Intelligence, 2020[29]). Box 3.2 uses a quick-and-dirty approximation to check the validity of this estimate.

Taking an average weight of 2.7 grams per surgical mask (Graulich et al., 2021[27]), this amounts to 140 kt of plastics use. However, this is a conservative estimate since other face masks such as N95 respirators weigh more. To account for this and for the fact that the estimate of 52 billion masks seems conservative, a reasonable approximation is to double that weight to 280 kt. Finally, it was estimated that 12 kt of plastic residues from PT-PCR diagnostic tests were generated by August 2020 worldwide (Celis et al., 2021[19]); a rough estimate for 2020 is 20 kt. Thus, plastics use for PPE has clearly increased in 2020 compared to earlier years: total additional plastics use for PPE purposes is estimated to equal around 300 kt.

Box 3.2. Tens of billions of face masks are likely to have been produced in 2020

China produced 9 million face masks per day in January, 110 million in February (Ren, 2020[22]) and 200 million by the end of April (SCIO, 2020[23]). Using the very bold assumption that production after April remained constant, total production for 2020 in China is estimated at 63 billion masks. In 2019, China represented around 50% of the global market (Bown, 2020[30]; Subramanian, 2020[21]), but it is clear that its market share went up considerably in 2020 (Section 3.2.1). Adopting a rough estimate of 75% global market share, global production would be estimated at 85 billion masks; at a constant 50% share the estimate becomes 126 billion masks. Thus, the estimate of 52 billion masks cited above seems conservative, but of the right order of magnitude.

Source: Own calculations based on data from Ren (2020[22]), SCIO (2020[23]) and Subramanian (2020[21]).

3.2.3. Plastics use for packaging shifted across sectors

In normal circumstances, almost one-third of global annual plastics use can be attributed to packaging (Chapter 2). The COVID-19 pandemic had mixed effects on the demand for packaging in the year 2020. On the one hand, the shift towards take-away, food delivery and e-commerce increased demand for plastic packaging. The demand for hygiene products, including disinfectant gel – which mostly comes in plastic packaging – also increased. On the other hand, the closure of shops and workplaces and other limitations to economic activity translated into reduced demand for packaging.

Graulich et al. (2021[27]) report that EU production of plastic packaging declined rapidly at the beginning of the pandemic, but picked up later in October as restrictions were lifted by many countries. The result was a reduction of 227 kt between April and October 2020 on the pre-COVID trend (Figure 3.1). This reflects roughly 1.5% of total use of packaging plastics in the European Union. Plastics Europe (2021[6]) suggests a somewhat larger drop in packaging plastics use, estimating that almost 500 kt fewer plastics were used in Europe's packaging sector in 2020 – just over a 2.5% decrease. The reduction is attributed to lower production levels in sectors that demand packaging plastics, which significantly reduced the market of commercial and industrial packaging. The Italian National consortium for the Collection and Recycling of Plastic Packages (COREPLA) reports that in Italy plastic packaging use was 5% lower than 2019 levels in terms of weight (COREPLA, 2021[31]).[2]

Figure 3.1. Production of plastic packaging in the European Union temporarily dropped

Tonnes

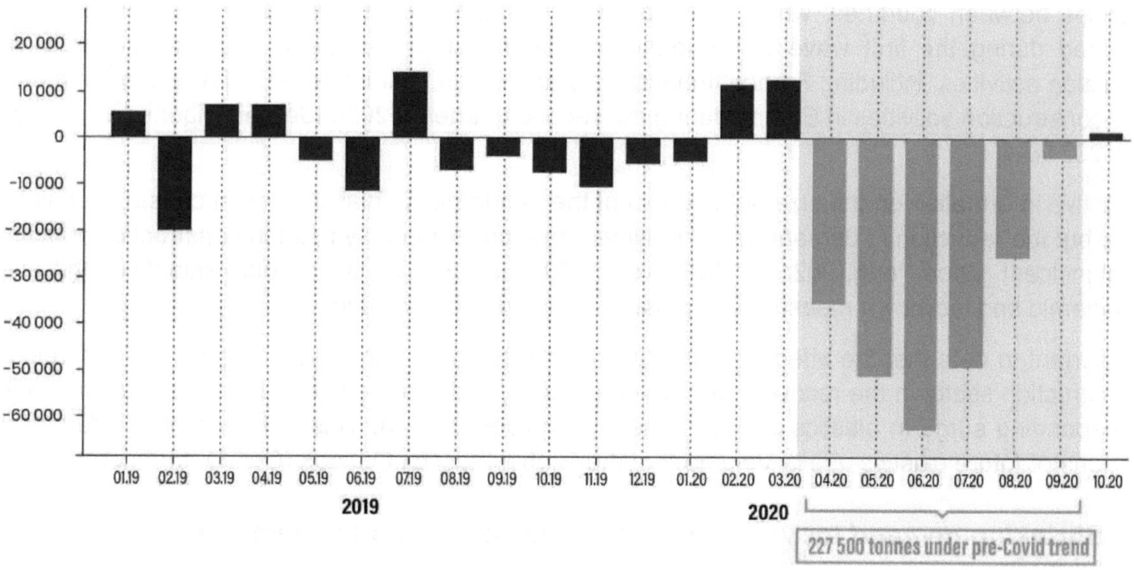

Note: The deviations represent short-term fluctuations from a long-term trend. These fluctuations were exacerbated from April 2020 by COVID-19 in Europe.
Source: Own elaboration based on Graulich et al. (2021[27]), "Impact of Covid-19 on single-use plastics and the environment in Europe".

While plastic packaging production declined overall, the use of plastics for packaging in online sales (e-commerce) increased substantially in 2020. Preliminary calculations by Graulich et al. (2021[27]) indicate that e-commerce used an additional 11.5 to 17.5 kt of plastics in the European Union compared to business-as-usual expectations. In China, where a relatively large share of consumer spending is conducted online, online sales of consumer goods increased by 14.8% in 2020 compared to 2019. By contrast, total retail sales of consumer goods decreased by 4.1% in 2020 (National Bureau of Statistics of China, 2021[32]).

Food packaging was a source of additional plastics use in 2020 as well, as take-away and e-commerce use significantly more single-use plastics than restaurant visits. Indeed, an increase of around 15% has been estimated in the demand for food delivery services and in the associated plastics use and waste

(Oliveira et al., 2021[33]). However, the decline in food packaging for shops and restaurants, which in normal years tends to reflect a substantially larger share of the total food market, mitigates this.

Finally, there were some incentives – and in some cases even regulations (Section 3.3.3) – to switch to single-use plastics as a perceived safer alternative to reusable bags that can be washed. For instance, the Governor of New Hampshire issued a health order requiring stores to use single-use bags (paper or plastic) (Tabuchi, 2020[34]). The evidence to support this push from a public health perspective is, however, weak (Laubinger and Varghese, 2020[35]).

This anecdotal evidence suggests that while there was a visible increase in some uses of packaging plastics, notably related to e-commerce and food delivery services, there were reductions in the use of packaging plastics throughout the economy in sectors whose production was disrupted. Thus, although the net effect of the COVID-19 pandemic and lockdown measures on plastics use for packaging in 2020 is unclear, it is unlikely to be large.

3.2.4. The temporary halt to construction had a large effect on plastics demand

The construction sector uses around one-sixth of all plastics globally (Chapter 2). In many countries, construction activities were shut down for several months to avoid health risks. There were important differences between countries: while for instance in Germany construction activities continued almost unhindered during the first wave of the pandemic, many other European countries severely limited construction activities, including France, Ireland, Italy and Spain, leading to a total reduction of more than 25% in construction activities in Europe during the second quarter of 2020 (de Vet, Nigohosyan and Nunez Ferrer, 2021[36]).

Quantitative information on the size of the effect of the pandemic on plastics use in construction is largely lacking, but the reduction in demand for all polymers that are commonly used in construction is estimated to be significant (Zhou Peng, 2021[37]; S&P Global, 2020[38]). Section 3.4.1 below quantifies the effect of the pandemic and lockdown measures on plastics demand in construction.

It is important to note that the effect on construction is likely to be short-lived: a large role is foreseen for the construction sector in the recovery from the pandemic, and it is likely that this will be accompanied by a corresponding surge in plastics use for construction (Section 3.5). This will be explored further in the projections of future plastics use in Volume 2 of the Global Plastics Outlook (OECD, forthcoming[39]).

3.2.5. Shrinking demand for vehicles also drove down plastics demand

The demand for plastics by the motor vehicles sector was directly impacted by lower demand for cars and supply chain disruptions. The European Automobile Manufacturers Association (2021[40]) reports that the number of cars sold globally fell by more than 15% in 2020, compared to 2019. The decline was more significant in Europe (-21%) than in Russia (-8%) or China (-7%) for example. North American car sales fell in the three first quarters of 2020, but rebounded slightly in the fourth quarter, resulting in an overall sales decline of 18% on 2019 levels. Car sales contracted the most in South America (-29%), primarily due to the large number of COVID-19 cases and severity of lockdowns.

More than ten different plastic polymers are used to make a vehicle on average. This adds up to more than 100 kilogrammes for an average vehicle, with PP accounting for more than one-quarter (Patil, Patel and Purohit, 2017[41]). Thus, the significant reduction in the sale of motor vehicles had a significant downward effect on global plastics use, as shown in Section 3.4.1 below.

3.2.6. The synthetic fibres and textiles sectors were disrupted

The clothing sector was heavily hit by the COVID-19 pandemic as many retail outlets were forced to close their doors when lockdowns were implemented in many countries. Moreover, there were multiple factory closures and supply chain disruptions in Asia, where the largest producers and exporters in the textile industry are located (Sabanoglu, 2020[42]). Martin et al. (2020[43]) report that global production of polyester fibres decreased by almost 9% in 2020 compared to the year before, whereas IHS Markit estimates that polyester fibre production contracted by 1.2% in 2020, corresponding to around 500-750 kt (Clark, 2021[44]; IHS Markit, 2020[45]).

Cloth masks and other uses of textiles and synthetic fibres for PPE have increased demand for plastics, specifically PP fibres. Nonetheless, the overall effect on the synthetic fibres and textiles sectors is estimated to have been negative in 2020 (Martin et al., 2020[43]).

3.3. Effects on plastic waste and recycling are not clear cut

Reductions in industrial and commercial plastic waste were compensated for by increases in household plastic waste. Even before the pandemic, 77 million tonnes (Mt) of plastic waste were being mismanaged annually (Chapter 2). COVID-19 contributed further to the challenge of managing municipal waste properly, especially in developing countries where resources and infrastructure are largely lacking (Das et al., 2021[46]; AIT/UNEP, 2021[47]). Many countries faced significantly increased physical and financial challenges in managing their solid waste. Rural regions were more affected than urban regions, as waste treatment facilities are not evenly distributed and tend to be located near populated areas (IGES, 2020[48]). New logistical considerations due to the shift in the origin and composition of waste, additional requirements for performing sanitation activities and increased spending on protective gear all contributed to these challenges (AIT/UNEP, 2021[47]). Furthermore, many waste treatment facilities were temporarily shut down (AIT/UNEP, 2021[47]). There was a significant increase in uncontrolled landfilling and local burning strategies, for example in India, which also reflected an attempt to prevent virus contagion (Patrício Silva et al., 2020[12]). Illegal dumping of municipal solid waste was also recorded in OECD countries, such as Australia, Belgium, Ireland, the Netherlands, and the United Kingdom (AIT/UNEP, 2021[47]). Many cities, however, continued to guarantee solid waste collection, even if not necessarily separated by type of waste (OECD, 2020[49]). Overall, a larger share than usual of plastic waste was incinerated or landfilled rather than recovered.

Anecdotal evidence presented below suggests that municipal plastic waste increased in 2020, due to changes in consumer behaviour. Moreover, there is evidence of an alteration of the composition of municipal solid waste, reflecting larger shares of single-use plastics and – unsurprisingly – PPE (Yousefi et al., 2021[50]). These increases are, however, mitigated by decreases in municipal plastic waste from commercial activities such as accommodation and food services, as many businesses were shut down at least temporarily. The net effect on municipal waste generation in 2020 is therefore not clear but likely relatively small (AIT/UNEP, 2021[47]).

In Bangkok, municipal solid waste declined by 12% during the lockdown while household plastic waste increased by 62% (Promchertoo, 2020[51]). Households in Singapore and Hong Kong, China, were also recorded to have increased their plastic waste generation, mainly due to takeaway and online food delivery, with single-use plastics from take-aways more than doubling in Hong Kong, China, in April 2020 compared to 2019, for example (CGTN, 2020[52]; NUS, 2020[53]). Although no specific data on plastics are available, households in New York and Ireland also increased their waste generation by 21% and 3.3% respectively (RWMO, 2020[54]; Staub, 2020[55]). Finally, in Kobe, a Japanese city, household plastic waste increased by 10.3% (AIT/UNEP, 2021[47]).

Reduced industrial activity is likely to have decreased industrial plastic waste generation in 2020 (Section 3.4.2). While there is no robust evidence yet that the combined decline in industrial and commercial waste outweighed the increase in household waste, if their waste streams declined in line with their production levels, the decrease could be substantial. The reported increase in municipal waste is not sufficient evidence, as many industrial waste streams are collected separately to municipal solid waste.

The nature of medical waste, including PPE waste, changed drastically: before 2020, most PPE was used in controlled medical facilities, which tend to have strict waste management protocols. But from 2020, a large volume of PPE, and especially face masks, was used by individuals in public settings and ended up as household waste. Some countries recommended double-bagging potentially infectious waste, which may also have led to additional plastics use (IGES, 2020[48]).

Most health facilities incinerate medical waste to ensure that pathogens do not spread further (Ghodrat, Rashidi and Samali, 2017[56]; Joseph et al., 2021[15]). This practice has been further strengthened during the pandemic (AIT/UNEP, 2021[47]; Peng et al., 2020[57]). Medical waste in Wuhan, China, amounted to 110 to 150 tonnes per day in mid-February, and increased to 247 tonnes as the number of cases worsened. The government of Wuhan was able to face the surge in medical plastic waste to some extent by building a waste management facility with a capacity of 30 tonnes per day in less than two weeks (Wei, 2020[58]). In a review of five hospitals in Iran, it was found that medical waste more than doubled compared to pre-COVID levels (Kalantary et al., 2021[59]). Medical waste generation in India averaged 163 tonnes in the second half of 2020, peaking in September (at 183 tonnes) when the number of cases significantly increased (Central Pollution Control Board, 2021[60]). In Manila, Jakarta, Bangkok, Ha Noi and Kuala Lumpur, medical waste was reported to be six times higher in the first quarter of 2020 than pre-COVID levels (ADB, 2020[61]). On the other hand, medical waste in New York was found to have declined in the first five months of 2020. This could have been partly due to the supply shortage of PPE and the halting of non-COVID related medical procedures; it could also reflect the fact that much of the used household and hospital PPE was not labelled as medical waste (Wei, 2020[58]).

3.3.1. Plastics littering worsened

Littering of disposable PPE items, particularly face masks, gloves and cleaning wipes, increased in many countries almost immediately after governments started recommending their use – around March 2020 in many countries (Prata et al., 2020[28]; Roberts et al., 2021[62]). It seems likely that this increased stream of littered PPE plastics continued in 2021 and will do so for much longer. This loss of plastics to the environment causes a number of environmental and economic problems, as discussed in Chapter 2.

Reports and news articles describing the littering of PPE in coastal environments began accumulating early on in the pandemic and increased throughout 2020 (e.g. (BBC News, 2020[63]; Bondaroff and Cooke, 2020[64]; Chapman and Bomford, 2020[65]). Bondaroff and Cooke (2020[64]) document the large numbers of face masks and gloves that have littered beaches across Asia, even those that are remote. For instance, on the small beach of Tai A Chau in the Soko Islands in Hong Kong, China, a marine conservation organisation found 70 masks spread along a short 100-metre stretch as early as February 2020. The composition of litter has also changed with the advent of health concerns. In two rivers in Indonesia, approximately 15% of littered items that were collected between March and April 2020 were PPE items (Cordova et al., 2021[66]).

Bondaroff and Cooke (2020[64]) estimate that in 2020 1.56 billion face masks entered the ocean (corresponding to a 3% leakage assumption except for masks used in controlled medical facilities which have lower leakage rates), resulting in 5 to 6 kt of marine plastic leakage. A higher value was reported by Chowdhury et al. (2021[67]) who find that 150 to 390 kt may enter global oceans by the end of 2021.[3] While both values are small compared to the estimated 22 Mt of total leakage of plastics to the environment in 2019 in Chapter 2 of this report, littering as a direct result of the pandemic adds to the existing issues of environmental pollution.

Leakage does not only occur in marine environments – it also occurs on land. A recent analysis of land-based litter as reported by citizens of 11 OECD countries between September 2019 and October 2020 shows that face mask litter especially increased after the official onset of the pandemic. It amounted to less than 0.01% of total litter in October 2019, but made up 0.80% of total litter a year later (Roberts et al.,

2021[62]). While this highlights that face mask littering increased significantly due to COVID-19, it also indicates that the share of PPE volumes in total littering remains small.

A number of reports highlight PPE littering in cities (BBC News, 2020[68]; Fazio, 2020[69]; Tesfaldet et al., 2021[70]). This was found to have harmed some urban drainage systems, which were clogged by face masks and gloves. This increased cleaning and replacement costs for equipment in affected areas and heightened the risk of flooding and water pollution (Geberemariam, 2021[71]). Face masks and other PPE litter can also be transported by drainage systems to the marine environment (Fadare and Okoffo, 2020[72]).

One study found that 170 face masks were littered on a 13-km stretch covering three streets in Bangkok over 42 days of 5 hours of observation per day (Tesfaldet et al., 2021[70]). Another study reported that more than one-third of 140 50-metre stretches of roads that were inspected in September and October 2020 in Essex (United Kingdom) contained at least one PPE item, mostly face masks (Chapman and Bomford, 2020[65]). A Canadian study conducted in Toronto reports that on average 1 010 PPE items were found for every squared kilometre of residential, commercial and hospital districts (Ammendolia et al., 2021[73]).[4]

While additional littering on land is aesthetically unpleasant, it is less likely to be environmentally harmful in OECD countries, which are likely to respond by spending more on litter collection, than in non-OECD countries. In Toronto, for instance, the cleaning costs for managing litter amounted to almost USD 113 500 (CAD 146 614) between March and the end of July 2020, most of which was directly due to the increased amount of litter (Solid Waste Management Services, 2020[74]).[5] In developing countries, however, where litter may not be collected, this additional littering could lead to environmental degradation.

3.3.2. *Plastics recycling was disrupted*

Recycling of plastics was affected by the COVID-19 pandemic in various ways. First, disruptions to waste management, including the reduced collection of separated waste and the reduced trade in waste, lessened the supply of materials available for recycling (Laubinger and Varghese, 2020[35]).

Second, recycling companies were affected by the restrictions on economic activity. Recycling programmes were suspended in many regions and informal waste collectors reduced their activities (GMCA, 2020[75]; Martin et al., 2020[43]). Some cities in the United States suspended recycling programmes for fear that the virus would spread by the collected items (Zambrano-Monserrate, Ruano and Sanchez-Alcalde, 2020[76]; Staub, 2020[77]). A survey conducted in the United States indicates that 34% of recycling companies were partially or completely closed in April 2020 (Toto, 2020[78]). During the lockdown in Shanghai, centrally located neighbourhoods no longer had the option to separate recyclables (Bloomberg News, 2020[79]).

Third, the global oil price dropped significantly in the first quarter of 2020 (IEA, 2020[7]; US Bureau of Labor Statistics, 2020[8]). This reduced production costs for primary plastics, and thus the price of plastic products, while the production costs of secondary plastics were not reduced to the same extent. Although the price of secondary plastics has historically correlated with that of primary plastics, there is no spot market for secondary plastics (OECD, 2018[80]) and it is unclear how much the profitability of secondary production suffered. But it is likely that the competitiveness of the secondary plastics sector deteriorated (Brock, 2020[81]); see also Chapter 4. In Europe, many plastics recyclers temporarily shut down production in 2020 in response to government restrictions and deteriorating market conditions (PRE, 2020[82]).

The oil price picked up later in 2020, which pushed the price of primary plastics back up (IEA, 2020[7]; US Bureau of Labor Statistics, 2020[8]). At the same time, most governments began to manage lockdown measures better and in many countries municipalities ensured that separated waste collection was maintained or restored. This revived the recycling industry, although regional differences remained large. The overall effect on recycling volumes and the volumes of secondary plastics produced remain unclear, as there were no robust data available at the time of writing to identify which trend dominated over the course of the year.

Global recycling volumes have not only been influenced by the COVID-19 pandemic – the market has also been influenced by recent changes in national policies. These include mandatory minimum recycled content standards (Chapter 6), voluntary commitments by firms, and the broader international policy context, such as the recent amendments to the Basel Convention and China's ban on the import of waste (Chapter 4).

3.3.3. Waste and recycling policies changed temporarily

The government response measures to the COVID-19 pandemic have also affected plastics use and waste, as well as recycling policies. In the wake of growing sanitary concerns, government actions to reduce single-use plastic items were delayed in numerous places (Murphy, 2020[83]; Tabuchi, 2020[84]; US State of Maine, 2020[85]). For instance, India, Portugal, Senegal and multiple states in the United States as well as certain states and territories in Australia delayed their bans on single-use plastics, while Scotland and the Netherlands delayed the implementation of deposit-refund schemes (da Costa, 2021[86]). Italy delayed the implementation of its tax on plastic packaging several times; it is currently planned to take effect in 2023 (Zecchini, 2021[87]). Several local and national governments have now proceeded to implement these policies. For instance, New York started enforcing its ban on plastic bags in October 2020, after a seven-month delay (Associated Press, 2020[88]). In 2021, Commonwealth, state and territory environment ministers identified eight single-use plastic products that have to be phased out nationally by 2025 (or sooner in some cases) under the National Waste Policy Action Plan (Government of Australia, 2021[89]; ACT Government, 2021[90]; Government of South Australia, 2021[91]). And despite pressure on the EU to delay the implementation of its plastics tax, it went ahead as scheduled in July 2021 (EC, 2021[92]; Simon, 2020[93]).

As a response to the increase in illegal dumping in the early months of the pandemic, the Irish Government provided EUR 1 million of additional funding to support efforts to tackle this issue (Government of Ireland, 2020[94]).

Recycling policies were also affected by the pandemic. For instance, Fort Collins, a municipality in Colorado, temporarily put on hold plans to start a "community recycling ordinance" which would require that recycling services be provided by trash haulers to most multi-family and commercial properties by the end of 2020; it finally entered into force in July 2021 (City of Fort Collins, 2021[95]; Staub, 2020[96]). Because of social distancing recommendations from local governments, some recycling centres reduced their activity or even temporarily closed in the early months of the pandemic (Staub, 2020[77]). Moreover, as some cities were experiencing collection delays due to the impacts of COVID-19 on the workforce, garbage collection was prioritised over recycling (Staub, 2020[77]). Finally, waste pickers and other informal waste workers were also affected by COVID-19 containment measures (Sarkodie and Owusu, 2020[97]).

Laubinger and Varghese (2020[35]) warned early on that the initially temporary reversal or halting of some of the policy measures to reduce plastics use and waste could become permanent. This would hold back the smooth transition towards a more resource-efficient, circular economy.

3.4. OECD modelling suggests COVID-19 on balance reduced plastics use in 2020

The anecdotal and partial evidence presented above is insufficient to assess the overall effect of the COVID-19 pandemic and associated government response measures on global plastics use. Beyond the selected plastics applications where a direct effect occurred, there are indirect effects on plastics use that are driven by changes in economic activity and household consumption and by linkages between sectors. Many sectors have reduced their production in response to a lockdown, trade barriers or falling demand, and these have generally scaled down their plastics use accordingly.

For a complete picture, an economy-wide assessment is needed that connects plastics use to specific economic activities, and that connects the different sectoral and regional economic activities to each other.

As part of this *Global Plastics Outlook*, the ENV-Linkages modelling framework described in Chateau, Dellink and Lanzi (2014[98]) has been used for this broad assessment.[6] This section presents the results of that modelling, while Annex B describes the economic impacts assessed in the modelling framework.

These modelling results need to be interpreted with care. First, estimates of economic activity and plastics use for 2020 are not final at the time of writing, and updates of official statistics can be expected. Second, the modelling assumes that plastics use by production sectors scales down roughly in proportion to output changes.[7] This excludes shifts in production technology within the sector or shifts between different parts of the same sector, such as from eating in restaurants to take-away or from shop retail to e-commerce. Thus, these results are more indicative of the general implications of the economic effects of the pandemic on plastics use than of detailed use of specific polymers in specific subsectors. Nonetheless, the modelling assessment captures most of the major trends described in Section 3.2 and emphasises that indirect effects may be more important than the very visible direct effects for relatively small applications.

3.4.1. Plastics use declined in 2020, but less than economic activity

At the global level, the reduced scale of economic activity dominates the increased demand for specific plastic applications that were outlined above. Our modelling estimates that global plastics use declined by 2.2% from 2019 levels, or 4.5% below the pre-COVID projection for 2020 (Figure 3.2 and Figure 3.3). That is a drop of around 10 Mt from 2019 levels. Given that global GDP declined by almost 3.5% below 2019 levels (6.5% below the pre-COVID projection), the plastics intensity of the global economy actually increased. This contrasts with the recent declining trend in the plastics intensity of the economy: i.e. between 2015 and 2019 the growth in global plastics use was smaller than the growth in global GDP.

Some regions have seen a larger economic downturn than others, and this is reflected in their regional plastics use (Figure 3.2). For example, the Indian economy shrunk by 6% in 2020 (13% below the pre-COVID projection), leading to a reduction in plastics use of around 12.9% compared to the pre-COVID projection. This is equivalent to a 7% drop in 2020 compared to 2019, or 1.9 Mt.

Figure 3.2. Global plastics use declined by more than 10 Mt in 2020, affecting almost all regions

Regional plastics use in 2020 compared to 2019 and the pre-COVID 2020 projection

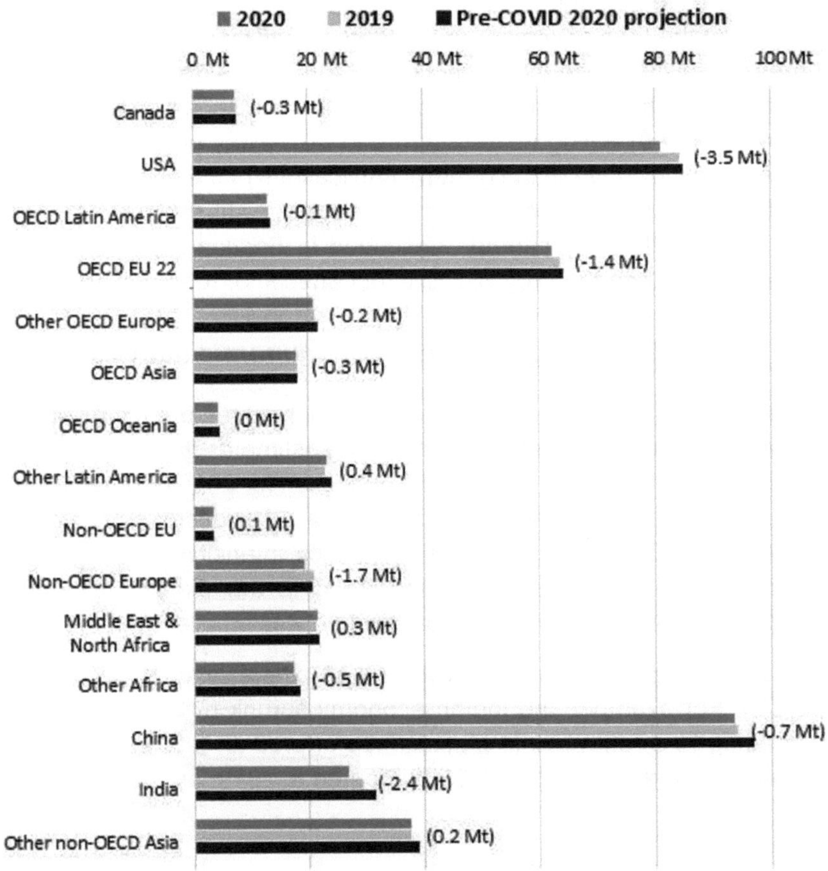

Note: The change in plastics use between 2019 and 2020 is indicated in brackets.
Source: OECD Global Plastics Outlook Database, Dellink et al. (2021[3]).

StatLink https://stat.link/4e89qc

Regional changes in plastics use in 2020 are also determined by the structure of the economy, which varies significantly across regions. Countries that specialise in sectors that use large volumes of plastics, not least India and the Non-OECD Europe region, will have larger reductions in plastics use, just as countries that specialise in sectors that are most severely hit by the pandemic tend to have larger reductions in economic activity. Reductions in plastics use are smaller than GDP losses in many countries, especially those in the EU (-3% versus -8% when compared to the pre-COVID projection) and in the OECD Latin America region (-2% versus -9%). This reflects the fact that the substantial economic costs in these regions are largely caused by disruptions to sectors that do not use a lot of plastics.

Figure 3.3. Global plastics use declined by more than 10 Mt in 2020, affecting almost all sectors

Sectoral plastics use in 2020 compared to 2019 and the pre-COVID 2020 projection

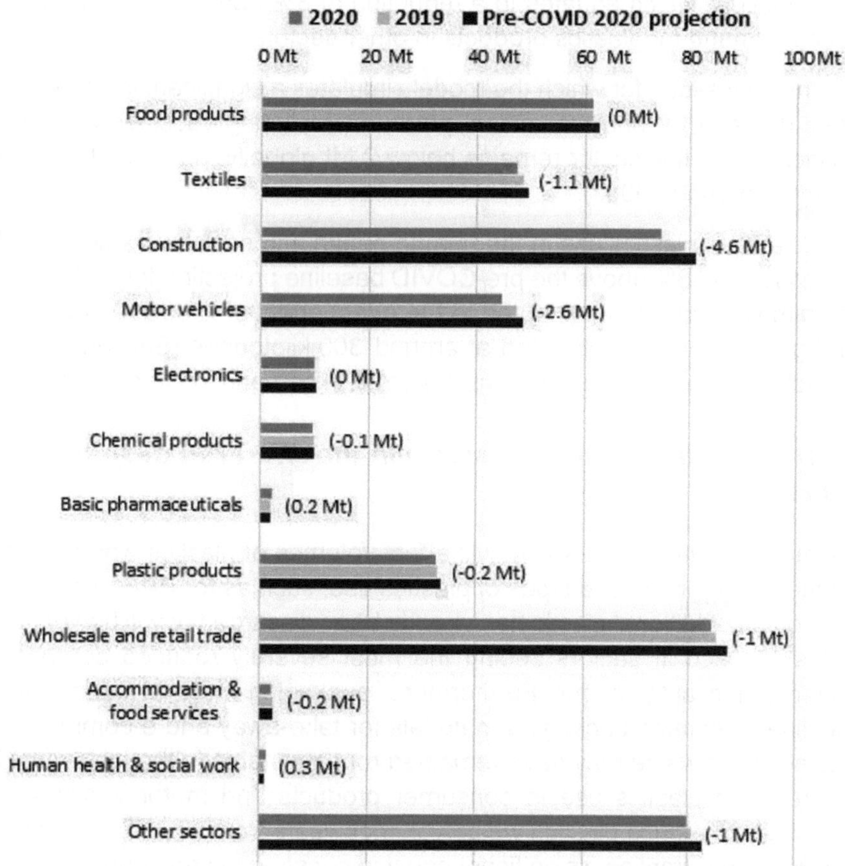

Note: Direct effects of consumption changes other than human health (including PPE) as discussed in Section 3.2.2 are not included in these calculations due to lack of robust global data. The change in plastics use between 2019 and 2020 is indicated in brackets.
Source: OECD Global Plastics Outlook Database , Dellink et al. (2021[3]).

StatLink https://stat.link/gr3e8a

Sectoral plastics use declined overall, except in health-related sectors

In line with the anecdotal evidence presented in Section 3.2, the impacts of the pandemic and lockdown measures on plastics use differ widely across sectors (Figure 3.3). Plastics use for food products is estimated to have remained roughly unchanged from 2019 (less than 200 kt) and declined by only a few percent below the pre-COVID projected levels for 2020. As explained above, the lockdown measures primarily affected the way in which food was consumed, rather than the overall volume of food consumption. Nonetheless, home delivery and take-away may have made this sector more intensive in its use of specific plastic polymers, something which could not be accounted for in this calculation as robust data are not (yet) available.

The big negative impact of the lockdown measures on construction activity and motor vehicles demand has led to a reduction in plastics use in these sectors by around 4.6 Mt and 2.6 Mt, respectively, according to the model simulations, compared to 2019 levels. This is driven by the substantial production declines in these sectors. Each of these sectors accounts for more than 10% of total plastics use, and together with food products, textiles and wholesale and retail trade, these reductions largely drive the total effects of the pandemic on plastics use.

Plastics use in the plastics and rubber production sector itself, and in the chemical sector, remain roughly unchanged from 2019 levels, which equates to a reduction of 3% from the pre-COVID projection. This is driven by the reduced demand for plastics products in other sectors.

Pharmaceuticals is the only sector for which the model simulates a significant increase in plastics use. The pandemic increased demand for pharmaceutical products, including vaccines and other medicaments. However, total plastics use in this sector remains below 2 Mt globally, and thus this increase is relatively minor in absolute terms (around 200 kt).

According to the simulations, plastics use in the human health and social work sector (which includes the medical sector) increased by 33% above the pre-COVID baseline projection for 2020 and 37% above 2019 levels. This can be almost completely attributed to the direct effect of PPE use in the health sector, such as face masks and gloves, roughly estimated at around 300 kilotonnes (Section 3.2.2). However, while this is large at the sectoral level, in absolute terms it is small in comparison to the changes in other sectors.

3.4.2. Plastic waste may have remained stable in the short run despite the switch to single-use plastics

The changes in plastics use discussed above will affect volumes of plastics waste for a long time. In the short run, much of the new or increased types of plastics use, such as for PPE, are single-use and have a short lifespan. Much of this additional plastic has already been discarded or will be very shortly. In contrast, the lifespans of plastics used in sectors seeing the most severely reduced demand, such as vehicle manufacture, is often significantly longer. Furthermore, packaging material used in e.g. wholesale and retail trade also declined, whereas packaging materials for take-away and e-commerce increased. Thus, although in 2020 total plastic waste may have remained roughly stable (although robust information is not yet available), the reduced plastics use in consumer products and motor vehicles, and especially in construction, is only likely to reduce plastics waste volumes years from now. This could change, however, if recovery from the pandemic implies a significant boost in construction and durable goods. These longer-term projections will be explored in more detail in Volume 2 of the *Global Plastics Outlook* (OECD, forthcoming[39]).

3.5. The longer-term implications of the COVID-19 pandemic remain unclear

Despite worries over the continued spread of COVID-19 for human health, and prolonged measures that restrict economic activity, economic activity in 2021 was significantly up from 2020 levels (OECD, 2021[1]). With a rebounding economy, plastics use is also projected to pick up again. But there are big variations in how fast different sectors and countries will recover (Dellink et al., 2021[3]), and there is considerable uncertainty around how the pandemic, economic activity and plastics use will evolve.

One major uncertainty that is directly relevant for plastics use and waste is the size of government recovery packages and the extent to which they are green. For instance, if there is large-scale investment in infrastructure boosted by these recovery packages, this will drive fast growth in construction activity, with an associated increase in plastics use as this sector accounts for more than 10% of total plastics use. If recovery packages are aimed at accelerating the transition towards a more resource-efficient and circular economy (OECD, 2021[99]), fast economic recovery does not need to imply a fast increase in plastics use. Instead, recycling and secondary use of plastics could be spearheaded, and the plastics intensity of the economy could be reduced.

Another key uncertainty is whether behavioural changes that emerged during the lockdown periods will become permanent, or whether things will "go back to normal". It remains to be seen whether the fast growth in e-commerce will continue, and whether it increases short-lived plastics use for packaging. That face masks and other PPE will continue to be used in the coming years is perhaps a little less uncertain, but the amount of littered plastics resulting from this depends on how the pandemic evolves as well as on whether behavioural changes turn out to be permanent or temporary.

The backward-looking exercise in this chapter sheds light on how interactions in the economic system are crucial for a broad assessment of the implications of COVID-19 on plastics use. It has highlighted a widespread reduction in plastics use in 2020 in many economic sectors, but increases in selected applications and a shift towards more single-use plastics. Forward-looking analysis, as envisaged in Volume 2 of the *Global Plastics Outlook* (OECD, forthcoming[39]), will be able to shed light on the longer-term consequences.

References

ACEA (2021), *Economic and Market Report: EU Automotive Industry Full-year 2020*, European Automobile Manufacturers Association, https://www.acea.auto/files/Economic_and_Market_Report_full-year_2020.pdf. [40]

ACT Government (2021), *https://www.cityservices.act.gov.au/recycling-and-waste/single-use-plastics*. [90]

ADB (2020), *Managing Infectious Medical Waste during the COVID-19 Pandemic*, https://www.adb.org/publications/managing-medical-waste-covid19. [61]

AIT/UNEP (2021), *Covid-19 & Plastic Plight: a Reflection from One Year of the Pandemic*, http://www.circular-economy.ait.ac.th/downloads/COVID-19%20&%20Plastic%20Plight%20Report.pdf. [47]

Ammendolia, J. et al. (2021), "An emerging source of plastic pollution: Environmental presence of plastic personal protective equipment (PPE) debris related to COVID-19 in a metropolitan city", *Environmental Pollution*, Vol. 269, p. 116160, http://dx.doi.org/10.1016/j.envpol.2020.116160. [73]

Arizton Advisory and Intelligence (2020), *Medical Face Mask Market - Global Outlook and Forecast 2020-2025*, Market Research.com, https://www.marketresearch.com/Arizton-v4150/Medical-Face-Mask-Global-Outlook-13345767/. [29]

Associated Press (2020), *Plastic Bag Ban Starts in New York After Months of Delay*, Associated Press, https://apnews.com/article/business-new-york-75d5e594b00090ae7263efc70f8a33f5b. [88]

Basmage, O. and M. Hashmi (2020), "Plastic Products in Hospitals and Healthcare Systems", in *Encyclopedia of Renewable and Sustainable Materials*, Elsevier, http://dx.doi.org/10.1016/b978-0-12-803581-8.11303-7. [18]

BBC News (2020), *Coronavirus: Discarded disposable gloves on the street*, BBC News, https://www.bbc.com/news/in-pictures-52188627. [68]

BBC News (2020), *Coronavirus: French alarm at Covid-linked Med pollution*, BBC News, https://www.bbc.com/news/world-europe-52807526. [63]

Bloomberg News (2020), *China's War on Garbage Faces a Major Coronavirus Setback*, Bloomberg Quint, https://www.bloombergquint.com/business/china-s-war-on-garbage-faces-a-major-coronavirus-setback. [79]

Bondaroff, T. and S. Cooke (2020), *Masks on the Beach: The Impact of COVID-19 on Marine Plastic Pollution*, OceansAsia, https://oceansasia.org/wp-content/uploads/2020/12/Marine-Plastic-Pollution-FINAL.pdf. [64]

Bown, C. (2020), *COVID-19: China's exports of medical supplies provide a ray of hope*, Peterson Institute for International Economics, https://www.piie.com/blogs/trade-and-investment-policy-watch/covid-19-chinas-exports-medical-supplies-provide-ray-hope. [30]

Brock, J. (2020), *A Reuters Special Report: The Plastic Pandemic. Covid-19 trashed the recycling dream.*, Reuters, https://www.reuters.com/investigates/special-report/health-coronavirus-plastic-recycling/. [81]

Celis, J. et al. (2021), "Plastic residues produced with confirmatory testing for COVID-19: Classification, quantification, fate, and impacts on human health", *Science of The Total Environment*, Vol. 760, p. 144167, http://dx.doi.org/10.1016/j.scitotenv.2020.144167. [19]

Central Pollution Control Board (2021), *COVID-19 Waste Management*, Ministry of Environment, Forest and Climate Change. Government of India, https://cpcb.nic.in/covid-waste-management/. [60]

CGTN (2020), *Hong Kong plastic waste: Food delivery and takeouts bring surge in plastic pollution*, CGTN, https://news.cgtn.com/news/7a497a4d33514464776c6d636a4e6e62684a4856/index.html. [52]

Chapman, C. and K. Bomford (2020), *Litter in lockdown: A study of litter in the time of coronavirus*, CPRE, https://www.cpre.org.uk/wp-content/uploads/2020/12/Litter-in-lockdown-full-report-December-2020.pdf. [65]

Chateau, J., R. Dellink and E. Lanzi (2014), "An Overview of the OECD ENV-Linkages Model: Version 3", *OECD Environment Working Papers*, No. 65, OECD Publishing, Paris, http://dx.doi.org/10.1787/5jz2qck2b2vd-en. [98]

Chowdhury, H., T. Chowdhury and S. Sait (2021), "Estimating marine plastic pollution from COVID-19 face masks in coastal regions", *Marine Pollution Bulletin*, Vol. 168, p. 112419, http://dx.doi.org/10.1016/j.marpolbul.2021.112419. [67]

City of Fort Collins (2021), *Recycling: Recycling & Trash Ordinances*, https://www.fcgov.com/recycling/ordinances. [95]

Clark, D. (2021), *Recovery for the paraxylene industry or temporary reprieve?*, IHS Markit, https://ihsmarkit.com/research-analysis/recovery-for-the-paraxylene-industry-or-temporary-reprieve.html?ite=997087&ito=1274&itq=3b1f1db2-19e0-4d34-b496-811584ab7ccb&itx%5Bidio%5D=771816356. [44]

Cordova, M. et al. (2021), "Unprecedented plastic-made personal protective equipment (PPE) debris in river outlets into Jakarta Bay during COVID-19 pandemic", *Chemosphere*, Vol. 268, p. 129360, http://dx.doi.org/10.1016/j.chemosphere.2020.129360. [66]

COREPLA (2021), *I risultati 2020 di corepla: raccolta in aumento nonostante l'emergenza sanitaria (+4%) e dati più omogenei tra le regioni.*, Consorzio Nazionale Per La Raccolta, Il Riciclo E Il Recupero Degli Imballaggi In Plastica, https://www.corepla.it/news/i-risultati-2020-di-corepla-raccolta-aumento-nonostante-l-emergenza-sanitaria-4-e-dati-pi-omoge. [31]

da Costa, J. (2021), "The 2019 global pandemic and plastic pollution prevention measures: Playing catch-up", *Science of The Total Environment*, Vol. 774, p. 145806, http://dx.doi.org/10.1016/j.scitotenv.2021.145806. [86]

Das, A. et al. (2021), "COVID-19 and municipal solid waste (MSW) management: a review", *Environmental Science and Pollution Research 2021 28:23*, Vol. 28/23, pp. 28993-29008, http://dx.doi.org/10.1007/S11356-021-13914-6. [46]

de Vet, J., D. Nigohosyan and J. Nunez Ferrer (2021), *Impacts of the Covid-19 pandemic on EU industries*, European Parliament, https://www.europarl.europa.eu/RegData/etudes/STUD/2021/662903/IPOL_STU(2021)662903_EN.pdf. [36]

Dellink, R. et al. (2021), "The long-term environmental implications of COVID-19", *OECD Environment Working Papers*, No. 176, OECD Publishing, Paris, http://dx.doi.org/10.1787/123dfd4f-en. [3]

EC (2021), *Single-use plastics*, European Commission, https://ec.europa.eu/environment/topics/plastics/single-use-plastics_en. [92]

ESDO (2020), *ESDO's Online Press Briefing on COVID-19 Pandemic Outbreak 14,500 Tons of Hazardous Plastic Waste in a Month*, Environment and Social Development Organization (ESDO), https://esdo.org/esdos-online-press-briefing-on-hazardous-plastic-waste-generation-in-a-month-during-covid-19-pandemic/. [26]

Eurostat (2021), *Manufacture of rubber and plastic products, Calendar adjusted data, 2019-2020*, Eurostat. [10]

Fadare, O. and E. Okoffo (2020), "Covid-19 face masks: A potential source of microplastic fibers in the environment", *Science of The Total Environment*, Vol. 737, p. 140279, http://dx.doi.org/10.1016/j.scitotenv.2020.140279. [72]

Fazio, M. (2020), *Your Used Mask Needs to Make It to the Trash Can*, The New York Times, https://www.nytimes.com/2020/07/25/climate/covid-masks-discarded.html. [69]

Geberemariam, T. (2021), "The Potential Indirect Impact of COVID-19 on Urban Drainage Systems", *Journal of Irrigation and Drainage Engineering*, Vol. 147/10, p. 02521001, http://dx.doi.org/10.1061/(asce)ir.1943-4774.0001606. [71]

Ghodrat, M., M. Rashidi and B. Samali (2017), "Life Cycle Assessments of Incineration Treatment for Sharp Medical Waste", in *The Minerals, Metals & Materials Series, Energy Technology 2017*, Springer International Publishing, Cham, http://dx.doi.org/10.1007/978-3-319-52192-3_14. [56]

GMCA (2020), *All Household Waste Recycling Centres closed from today*, Greater Manchester Combined Authority, https://www.greatermanchester-ca.gov.uk/news/all-household-waste-recycling-centres-closed-from-today/. [75]

Government of Australia (2021), *Commonwealth%20Department%20of%20Agriculture,%20Water%20and%20the%20Environment.pdf*. [89]

Government of Ireland (2020), *Funding ringfenced to tackle illegal dumping during COVID-19*, Department of the Environment, Climate and Communications, https://www.gov.ie/en/press-release/46f2f8-funding-ringfenced-to-tackle-illegal-dumping-during-covid-19/. [94]

Government of South Australia (2021), *https://www.replacethewaste.sa.gov.au/.* [91]

Graulich, K. et al. (2021), *Impact of COVID-19 on single-use plastics and the environment in Europe*, European Environment Agency. [27]

Hamann, C., K. Sullivan and P. Wright (2014), "Protective Gloves", in *Textbook of Hand Eczema*, Springer Berlin Heidelberg, Berlin, http://dx.doi.org/10.1007/978-3-642-39546-8_28. [4]

Henneberry, B. (2021), *How to Make Personal Protective Equipment (PPE) for COVID-19 (Manufacturing and Sourcing Guide)*, THOMAS for Industry, https://www.thomasnet.com/articles/plant-facility-equipment/how-to-make-ppe/. [14]

IEA (2020), *World Energy Outlook 2020*, OECD Publishing, Paris, https://dx.doi.org/10.1787/557a761b-en. [7]

IGES (2020), *Waste Management during the COVID19 Pandemic: From Response to Recovery*, United Nations Environment Programme, https://www.iges.or.jp/jp/pub/waste-management-during-covid-19-pandemic-response-recovery/en. [48]

IHS Markit (2020), *COVID-19 Has Impacted the Global Fibers Growth Trend*, IHS Markit, https://cdn.ihsmarkit.com/www/pdf/1020/IHS-Markit-Annual-Global-Fibers-Infographic.pdf. [45]

IMF (2020), *World Economic Outlook, October 2020: A Long and Difficult Ascent*, International Monetary Fund, Washington, D.C., https://www.imf.org/en/Publications/WEO/Issues/2020/09/30/world-economic-outlook-october-2020 (accessed on 22 January 2021). [2]

Institute of Medicine (2006), *Reusability of Facemasks During an Influenza Pandemic: Facing the Flu*, The National Academies Press, Washington, D.C., http://dx.doi.org/10.17226/11637. [13]

Japan Plastics Industry Federation (2021), *Plastics production, 1999 to 2000*, http://www.jpif.gr.jp/3toukei/conts/nenji/y_seihin_c.htm. [11]

Joseph, B. et al. (2021), "Recycling of medical plastics", *Advanced Industrial and Engineering Polymer Research*, http://dx.doi.org/10.1016/j.aiepr.2021.06.003. [15]

Kalantary, R. et al. (2021), "Effect of COVID-19 pandemic on medical waste management: a case study", *Journal of Environmental Health Science and Engineering*, Vol. 19/1, pp. 831-836, http://dx.doi.org/10.1007/s40201-021-00650-9. [59]

Laubinger, F. and N. Varghese (2020), *COVID-19 and the looming plastics pandemic*, OECD Environment Focus, https://oecd-environment-focus.blog/2020/07/07/covid-19-and-the-looming-plastics-pandemic/. [35]

Marsh, K. and B. Bugusu (2007), "Food Packaging? Roles, Materials, and Environmental Issues", *Journal of Food Science*, Vol. 72/3, pp. R39-R55, http://dx.doi.org/10.1111/j.1750-3841.2007.00301.x. [5]

Martin, P. et al. (2020), *Can the polyester industry recover from Covid-19's shockwaves?*, Wood Mackenzie, https://www.woodmac.com/news/opinion/can-the-polyester-industry-recover-from-covid-19s-shockwaves/full-report/. [43]

McKeen, L. (2014), "Plastics Used in Medical Devices", in *Handbook of Polymer Applications in Medicine and Medical Devices*, Elsevier, http://dx.doi.org/10.1016/b978-0-323-22805-3.00003-7. [16]

METI (2020), *METI to Convey Information on Menu of Support Measures for Businesses Affected by Novel Coronavirus Disease Utilizing LINE Application*, Ministry of Economy, Trade and Industry (METI), Government of Japan, https://www.meti.go.jp/english/covid-19/mask.html. [25]

Murphy, H. (2020), *California Lifts Ban on Plastic Bags Amid Virus Concerns*, The New York Times, https://www.nytimes.com/2020/04/24/us/california-plastic-bag-ban-coronavirus.html. [83]

National Bureau of Statistics of China (2021), *Total Retail Sales of Consumer Goods Went Up by 4.6 percent in December 2020*, National Bureau of Statistics of China, http://www.stats.gov.cn/English/PressRelease/202101/t20210119_1812515.html. [32]

National News Bureau of Thailand (2020), *Covid-19 has positive impact on ecosystem*, National News Bureau of Thailand, https://thainews.prd.go.th/en/news/detail/TCATG200418155259223. [24]

NUS (2020), *The poison of disposables*, NUS, https://blog.nus.edu.sg/poisonofconsumerism/2020/07/16/the-poison-of-disposables/. [53]

OECD (2021), *OECD Economic Outlook, Interim Report March 2021*, OECD Publishing, Paris, https://dx.doi.org/10.1787/34bfd999-en. [1]

OECD (2021), *The OECD Green Recovery Database : Examining the environmental implications of COVID-19 recovery policies*, https://www.oecd.org/coronavirus/en/policy-responses. [99]

OECD (2020), *Cities policy responses*, https://www.oecd.org/coronavirus/policy-responses. [49]

OECD (2020), *The face mask global value chain in the COVID-19 outbreak: Evidence and policy lessons*, OECD Publishing, Paris, https://dx.doi.org/10.1787/a4df866d-en. [20]

OECD (2018), *Improving Markets for Recycled Plastics: Trends, Prospects and Policy Responses*, OECD Publishing, Paris, https://dx.doi.org/10.1787/9789264301016-en. [80]

OECD (forthcoming), *Global Plastics Outlook, Volume 2*, OECD. [39]

Oliveira, W. et al. (2021), "Food packaging wastes amid the COVID-19 pandemic: Trends and challenges", *Trends in Food Science & Technology*, http://dx.doi.org/10.1016/J.TIFS.2021.05.027. [33]

Oral, E., S. Kurtz and O. Muratoglu (2017), "7.3 Ultrahigh Molecular Weight Polyethylene Total Joint Implants", in *Comprehensive Biomaterials II*, Materials Science and Materials Engineering, http://dx.doi.org/10.1016/b978-0-12-803581-8.10219-x. [17]

Patil, A., A. Patel and R. Purohit (2017), "An overview of Polymeric Materials for Automotive Applications", *Materials Today: Proceedings*, Vol. 4/2, pp. 3807-3815, http://dx.doi.org/10.1016/j.matpr.2017.02.278. [41]

Patrício Silva, A. et al. (2020), "Rethinking and optimising plastic waste management under COVID-19 pandemic: Policy solutions based on redesign and reduction of single-use plastics and personal protective equipment", *Science of The Total Environment*, Vol. 742, p. 140565, http://dx.doi.org/10.1016/j.scitotenv.2020.140565. [12]

Peng, J. et al. (2020), "Medical waste management practice during the 2019-2020 novel coronavirus pandemic: Experience in a general hospital", *American Journal of Infection Control*, Vol. 48/8, pp. 918-921, http://dx.doi.org/10.1016/J.AJIC.2020.05.035. [57]

PlasticsEurope (2021), *EU Plastics Production and Demand: First Estimates for 2020*, PlasticsEurope Association of Plastics Manufacturers, https://www.plasticseurope.org/en/newsroom/news/eu-plastics-production-and-demand-first-estimates-2020. [6]

Prata, J. et al. (2020), "COVID-19 Pandemic Repercussions on the Use and Management of Plastics", *Environmental Science & Technology*, Vol. 54/13, pp. 7760-7765, http://dx.doi.org/10.1021/ACS.EST.0C02178. [28]

PRE (2020), *Plastics recyclers cease production*, Plastics Recyclers Europe, https://www.plasticsrecyclers.eu/post/plastics-recyclers-cease-production. [82]

Promchertoo, P. (2020), *Food delivery services add tonnes of plastic to Thailand's landfills during COVID-19 crisis*, https://www.channelnewsasia.com/news/asia/food-delivery-increases-thailand-plastic-waste-during-COVID-19-12711692?cid. [51]

Ren, D. (2020), *China boosts face mask production capacity by 450 per cent in a month, threatening a glut scenario*, South China Morning Post, https://www.scmp.com/business/companies/article/3075289/china-boosts-face-mask-production-capacity-450-cent-month. [22]

Roberts, K. et al. (2021), "Increased personal protective equipment litter as a result of COVID-19 measures", *Nature Sustainability*, http://dx.doi.org/10.1038/s41893-021-00824-1. [62]

RWMO (2020), *Interim Report: Performance of the Waste Sector in Ireland: Covid 19 - Initial Restrictions Phase 12th March - 18th May 2020*, Regional Waste Management Offices, https://acrplus.org/images/project/Covid-19/RWMO_Ireland_Covid_19_Interim_Report_Waste.pdf. [54]

S&P Global (2020), *Global petrochemical trends: H2 2020*, S&P Global, https://www.spglobal.com/platts/en/market-insights/special-reports/petrochemicals/global-petrochemical-outlook-h2-2020. [38]

Sabanoglu, T. (2020), *Top textile exporting countries worldwide 2019*, Statista, https://www.statista.com/statistics/236397/value-of-the-leading-global-textile-exporters-by-country/. [42]

Sarkodie, S. and P. Owusu (2020), "Impact of COVID-19 pandemic on waste management", *Environment, Development and Sustainability 2020 23:5*, Vol. 23/5, pp. 7951-7960, http://dx.doi.org/10.1007/S10668-020-00956-Y. [97]

SCIO (2020), *Fighting COVID-19: China in Action*, The State Council, The People's Republic of China, http://english.scio.gov.cn/whitepapers/2020-06/07/content_76135269.htm. [23]

Simon, F. (2020), *EU dismisses industry calls to lift ban on single-use plastics*, euractiv.com, https://www.euractiv.com/section/circular-economy/news/eu-dismisses-industry-calls-to-lift-ban-on-single-use-plastics/. [93]

Solid Waste Management Services (2020), *Impact of Covid-19 on Waste Collection and LItter in Greenspaces and Parks*, Solid Waste Management Services, Toronto, https://www.toronto.ca/legdocs/mmis/2020/ie/bgrd/backgroundfile-156330.pdf. [74]

Staub, C. (2020), *City data shows COVID-19 impacts on recycling tonnages*, Resource Recycling, https://resource-recycling.com/recycling/2020/04/28/city-data-shows-COVID-19-impacts-on-recycling-tonnages/#:~:text=Recycling%20programs%20are%20reporting%20greater. [55]

Staub, C. (2020), *Coronavirus pandemic disrupts recycling sector*, Resource Recycling, https://resource-recycling.com/recycling/2020/03/17/coronavirus-pandemic-disrupts-recycling-sector/. [77]

Staub, C. (2020), *How programs in NY, Texas and Colorado are handling COVID-19*, Resource Recycling, https://resource-recycling.com/recycling/2020/08/25/how-programs-in-ny-texas-and-colorado-are-handling-covid-19/. [96]

Subramanian, S. (2020), *How the face mask became the world's most coveted commodity*, The Guardian, https://www.theguardian.com/world/2020/apr/28/face-masks-coveted-commodity-coronavirus-pandemic. [21]

Tabuchi, H. (2020), *In Coronavirus, Industry Sees Chance to Undo Plastic Bag Bans*, The New York Times, https://www.nytimes.com/2020/03/26/climate/plastic-bag-ban-virus.html. [84]

Tabuchi, H. (2020), *In Coronavirus, Industry Sees Chance to Undo Plastic Bag Bans*, The New York Times, https://www.nytimes.com/2020/03/26/climate/plastic-bag-ban-virus.html. [34]

Tesfaldet, Y. et al. (2021), "Assessing face mask littering in urban environments and policy implications: The case of Bangkok", *Science of The Total Environment*, p. 150952, http://dx.doi.org/10.1016/j.scitotenv.2021.150952. [70]

Toto, D. (2020), *Challenges of the unknown*, Waste Today, https://www.wastetodaymagazine.com/article/covid-19-recycling-industry-survey-responses/. [78]

US Board of Governors of the Federal Reserve System (2021), *Industrial Production: Manufacturing: Non-Durable Goods: Plastics and Rubber Products (NAICS = 326) [IPG326S]*, Federal Reserve Bank of St. Louis, https://fred.stlouisfed.org/series/IPG326S. [9]

US Bureau of Labor Statistics (2020), *From the barrel to the pump: the impact of the COVID-19 pandemic on prices for petroleum products*, US Bureau of Labor Statistics, https://www.bls.gov/opub/mlr/2020/article/from-the-barrel-to-the-pump.htm. [8]

US State of Maine (2020), *Governor Mills, Legislature Spearhead Emergency Legislative Package to Respond to COVID-19*, State of Maine: Office of Governor Janet T. Mills, https://www.maine.gov/governor/mills/news/governor-mills-legislature-spearhead-emergency-legislative-package-respond-covid-19-2020-03-17. [85]

Wei, G. (2020), *Medical Waste Management Experience and Lessons in COVID-19 Outbreak in Wuhan*, https://www.waste360.com/medical-waste/medical-waste-management-experience-and-lessons-covid-19-outbreak-wuhan. [58]

Yousefi, M. et al. (2021), "Municipal solid waste management during COVID-19 pandemic: effects and repercussions", *Environmental Science and Pollution Research*, Vol. 28/25, pp. 32200-32209, http://dx.doi.org/10.1007/s11356-021-14214-9. [50]

Zambrano-Monserrate, M., M. Ruano and L. Sanchez-Alcalde (2020), "Indirect effects of COVID-19 on the environment", *Science of The Total Environment*, Vol. 728, p. 138813, http://dx.doi.org/10.1016/j.scitotenv.2020.138813. [76]

Zecchini, F. (2021), *Italy delays contested new sugar and plastic taxes until 2023*, Reuters, https://www.reuters.com/world/europe/italy-delays-contested-new-sugar-plastic-taxes-until-2023-2021-10-21/. [87]

Zhou Peng, T. (2021), *Petrochemicals 2020: A year of resilience and the road to recovery*, McKinsey & Company, https://www.mckinsey.com/~/media/mckinsey/industries/chemicals/our%20insights/petrochemicals%202020%20a%20year%20of%20resilience%20and%20the%20road%20to%20recovery/petrochemicals-2020-a-year-of-resilience-and-the-road-to-recovery-vf.pdf?shouldIndex=false. [37]

Notes

[1] This chapter focuses on the implications of the pandemic as they emerged in 2020. The longer-term consequences are included in the baseline projections presented in Volume 2 of the Global Plastics Outlook (OECD, forthcoming[39]).

[2] Despite the lower input onto the market, separate collection of plastic packaging waste increased by 4% compared to 2019 levels, mostly reflecting improvements in waste management systems in parts of the country.

[3] To reach these figures, they multiplied one face mask per day with the share of people who accept face masks in each region (a share varying widely across countries – from 5% in Sweden to 95% in Spain, with China at 84% and the USA at 73%). This leads to a global estimate of 140 billion face masks used per year. They then calculated the plastic pollution using the regional shares of mismanaged waste.

[4] In comparison, 4 750 items of PPE were found for every km^2 of grocery store parking lots and 1 330 items per km^2 in hospital districts (Ammendolia et al., 2021[73]).

[5] One quarter of the costs were attributed to the loss of labour due to COVID-19 related illness and medical recommendations for self-isolation (Solid Waste Management Services, 2020[74]).

[6] The projections of plastics use to 2060 presented in Volume 2 of the *Global Plastics Outlook* (OECD, forthcoming[39]) build on these impacts in 2020 as well as on the recovery pathway laid out in Dellink et al. (2021[3]).

[7] Changes in relative prices will affect production methods and lead to some substitution effects between various inputs in production, but the effect is relatively small compared to the effects of output changes.

4. Trends in the secondary plastics markets

This chapter discusses recycling and explores the structure of the secondary plastics market, tracking its expansion in recent decades. It also analyses recent developments in policy, investment, and trade in waste and their impacts on secondary markets.

KEY MESSAGES

- Recycling has an important role to play in lowering plastics' environmental footprint alongside strategies to reduce plastic waste through reduced consumption and reuse systems. Recycling diverts material from more harmful waste management practices, and the availability of secondary (recycled) plastics can help lower demand for primary (virgin) plastics.
- The production of secondary plastics has more than quadrupled in weight in the last 20 years and is growing more quickly than primary plastic production. However secondary plastic markets remain small and in 2019, secondary plastics production accounted for only 6% of total plastic production. Most sectors continue to rely on primary plastics for economic or quality reasons.
- Markets for secondary plastics remain vulnerable. Historically, secondary material has often been used as a substitute for primary plastic. As a result, the price of secondary plastics correlated with the price of primary plastic equivalents. This absence of a separate demand for secondary material affects the viability of recycling, since secondary prices do not fully reflect the costs of secondary production (e.g. collection, sorting, and processing), but follow price patterns of primary plastics and their inputs (e.g. oil prices). As well, compared with firms that produce primary plastics, recycling firms produce less material, are less capital-intensive and have fewer sales making them less resilient.
- There are positive signs for secondary plastics markets. Recent policies in some countries have strengthened policies to "push" supply through taxes on non-recycled plastic waste, and "pull" demand for secondary plastic through recycled content targets. An emerging differentiation in price with primary equivalents in some markets for some polymers, and growing innovation in recycling technologies, are positive signs.
- Since January 2021, amendments to the Basel Convention and OECD Decision on Transboundary Movements of Waste have set new requirements for plastic waste trade. These measures are expected to prolong a trend of diminishing trade volumes, increasing domestic processing and recycling, as well as exports shifting to new countries, initiated when the People's Republic of China introduced its National Sword policy in 2017, which banned most imports of plastic waste.

4.1. Markets for secondary plastics contribute to a more circular use of plastics

As highlighted by the "3 R framework" (reduce, reuse, recycle), policies should seek first to reduce plastic consumption and maintain plastic material in higher value loops, prior to recycling. Reducing plastics can be done by optimising product design and reusing can be done by shifting from single-use to more durable plastic products, which can lower the energy use per consumption cycle. Recycling plastics and using this "secondary" plastic material can reduce environmental pressures when reduction or substitution away from plastics is not feasible, or would lead to greater environmental impacts and when durable plastic product reach their end of life. Recycling plastics is thus an important component of the circular economy.

As far as it displaces primary plastic production and does not induce additional plastic consumption, recycling provides environmental benefits (Zink and Geyer, 2018[1]). The separate collection of plastics for recycling helps to keep plastic waste out of landfills (where plastics can emit harmful compounds and leachates), and incineration, during which plastics generate flue gases and other harmful emissions (Ilyas et al., 2018[2]). Moreover, revenues from recycling encourage valuable materials to be collected and adoption of measures for reducing the volume of mismanaged waste. Finally, recycling provides feedstock for secondary plastics, which can be used to make products with a reduced carbon footprint (Benavides et al., 2018[3]; Zheng and Suh, 2019[4]).

4.2. Plastic waste streams, collection, separation and recycling methods determine the value of secondary plastics

Recycling plastics requires several costly upstream steps, including collecting, sorting and transporting waste. The organisation of these activities differs structurally across countries (Table 4.1). Most high-income countries have a formal system of separate collection organised by the government. The collected material is frequently sorted using capital-intensive processing. In contrast, in low-income countries, separate collection and sorting of high value recyclables such as PET (polyethylene terephthalate) are often performed by low-skilled workers or by an informal recycling sector (i.e. waste pickers). While informal workers can perform key functions in collecting and sorting wastes, there are serious concerns that informal recycling processes are relatively inefficient and environmentally harmful, often failing to prevent emissions of hazardous substances and resulting in health and environmental risks (Box 4.1).

Table 4.1. Collection and sorting processes differ by country income level

	Low-income countries	High income countries
Collection	• Only partial coverage of public waste collection in cities and almost none in the countryside. • Informal sector plays a key role in collecting and sorting recyclables. • High-quality sorting achieved, but only for some high value streams such as PET.	• Municipal-led plastics recycling schemes are common. • Quality of sorting depends on local habits, collection facilities for recyclables and financial incentives. • Collection systems are highly mechanised.
Sorting	• Manual sorting is common. • Mechanical equipment limited to balers for compaction.	• Highly mechanised and capital-intensive facilities to maximise recovery of valuable plastics.
International transport	• Low- value collected waste is usually dumped. • Local recycling industry can attract flows of international waste plastics, e.g. South-East Asian States are net-importers.	• High-value plastics are recycled locally. • Low value plastics are exported for recycling elsewhere.

Source: Adapted from (OECD, 2018[5]). *Improving Markets for Recycled Plastics: Trends, Prospects and Policy Responses*, https://dx.doi.org/10.1787/9789264301016-en.

Box 4.1. Formalising informal recycling remains a challenge

Informal recycling refers to waste recovery activities that are not supported or recognised by the public sector's waste management authorities. Activities range from waste collection and separation (i.e. "waste picking"), to more "downstream" recycling and processing. At least 15 million people worldwide work in the informal waste sector, collecting and recovering recyclable material from waste, which demonstrates the prevalence of the informal sector (Medina, 2008[6]).

The impacts of the informal sector on recycling are complex and context-dependent. In developed countries with formal waste management systems, "waste-picking" can undermine the financing of these systems by removing valuable materials from the waste stream. However, in low-income countries with limited formal collection and sorting, the informal waste sector can collect and sort high value recyclables effectively (Gunsilius, 2011[7]; CWG and GiZ, 2011[8]).

Nevertheless, there are serious environmental concerns over informal "downstream" operations such as the recycling and treatment of waste. These operations often use crude processes that are not environmentally sound. For instance, informal recycling processes for e-waste often involve burning products to recover valuable metals. Informal waste processers may also discard, dump, burn or otherwise improperly manage residual waste of insufficient economic value, causing leakage of plastics or pollutants into the environment.

There are also serious social and public health concerns surrounding informal waste management. It is often marginalised or vulnerable groups, including migrants, women, the unemployed, disabled and children, who engage in waste picking, sometimes both working and living in dreadful circumstances on dumpsites (Medina, 2008[6]). Other health impacts include exposure to hazardous emissions from open burning (Velis and Cook, 2021[9]). The occupation is particularly socially precarious as workers are rarely covered by social protection or health insurance. Informal enterprises are, by definition, unregistered, which makes them vulnerable to exploitation, while their lack of proper inventories leave operators vulnerable to theft.

A challenge for lower- and middle-income countries is therefore to find ways to formally integrate workers engaged in the informal waste sector to secure their positive contribution, while mitigating the environmental, health and social impacts (Wilson, Velis and Cheeseman, 2006[10]).

The origin of a plastic waste stream determines the level of purity that can be attained after recycling, and thus the value of the resultant secondary plastic (Table 4.2). Post-industrial waste and post-consumer commercial waste can be collected in large containers to minimise logistic costs. Moreover, control mechanisms (e.g. training employees and visual inspection during pickup) can help to achieve high-quality streams and high market prices. In contrast, post-consumer household waste has a high cost of collection (e.g. kerbside collection is expensive) and often contains a substantial share of impurities. Consequently, the collection of most household waste streams tends to generate a net cost for the municipalities in charge. The high-income countries with the highest recycling rates tend to use Extended Producer Responsibility schemes to finance the collection of recyclable plastics from households (explained in Chapter 6) in order to compensate these costs.

Table 4.2. Post-industrial and post-consumer waste streams vary in value and handling routes

	Post-industrial waste	Post-consumer commercial waste	Post-consumer household waste
Definition	Waste generated during the manufacturing process (ISO, 2016[11]).	Waste generated by commercial, industrial, or institutional facilities (ISO, 2016[11]).	Waste generated by households as end-users of a product (ISO, 2016[11]).
Example(s)	Waste generated in plastic production and conversion (Plastics Europe, 2019[12]).	Waste packaging generated in the distribution chain or waste generated by consumers at a business' premises (Toowoomba Region, 2020[13]).	A used plastic yoghurt pot or soft drink bottle.
Collection	Via negotiated contracts with waste management companies.	Via negotiated contracts with waste management companies to collect high volume containers. Municipalities are sometimes also involved in collecting this stream.	Typically operated or subcontracted by municipalities. Collection through kerbside and communal collection, deposit-refund schemes, and the informal sector.
Sorting	Relatively homogeneous waste stream.	If properly sorted at source, a homogenous waste streams can be achieved.	Intensive sorting and separation required. Impurities often lead to downcycling.
Transport/ trade	Tends to be processed domestically.	Can be processed domestically or exported for recycling elsewhere.	Pure streams are domestically recycled but other streams may be exported for recycling.

Currently, only mechanical recycling[1] of PET and polyethylene (PE) plastics demonstrates widespread commercial viability (Garcia and Robertson, 2017[14]). Mechanical recycling of polypropylene (PP) and polyvinyl chloride (PVC) also occurs, but to a lesser extent. Compared with other forms of plastics production and recycling (see below), mechanical recycling requires little capital investment and has fewer barriers to entry for new firms (Hundertmark et al., 2018[15]). However, it results in varying degrees of degradation and quality can only be maintained for a limited number of cycles involving the same material (Hatti-Kaul et al., 2020[16]). Therefore, manufacturers often use mechanically recycled plastics for lower value applications, known as downcycling (Ellen MacArthur Foundation, 2016[17]). Advances in design, separation (either separate collection or using technology to sort mixed waste), pre-treatment and recyclability can improve the output quality of mechanical recycling.

Chemical recycling operations[2] can complement mechanical recycling by expanding recycling opportunities to additional resins and waste streams (Ragaert et al., 2021[18]). However, chemical recycling facilities are still predominantly in the pilot or demonstration stages (Hann and Connock, 2020[19]). The primary barrier to expansion is economic feasibility. In addition, due to the high energy intensity of these processes and their production of toxic by-products, chemical recycling may not always be environmentally beneficial. However, the processes can produce particularly high-quality, pure material (in purification and plastic-to-monomer applications) that can meet the standards for food applications, potentially justifying the costs (Ragaert et al., 2021[18]). Plastic-to-fuel applications, in which plastic waste is transformed into fuels, can generate equally high-quality end products, but some countries and stakeholders do not consider this to be recycling. In the coming decades, industry is likely to increase investments in chemical recycling due to its potential role in future recycling markets.

4.3. Secondary plastics markets remain small and vulnerable despite recent growth

Recycling markets are the fora of exchange for the numerous actors involved at different points in the supply chain, including the public sector, firms, traders (exporters and importers), brokers, and ultimately manufacturers. Markets allocate recycled plastics to the use with the highest value and create a profit motive that incentivises higher recycling rates. The larger the scale and depth of the markets, the better secondary materials are able to compete with primary equivalents, in turn driving the environmental benefits of recycling.

Secondary plastics production has more than quadrupled in the last two decades, from roughly 6.7 Mt in 2000 to 29.1 Mt in 2019, but remains small compared to primary plastics production. Production of primary equivalents nearly doubled over the same period amounting to 431 Mt in 2019. Taken together, the continued growth in primary production and the relatively small size of secondary production suggests that there has not been a fundamental shift in the market to secondary plastics (Figure 4.1).

Figure 4.1. Secondary production is growing, but makes up only six percent of total plastic production

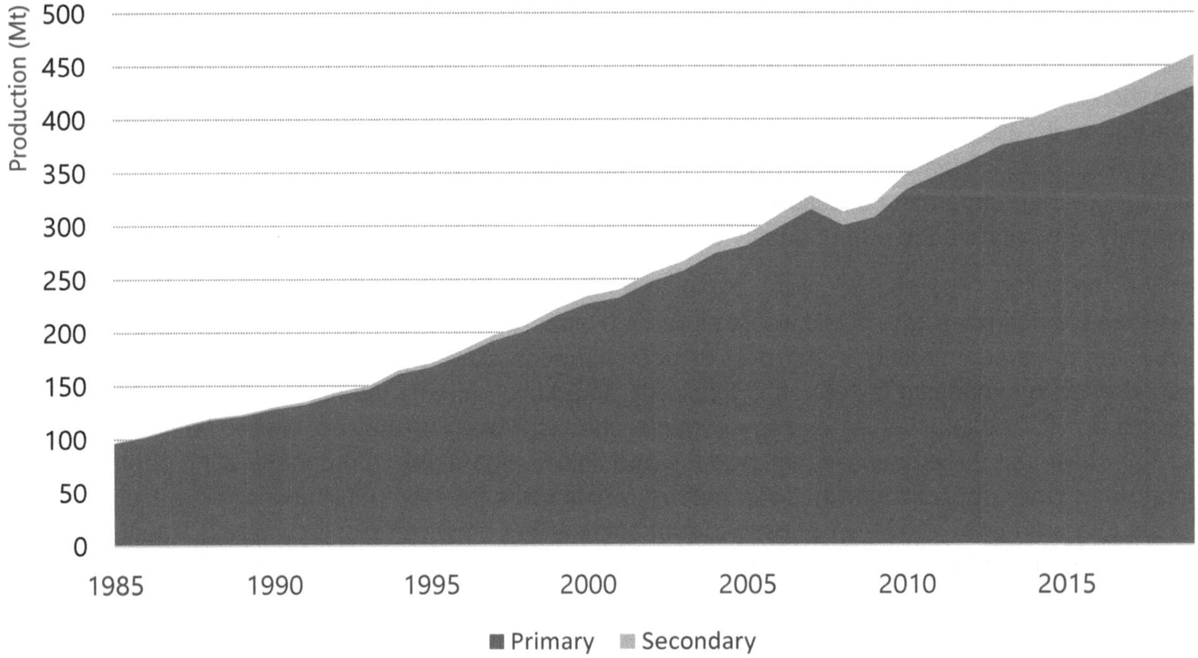

Source: OECD Global Plastics Outlook Database, https://doi.org/10.1787/c0821f81-en.

StatLink https://stat.link/9szph5

There are regional differences in secondary production capacity. The Asia-Pacific region is the largest producer by weight, followed by Europe and North America. Recycling is likely to continue increasing in Asia-Pacific due to growing infrastructure development as well as low labour costs. Introducing more advanced technology and upscaling operations could further improve the quantity and quality of the supply of secondary plastics in these markets. In Europe growth is expected due to policies such as recycled content standards that favour the production and use of secondary plastics (Grand View Research, 2020[20]).

Economically, there are several drivers of and barriers to secondary production. Historically, secondary material has often been used by manufacturers as a (low-cost) substitute for primary plastic. As a result the price of secondary plastics correlated with the price of primary plastic equivalents. This absence of a separate demand for secondary material affects the viability of recycling, since secondary material prices do not fully reflect the costs of secondary production (e.g. collection, sorting, and processing), but follow price patterns of primary plastics and their inputs (e.g. oil prices). This leaves secondary plastics markets exposed to price fluctuations in primary plastics markets. As well, compared with firms that produce primary plastics, recycling firms produce less material, are less capital-intensive and have fewer sales making them less resilient (Table 4.3). These differences between primary and secondary markets suggest that secondary markets are relatively small and vulnerable (OECD, 2018[5]).

Table 4.3. There are key differences in the economics of primary and secondary plastics

	Primary plastics	Secondary plastics
Business model	Turn petroleum or natural gas streams into a finished product through chemical processing	Reprocess used or otherwise discarded plastic material so it may serve another useful purpose
Resin production volumes in selected countries	• Canada: USD 8.3 billion in sales (Deloitte, 2019[21]) • Japan: 10 670 kt (Plastic Waste Management Institute, 2019[22]) • Global: 10 companies responsible for over USD 816 billion in sales (Polymer Properties Database, 2018[23])	• Canada: USD 290 million in sales (Deloitte, 2019[21]) • Japan: 760 kt (Plastic Waste Management Institute, 2019[22]) • Global: USD 35 billion in market value by entire industry (Locock et al., 2017[24])
Price drivers	• Prices of raw material feedstock such as natural gas and crude oil and refining costs (Clews, 2016[25])	• Prices of substitutes: primary polymers or other materials (e.g. cotton for fibre) • Quality (absence of impurities) • Opportunity costs of other forms of waste management; and • Costs of production in markets with a separate demand for secondary plastics (OECD, 2018[5])
Profile of typical firm	• Specialist company focused on a specific stage of production; or • Vertically integrated major energy and national oil companies (Clews, 2016[25])	• Operates at regional or local scale; and • Specialises in one or a few waste streams (Oestreich et al., 2020[26])

Note: kt = kilotonne.

Another barrier to the growth of secondary plastics is the quality of the plastic waste collected. The wide range of polymers and additives (including hazardous chemicals) used in the manufacture of plastics means that polymers in plastic waste are often co-mingled and contaminated (see Annex A for more details). Moreover, if not sorted properly and kept apart from other waste streams such as organic waste, collected plastic waste is of little value for secondary material production due to the difficulty of extracting impurities and the limited range of potential applications for low-grade recycled material.

Regulation strongly affects the business case for recycling activities and the market for secondary plastics. High landfill and incineration taxes are strong drivers of recycling, as are landfill bans. However, if not accompanied by strong environmental standards and enforcement, the risk is that waste will continue to be dumped, incinerated or mismanaged, weakening recycling rates (OECD, 2018[5]).

4.4. There are recent positive signs for secondary markets

4.4.1. Policy frameworks are being strengthened

Public authorities are strengthening policy frameworks to both restrain the demand for primary plastics (Chapter 6) and to replace primary plastics with secondary material in applications where plastics are the optimal material. Previous OECD work evaluated 51 policy interventions to improve secondary plastics markets (OECD, 2018[5]) that remain highly relevant. To summarise, policies can foster secondary markets and increase their resilience in three ways:

- Demand-"pull" measures, such as recycled content standards or green public procurement can increase the demand for secondary materials.
- Supply-"push" measures, such as extended producer responsibility (EPR) schemes or research and development funds for recycling technologies can lower costs and improve the quality of supply. Eco-design and information requirements, such as design standards for disassembly and information requirements or bans of hazardous substances can further improve the quality of supplied secondary materials (Box 4.2). Landfill and incineration taxes are further policies that incentivise recycling.

- Policies that aim to ensure that the price of primary plastic includes the external costs of primary production can level the playing field for recycling. Examples include taxes on primary production, and reforming support for fossil fuel production and consumption.

Box 4.2. Design requirements can either restrict or enable the use of secondary plastics

In many countries there are strict requirements on the use of recycled plastics for food-grade material. For example, in the European Union only recycled PET sourced from previous food contact material is allowed to be used for food-grade applications (European Union, 2008[27]). For PET[1] or high-density polyethylene (HDPE), these requirements can be met by selectively collecting beverage containers and milk bottles, but this is more challenging for many other polymer streams as they are often collected together with non-food-grade material (Victory, 2020[28]).

Current design and waste collection practices only provide small amounts of the high-quality material that meets the regulatory requirements. In the medium and long term, growing demand for secondary plastics and subsequent price increases can encourage better supply quality and quantity.

Design requirements can help to improve the quality of plastics, enabling recycling for higher end secondary use. Examples of such policies include bans or clear marking of hazardous additives. In addition, policies that incentivise design for disassembly can enable greater flexibility for both re-use and recycling.

Note: [1] PlasticsEurope considers all PET resin grades placed on the EU market to be food-contact approved (EFSA CONTAM Panel, 2016[29]).

Three recent policy developments are worth further consideration for their potential to shift the demand and supply from primary to secondary plastics:

- regulatory recycled content standards
- taxes on non-recycled waste generation, and
- extensive voluntary commitments by firms.

An increasing number of countries are introducing mandatory minimum recycled content standards or similar incentives. For instance, the EU's Single-Use Plastics Directive will require plastic bottles to contain at least 25% recycled content by 2025 and 30% recycled content by 2030 (European Union, 2019[30]). From 2022, California's Assembly Bill No. 793 will require a minimum share (up to 50% in 2030) of post-consumer recycled plastic in plastic beverage containers (California Legislative Information, 2020[31]). Also from 2022, the UK will apply a tax (GBP 200 per tonne) on plastic packaging with less than 30% recycled material (HM Revenue & Customs, 2020[32]). These policies aim to "pull" demand for secondary plastics though requirements or incentives for the composition of products or packaging. In turn, demand can help to instigate improved supply of secondary material as an input for regulated products.

In addition, several countries are planning to tax non-recycled plastic waste. The European Union introduced a levy on its Member States of EUR 0.8 for every kilogramme of non-recycled plastic packaging waste generated. This levy is in place since 1 January 2021 and is likely to lead to the introduction of a round of related national taxes in the coming years (European Commission, 2021[33]). For example, Italy and Spain have each announced they will introduce national taxes on non-recycled, single-use plastic packaging (KPMG, 2020[34]). Market-based instruments, such as these can help to increase the cost of waste management options that compete with recycling, lowering its relative cost. These measures can be a "push" for recycling by increasing the quantity of material collected for recycling.

Voluntary corporate commitments may help to generate significant additional demand for recycled post-consumer household polymers of high quality and purity. In recent years, leading brand-owners of fast-moving consumer goods and other sectors have made an increasing number of commitments to incorporate post-consumer recycled material in their products. Examples include the Ellen MacArthur Foundation's New Plastics Economy Global Commitment and the European Circular Plastics Alliance (Ellen MacArthur Foundation, 2021[35]; European Commission, 2021[36]). If these commitments are realised, they will substantially increase demand for recycled plastics, especially for food-grade secondary material.

4.4.2. The prices of some secondary plastic grades seems to be decoupling from primary equivalents

The European PET market suggests that the combination of policy instruments and recent industry commitments discussed above may be creating a specific demand for recycled polymers at prices that are less dependent on the prices of substitutes (Brown and Kinner, 2020[37]). From 2018, the difference between the reported price of secondary food-grade PET pellets and the spot price of a primary equivalent has grown to over EUR 600/tonne in 2020 (Victory, McGeough and Tudball, 2021[38]). The difference suggests some decoupling of primary and secondary prices in this market, especially for food-grade applications. This specific demand for secondary material should mean prices better reflect the underlying costs and should make demand less volatile, which should further boost recycling and secondary material supply.

4.4.3. Innovation in recycling is on the rise

The interest of entrepreneurs and investors in the circular use of plastics is also picking up. The total number of patents for environmentally relevant plastic innovation rose by a factor of 3.4 between 1990 and 2017 (for details see Chapter 5). In addition, new patents are increasingly focusing on waste prevention and recycling, with about half of all patented plastic innovations in 2017 having a focus on these areas. Changes in consumer priorities and an increasing policy emphasis on plastic recycling seem to have improved the business case for investments in new recycling technologies and projects (Box 4.3).

Box 4.3. Is the business case for investing in recycling improving?

The business case for investing more in recycling has until recently been undermined by the low prices of primary material (in part due to their external costs), the high cost of recycling and competition with other disposal options. The following emerging shifts should improve the viability of secondary plastics:

- Growing public awareness of plastic leakage is driving policy interventions and voluntary commitments from the private sector and strengthening the demand for recycled material.
- Technological advances are lowering recycling costs, improving the quality (i.e. price) of secondary plastic material and expanding commercial recycling to more polymers and waste streams.
- Demand for plastics (and demand for feedstock for plastic production) is starting to grow, especially in emerging economies.
- A growing use of policies internalises the external costs of primary plastic production and alternative waste disposal options.

However, the following developments could reduce the viability of secondary plastics:

- Investment in capital-intensive waste-to-energy infrastructure establishes a long-term constant demand for incineration, which could create a "lock-in" effect and lower the incentive to launch recycling projects.
- Technological advances in extraction or oversupply reduce the price of fossil fuels, driving down the relative price of primary plastics.

4.4.4. Trade in plastic waste is expected to keep falling in the near future

International trade in plastic waste and scrap can enable economic efficiencies by moving materials to countries with a comparative advantage in recycling plastic. For example, markets in Asia – particularly China and India – can produce secondary material cheaply due to lower labour costs and a well-developed recycling infrastructure (Locock et al., 2017[24]). China has historically been the predominant export destination for many OECD countries, largely for these reasons, as well as a high demand for (secondary) plastics by its manufacturing sector. In addition, the availability of inexpensive shipping to China, driven by the country's trade surplus and its prominent role in global manufacturing supply chains, has facilitated export flows to China (Wang et al., 2020[39]; Merrington, 2017[40]). The economies of scale that such trade enables are likely to be an essential tool for strengthening secondary markets and bridging (part of) the gap in production between primary and secondary plastics.

On the other hand, trade in waste may lead to environmental leakage, if it is motivated by differences in the stringency or enforcement of environmental regulation (e.g. lower environmental standards for contaminated or hazardous plastic waste treatment) (Yamaguchi, 2018[41]; Kellenberg, 2012[42]). Some export destinations have experienced a serious influx of plastic waste that is heavily contaminated and hard to recycle. A share of this waste is treated by the informal waste management sector, which can lead to environmental and health issues (Box 4.1).

Global waste trade peaked in 2014, but then started to decrease following the introduction of strict import requirements by China (Figure 4.2 and Box 4.4). Since 2013, China has imposed several drastic restrictions on imported plastic waste in order to increase quality, reduce waste leakage and promote recycling of domestically-collected waste. The "Green Fence" policy began in 2013 and banned imports of mixed plastic waste that contained more than 1.5% contamination with non-recyclables (Velis, 2014[43]). Since 2017, the "National Sword" policy has tightened this restriction to 0.5% contamination (Wang et al., 2020[39]; Brooks, Wang and Jambeck, 2018[44]). As these new levels are challenging for industry to meet, the policy effectively banned the vast majority of waste exports to China.

Figure 4.2. The fall in plastic waste exported to China has significantly reduced global trade

Global reported exports of plastic waste and scrap by weight and destination (2012-20)

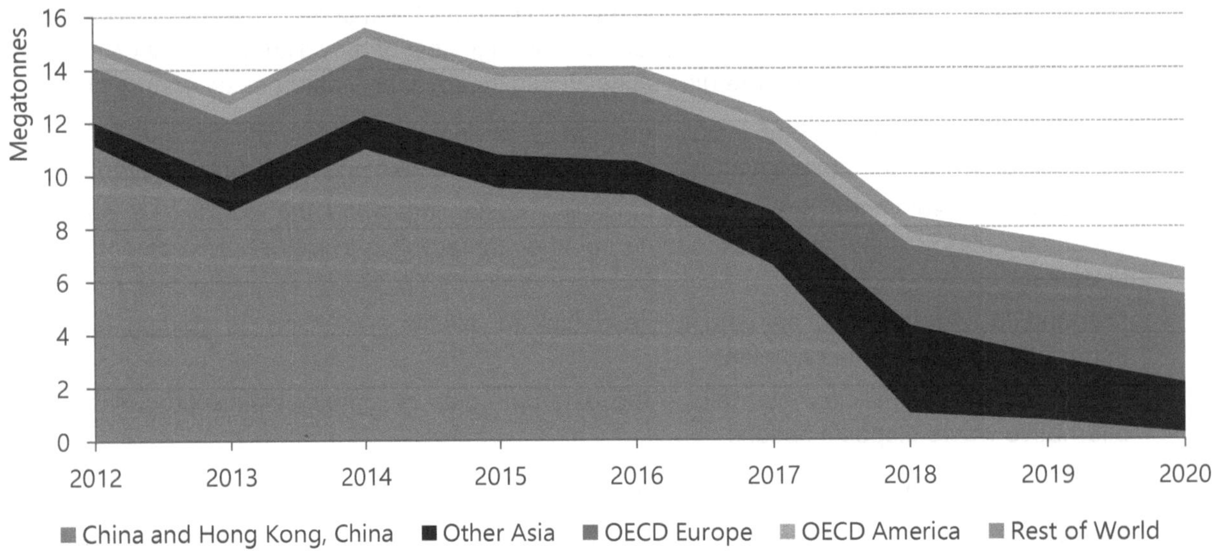

Note: Other Asia is based on country groupings in the OECD ENV-Linkages model and does not include OECD member countries Japan and Korea. OECD America includes Canada, USA, Chile, Colombia, Costa Rica and Mexico. See Table A.A.2 in Annex A for more information on regional aggregations. The graph shows annual data of Harmonised Code (HS) 3915 "Waste, parings and scrap, of plastics" from UN Comtrade. For 2016-18, the sum of monthly reported data for HS 391510, HS 391520, HS 391530 and HS 391590 are used for US reported exports. This is to address a possible gap in annual data, as described by Law et al (2020[45]).
Source: Authors' analysis based on *UN Comtrade Database*, https://comtrade.un.org, accessed 12 October 2021.

Box 4.4. Import restrictions have reduced the share of plastic waste traded

Between 2014 and 2020, the global share of plastic waste exported in overall plastic waste generated declined from about 5.3% (15.6 Mt exported out of 296.2 Mt waste generated) to roughly 1.8% (6.4 Mt exported out of 359.9 Mt generated). Changes in Chinese policy were especially disruptive for Australia and New Zealand, as well as for Japan and Korea, all of which were heavily reliant on exporting plastic waste (Figure 4.3).

The rapid reduction in waste trade, combined with the steady increase in plastic waste, has induced a sudden surge in other outlets: domestic recycling, domestic disposal, domestic stockpiling, or unreported trade. Initially, many companies stockpiled waste for domestic processing or for exporting at a later stage. However, the combination of the sudden restrictions in exports and the short-term recycling capacity limitations has likely lead to a significant amount of plastic waste being disposed of through incineration and landfilling.

Figure 4.3. The share of plastic waste exported has fallen drastically in some OECD regions

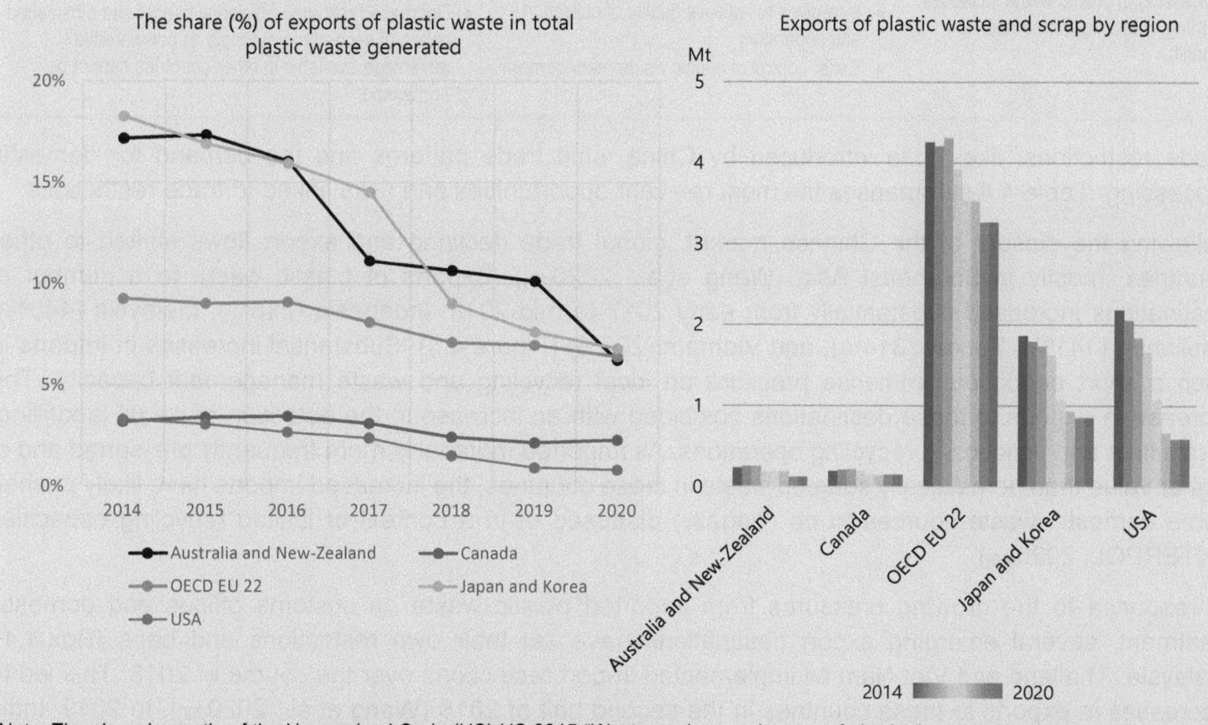

Note: The share is a ratio of the Harmonised Code (HS) HS 3915 "Waste, parings and scrap, of plastics" reported by exporters (reporters), organised by region, to the total weight of plastic waste generated estimated by the OECD ENV-linkages model. For 2016-2018, the sum of monthly reported data for HS 391510, HS 391520, HS 391530 and HS 391590 are used for US reported exports.

Source: Own analysis based on *UN Comtrade Database*, https://comtrade.un.org, accessed 12 October 2021; and OECD Plastics Outlook Database.

Table 4.4. Trade restrictions create both opportunities and risks

	Opportunities	Risks
National import bans lead to more exports to alternative emerging economies with relatively favourable trade terms.	• Building up recycling infrastructure and generating economic activity in alternative import markets	• Trafficking as well as illegal and potentially environmentally unsound waste management in emerging economies that are overwhelmed by imports (INTERPOL, 2020[46]). Especially relevant if enforcement and information campaigns to disseminate trade rules and environmental laws are insufficient
Multilateral trade restrictions (e.g. Amendments to the Basel Convention) lead to more exports to advanced economies within the OECD.	• More material likely to be efficiently recycled in an environmentally sustainable manner • Recycling processes covered by better governance compared with emerging economies • Incentives to improve quality of collection and separation	• Regional trade agreements create favourable trade conditions that could inhibit global movement to markets with comparative advantage (Leigh Mills, Van der Ven and Bodouroglou, 2020[47])
Overall more restrictions reduce international trade and domestic processing of plastic waste increases (sorting, recycling, incineration or landfill).	• Incentives to reduce plastic waste generation and to invest in circular economy business models and infrastructure • Incentives to improve quality of collection and separation • Better control of plastic waste management	• Increased disposal of plastic waste and reliance on incineration or landfilling • Increased illegal dumping where treatment capacity is lacking • Decreased resource efficiency overall and diminished prices of secondary materials as comparative advantage available in other countries cannot be harnessed

Trade restrictions, like those introduced by China, shift trade patterns and the demand for domestic processing. Table 4.4 summarises the most relevant opportunities and risks linked to trade restrictions.

Following the closure of the Chinese market, global trade declined and export flows shifted to other countries, mostly in Southeast Asia (Wang et al., 2020[39]). Exports of plastic waste to a number of destinations increased substantially from early 2017 to mid-2018: Indonesia (218%), Malaysia (440%), Thailand (1141%), Turkey (314%), and Vietnam (203%) (Figure 4.4). Substantial increases in imports in such a short period put immense pressure on local recycling and waste management capacity. The increase in exports to these destinations coincided with an increase in the detection of illegal landfilling, waste fires and unlicensed recycling operations. As imported material is more frequently pre-sorted and of higher value than domestically sourced waste in these countries, the increased imports have likely pushed some domestic waste sources to be (illegally) disposed of in a context of limited recycling capacities (INTERPOL, 2020[46]).

In response to the growing pressures from imported plastic waste on customs offices and domestic treatment, several emerging export destinations have set their own restrictions and bans (Box 4.4). Malaysia, Thailand and Viet Nam all implemented import restrictions over the course of 2018. This led to decreases in exports to these countries in the second half of 2018 (Wang et al., 2020[39]). In 2019, India also banned imports of plastic waste (Staub, 2019[48]). Exports to Malaysia, Viet Nam and most notably Turkey, continued to rise again in 2019. In spring 2021, Turkey introduced an import ban for some types of plastic waste, which was subsequently replaced by an enhanced licensing system (Republic of Turkey, 2021[49]).

Figure 4.4. Global exports of plastic waste have shifted to other countries

Monthly reported exports of HS 3915 by weight (in thousand tonnes) for 2016-2020

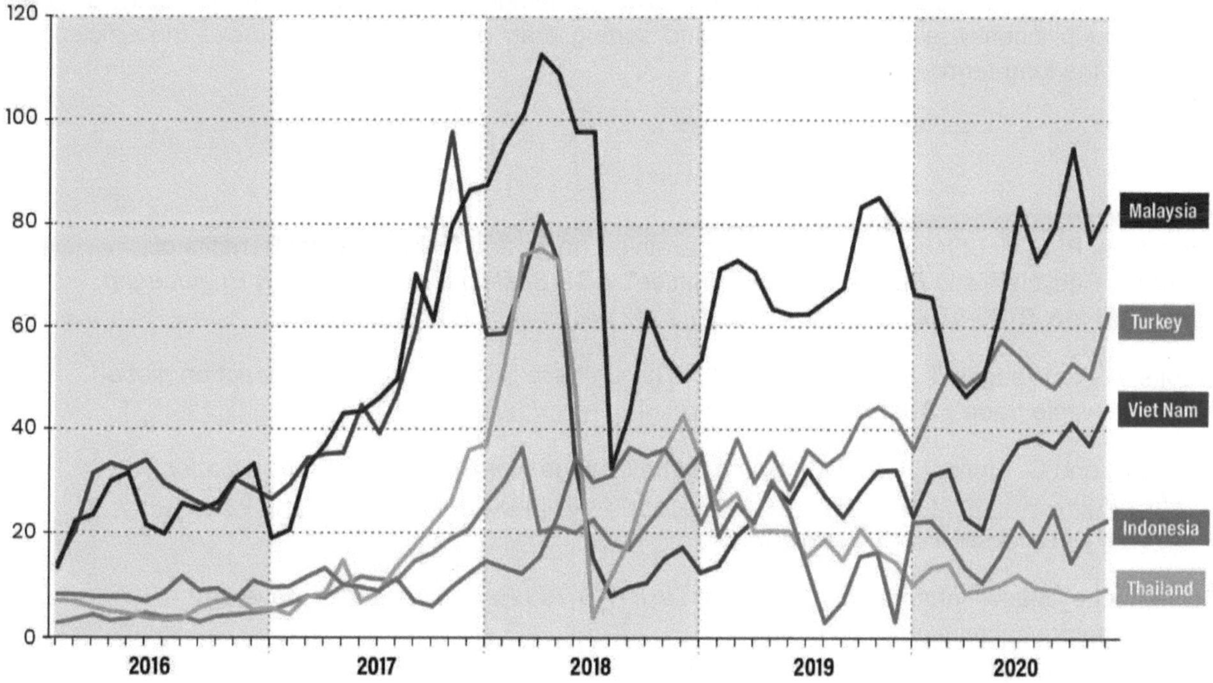

Source: Own analysis based on monthly data of Harmonised Code (HS) 3915 "Waste, parings and scrap, of plastics" from UN Comtrade (UN Comtrade, n.d.[50]), *UN Comtrade Database*, https://comtrade.un.org, accessed 12 October 2021.

The continued demand for feedstock materials in China has triggered foreign investment by Chinese recycling firms in other Asian states. Whilst waste processing has shifted to other countries, China often remains the ultimate destination for much of the processed secondary plastic material (Morita and Hayashi, 2018[51]; Toloken, 2020[52]). Exemplifying China's shift from an importer of plastic waste to an importer of processed secondary plastics, Chinese imports of secondary pellets grew from 10 000 tonnes per month before scrap import restrictions were introduced, to around 400 000 tonnes per month in 2018 (Taylor, 2018[53]).

In addition to unilateral trade restrictions, recent amendments to the Basel Convention and OECD Council Decision 0266 to address environmental concerns stemming from the lack of environmentally sound management of imported plastic waste came into force in 2021:

- The Conference of the Parties (COP) to the Basel Convention on the Control of Transboundary Movements of Hazardous Wastes and Their Disposal (the Basel Convention) adopted amendments to Annexes II, VIII and IX to restrict the transboundary movement of certain plastic waste unless it is almost free of contamination and destined for recycling in an environmentally sound manner (Secretariat of the Basel Convention, 2020[54]).
- The OECD Decision of the Council on the Control of Transboundary Movements of Wastes Destined for Recovery Operations [OECD/LEGAL/0266] (the OECD Decision), which is closely interlinked with the Basel Convention and allows for facilitated intra-OECD waste shipments, was subsequently also amended, enabling OECD Member Countries to control non-hazardous plastic waste in line with their domestic legislation and international law (OECD, 2020[55]).

These amendments have expanded the plastic waste types that are subject to trade restrictions and have also fragmented the rules for intra-OECD trade. The additional heterogeneity in trade rules will likely raise compliance costs for waste traders and increase complexity for enforcement organisations. Taken together these developments are likely to further reduce trade volumes of affected plastic waste in the short term. Conversely, the stricter rules could help to reduce trade in problematic and hard-to-recycle (i.e. highly mixed or contaminated) plastic waste, lowering plastic leakage to the environment. Indirectly, the trade rules also help incentivise better collection and sorting practices, which can improve the efficiency of recycling in the long-term.

References

Benavides, P. et al. (2018), "Exploring Comparative Energy and Environmental Benefits of Virgin, Recycled, and Bio-Derived PET Bottles", *ACS Sustainable Chemistry & Engineering*, Vol. 6/8, pp. 9725-9733, http://dx.doi.org/10.1021/acssuschemeng.8b00750. [3]

Brooks, A., S. Wang and J. Jambeck (2018), "The Chinese import ban and its impact on global plastic waste trade", *Science Advances*, Vol. 4/6, http://dx.doi.org/10.1126/sciadv.aat0131. [44]

Brown, A. and C. Kinner (2020), *Will Coronavirus Change The Course Of Plastic Circularity?*, https://www.woodmac.com/news/opinion/will-coronavirus-change-the-course-of-plastic-circularity/ (accessed on 5 October 2020). [37]

California Legislative Information (2020), *Bill Text - AB-793 Recycling: plastic beverage containers: minimum recycled content.*, https://leginfo.legislature.ca.gov/faces/billTextClient.xhtml?bill_id=201920200AB793 (accessed on 20 October 2021). [31]

Clews, R. (2016), *Project Finance for the International Petroleum Industry*, Elsevier Inc., http://dx.doi.org/10.1016/C2013-0-13683-5. [25]

CWG and GiZ (2011), "The Economics of the Informal Sector in Solid Waste Management: Economic Aspects of the Informal Sector in Solid Waste Management", https://www.giz.de/en/downloads/giz2011-cwg-booklet-economicaspects.pdf (accessed on 23 July 2021). [8]

Deloitte (2019), *Economic Study of the Canadian Plastic Industry, Market and Waste*, http://publications.gc.ca/collections/collection_2019/eccc/En4-366-1-2019-eng.pdf (accessed on 26 February 2021). [21]

EFSA CONTAM Panel (2016), "Statement on the presence of microplastics and nanoplastics in food, with particular focus on seafood", *EFSA Journal*, Vol. 14/6, p. 30, http://dx.doi.org/10.2903/j.efsa.2016.4501. [29]

Ellen MacArthur Foundation (2021), *Global Commitment - New Plastics Economy*, https://www.newplasticseconomy.org/projects/global-commitment (accessed on 21 September 2021). [35]

Ellen MacArthur Foundation (2016), "The New Plastics Economy: Rethinking the future of plastics", *Ellen MacArthur Foundation* January. [17]

European Commission (2021), *Circular Plastics Alliance*, https://ec.europa.eu/growth/industry/policy/circular-plastics-alliance_en (accessed on 21 September 2021). [36]

European Commission (2021), *Plastics own resource*, https://ec.europa.eu/info/strategy/eu-budget/long-term-eu-budget/2021-2027/revenue/own-resources/plastics-own-resource_en (accessed on 1 February 2022). [33]

European Union (2019), *DIRECTIVE (EU) 2019/904 OF THE EUROPEAN PARLIAMENT AND OF THE COUNCIL on the reduction of the impact of certain plastic products on the environment*, https://eur-lex.europa.eu/legal-content/EN/TXT/PDF/?uri=CELEX:32019L0904&from=EN (accessed on 21 September 2021). [30]

European Union (2008), *COMMISSION REGULATION (EC) No 282/2008 on recycled plastic materials and articles intended to come into contact with foods and amending Regulation (EC) No 2023/2006*, https://eur-lex.europa.eu/legal-content/EN/TXT/PDF/?uri=CELEX:32008R0282&from=EN (accessed on 21 September 2021). [27]

Garcia, J. and M. Robertson (2017), *The future of plastics recycling*, American Association for the Advancement of Science, http://dx.doi.org/10.1126/science.aaq0324. [14]

Grand View Research (2020), *Recycled Plastics Market: Market Analysis.* [20]

Gunsilius, E. (2011), "The role of the informal sector in solid waste management and enabling conditions for its integration experiences from GTZ". [7]

Hann, S. and T. Connock (2020), *Chemical Recycling: State of Play*, Eunomia, https://www.eunomia.co.uk/reports-tools/final-report-chemical-recycling-state-of-play/ (accessed on 21 September 2021). [19]

Hatti-Kaul, R. et al. (2020), "Designing Biobased Recyclable Polymers for Plastics", *Trends in Biotechnology*, Vol. 38/1, pp. 50-67, http://dx.doi.org/10.1016/j.tibtech.2019.04.011. [16]

HM Revenue & Customs (2020), *Plastic packaging tax - GOV.UK*, https://www.gov.uk/government/publications/introduction-of-plastic-packaging-tax/plastic-packaging-tax (accessed on 4 May 2021). [32]

Hundertmark, T. et al. (2018), *Recycling and the future of the plastics industry*, https://www.mckinsey.com/industries/chemicals/our-insights/how-plastics-waste-recycling-could-transform-the-chemical-industry (accessed on 21 September 2021). [15]

Ilyas, M. et al. (2018), *Plastic waste as a significant threat to environment - A systematic literature review*, De Gruyter, http://dx.doi.org/10.1515/reveh-2017-0035. [2]

INTERPOL (2020), *Emerging criminal trends in the global plastic waste market since January 2018*, INTERPOL, Lyon, http://www.INTERPOL.int. [46]

ISO (2016), *ISO 14021:2016 Environmental labels and declarations - Self declared environmental claims (Type II environmental labelling)*, https://www.iso.org/obp/ui/#iso:std:iso:14021:ed-2:v1:en:sec:7.8.1.1 (accessed on 2 March 2021). [11]

Kellenberg, D. (2012), "Trading wastes", *Journal of Environmental Economics and Management*, Vol. 64/1, pp. 68-87, http://dx.doi.org/10.1016/j.jeem.2012.02.003. [42]

KPMG (2020), *EU: Review of the proposal for plastic tax, environmental-related measures*, https://home.kpmg/us/en/home/insights/2020/09/tnf-eu-review-porposal-plastic-tax-environmental-related-measures.html (accessed on 4 May 2021). [34]

Law, K. et al. (2020), "The United States' contribution of plastic waste to land and ocean", *Science Advances*, Vol. 6/44, http://dx.doi.org/10.1126/sciadv.abd0288. [45]

Leigh Mills, S., C. Van der Ven and C. Bodouroglou (2020), *Sustainable Trade in Resources: Global Material Flows, Circularity, and Trade*, United Nations Environment Programme, Nariobi, Kenya, https://www.unep.org/resources/publication/sustainable-trade-resources-global-material-flows-circularity-and-trade (accessed on 10 December 2020). [47]

Locock, K. et al. (2017), *The Recycled Plastics Market: Global Analysis and Trends Copyright and disclaimer*, https://publications.csiro.au/rpr/pub?pid=csiro:EP19308 (accessed on 29 September 2020). [24]

Medina, M. (2008), *The informal recycling sector in developing countries*, https://ppp.worldbank.org/public-private-partnership/library/informal-recycling-sector-developing-countries (accessed on 23 July 2021). [6]

Merrington, A. (2017), "Recycling of Plastics", in *Applied Plastics Engineering Handbook: Processing, Materials, and Applications: Second Edition*, Elsevier Inc., http://dx.doi.org/10.1016/B978-0-323-39040-8.00009-2. [40]

Morita, Y. and S. Hayashi (2018), "Proposals to Strengthen Japan's Domestic Measures and Regional Cooperation on Stable and Environmentally Sound Plastic Scrap Recycling: Response to China's Ban on Imports of Plastic Scrap", *IGES Policy Brief*, Vol. 41, https://www.iges.or.jp/en/pub/proposals-strengthen-japan's-domestic-measures/en. [51]

OECD (2020), *Full summary of the amendments to the OECD Council Decision*, https://www.oecd.org/environment/waste/Full_summary_of_the_amendments_to_the_OECD_Council_Decision.pdf (accessed on 26 October 2020). [55]

OECD (2018), *Improving Markets for Recycled Plastics: Trends, Prospects and Policy Responses*, OECD Publishing, Paris, https://dx.doi.org/10.1787/9789264301016-en. [5]

Oestreich, J. et al. (2020), *Der Abfalls der Anderen – Über die Verantwortung für die Plastikflut in Asien*, https://polyproblem.org/wp-content/uploads/POLYPROBLEM-%E2%80%93-Wertsachen.pdf (accessed on 1 March 2021). [26]

Plastic Waste Management Institute (2019), *An introduction to plastic recycling 2019*, http://www.pwmi.or.jp/ei/plastic_recycling_2019.pdf (accessed on 26 February 2021). [22]

Plastics Europe (2019), *The Circular Economy for Plastics: A European Overview*, https://www.plasticseurope.org/en/resources/publications/1899-circular-economy-plastics-european-overview (accessed on 2 March 2021). [12]

Polymer Properties Database (2018), *Top 10 Plastic Resin Producers*, Polymer Database, https://polymerdatabase.com/Polymer%20Brands/Plastic%20Manufacturers.html (accessed on 6 October 2020). [23]

Ragaert, K. et al. (2021), "(forthcoming) A stock take on the technological state-of-the-art for the recycling of plastics ". [18]

Republic of Turkey (2021), *ÇEVRENİN KORUNMASI YÖNÜNDEN KONTROL ALTINDA TUTULAN ATIKLARIN İTHALAT DENETİMİ TEBLİĞİ (ÜRÜN GÜVENLİĞİ VE DENETİMİ: 2022/3)*, https://www.resmigazete.gov.tr/eskiler/2021/12/20211231M4-2.htm (accessed on 22 September 2021). [49]

Secretariat of the Basel Convention (2020), *Basel Convention Plastic Waste Amendments*, http://www.basel.int/Implementation/Plasticwaste/PlasticWasteAmendments/Overview/tabid/8426/Default.aspx (accessed on 22 December 2020). [54]

Staub, C. (2019), "Plastic shipments to India stall as ban draws near", *Plastics Recycling Update*, https://resource-recycling.com/plastics/2019/08/14/plastic-shipments-to-india-stall-as-ban-draws-near/ (accessed on 4 December 2020). [48]

Taylor, B. (2018), "Is China's shift to plastic pellet imports gaining steam?", *Recycling Today*, https://www.recyclingtoday.com/article/china-recycled-plastic-pellet-imports-2018/#:~:text=%E2%80%9CChina's%20imported%20%5Brecycled%2Dcontent,soared%2C%E2%80%9D%20states%20the%20group. [53]

Toloken, S. (2020), "New limits from China on recycled pellets 'real threat'", *Plastics News*, https://www.plasticsnews.com/news/new-limits-china-recycled-pellets-real-threat (accessed on 5 October 2020). [52]

Toowoomba Region (2020), *Definition of domestic waste versus commercial waste*, https://www.tr.qld.gov.au/environment-water-waste/waste-recycling/waste-facilities-rubbish-tips/7413-what-is-domestic-waste (accessed on 2 March 2021). [13]

UN Comtrade (n.d.), *Un Comtrade*, United Nations Statistical Office, https://comtrade.un.org/ (accessed on 5 October 2020). [50]

Velis, C. (2014), *Global recycling markets - plastic waste: A story for one player – China.* [43]

Velis, C. and E. Cook (2021), "Mismanagement of Plastic Waste through Open Burning with Emphasis on the Global South: A Systematic Review of Risks to Occupational and Public Health", *Environmental Science & Technology*, Vol. 55/11, pp. 7186-7207, http://dx.doi.org/10.1021/acs.est.0c08536. [9]

Victory, M. (2020), *Insight: recycling chain facing deeply challenging times but investment opportunities remain*, Independent Commodity Intelligence Services , London, https://www.icis.com/explore/resources/news/2020/05/19/10509185. [28]

Victory, M., H. McGeough and M. Tudball (2021), *2021 Global Market Outlook Sustainability*, https://www.icis.com/explore/resources/2021-global-market-outlook-sustainability-content/ (accessed on 28 January 2021). [38]

Wang, C. et al. (2020), "Structure of the global plastic waste trade network and the impact of China's import Ban", *Resources, Conservation and Recycling*, Vol. 153, http://dx.doi.org/10.1016/j.resconrec.2019.104591. [39]

Wilson, D., C. Velis and C. Cheeseman (2006), "Role of informal sector recycling in waste management in developing countries", *Habitat International*, Vol. 30/4, pp. 797-808, http://dx.doi.org/10.1016/j.habitatint.2005.09.005. [10]

Yamaguchi, S. (2018), "International Trade and the Transition to a More Resource Efficient and Circular Economy: A Concept Paper", *OECD Trade and Environment Working Papers*, No. 2018/03, OECD Publishing, Paris, https://dx.doi.org/10.1787/847feb24-en. [41]

Zheng, J. and S. Suh (2019), "Strategies to reduce the global carbon footprint of plastics", *Nature Climate Change*, Vol. 9/5, pp. 374-378, http://dx.doi.org/10.1038/s41558-019-0459-z. [4]

Zink, T. and R. Geyer (2018), "Material Recycling and the Myth of Landfill Diversion", *Journal of Industrial Ecology*, Vol. 23/3, pp. 541-548, http://dx.doi.org/10.1111/jiec.12808. [1]

Notes

[1] Mechanical recycling processes plastic waste by washing, shredding, melting, followed by re-moulding and is often blended with virgin material to form a finished product, typically in the form of pellets.

[2] Chemical recycling processes plastic waste by applying chemical agents that break down waste material into its building blocks (either polymers, monomers or fuels).

5. Innovation on plastics

Innovation can occur in the production, processing and recycling of plastics. This chapter first reviews the overall trends in innovation for environmentally relevant plastics technologies, before investigating the empirical link between circular economy policies and innovation. Finally, the chapter focuses on recent trends in specific technologies and the related policy implications.

KEY MESSAGES

- Innovation along the entire plastics value chain will be critical to reduce the environmental impacts of plastics. This chapter takes a novel approach to conceptualise and quantify this innovation on a global scale, drawing on patent and trademark data from the past three decades.
- Innovation in environmentally relevant plastics technologies has steadily increased – the total number of patents in this field rose by a factor of 3.4 between 1990 and 2017. In addition, our analysis of trademarks, which measure low-technological innovations that are not necessarily reflected by patents, indicates that every year between 1995 and 2017 innovation for reusing plastics increased by 23%, while innovation for repairing plastics rose by 12%.
- About half of all environmentally relevant innovations patented in 2017 focused on plastics circularity, i.e. on the prevention and recycling of plastic waste. One-third were related to biobased feedstock and the remainder were aimed at converting or disposing of waste as well as removing plastics leaked into the natural environment.
- The focus of patenting activity is shifting away from waste prevention to waste recycling, potentially due to consumer priorities and the policy emphasis on plastics recycling.
- Our quantitative evidence suggests that circular economy policies such as extended producer responsibility systems can encourage innovation in plastic waste recycling. However, innovation in plastic waste prevention and recycling remains limited, representing only 1.2% of total innovation on plastics in 2017 – largely unchanged since 1990 (1.1%). Much more ambitious policies are needed to direct technological change towards closing plastics loops and reducing leakage to the environment.
- Innovation activity is concentrated in OECD countries and the People's Republic of China, together accounting for more than 80% of all patents related to the circular use of plastics. Given the growing problems of plastic leakage in developing countries, there is a need to accelerate the international transfer of these technologies.
- Environmental relevant plastics innovation is evolving rapidly. For example, innovation in biodegradable plastics grew rapidly during the last decade but has recently slowed likely due to concerns over poor biodegradation in natural environments. Plastic-to-plastic chemical recycling technologies, which aim to recycle waste that cannot be processed with mechanical recycling, are only emerging but face significant challenges. Many other innovations across the life cycle of plastics are also emerging.
- Innovation will only lead to scalable solutions if the demand for circular plastics is strong. Consequently, investments in innovation should go hand in hand with education, environmental awareness, financial incentives for behavioural change and binding regulations that should be adapted to the local context.

5.1. What are the trends in environmentally relevant plastics innovation?

To answer this question, the present analysis measure environmentally relevant plastics innovation using patent and trademark data. A patent is an exclusive right granted to an inventor to use and sell his invention for a certain number of years. Patent counts are a common way to measure innovation because they capture detailed information on recent innovations of significant market value (Narin, 1995[1]). In contrast, trademarks measure low-technological innovations that are not necessarily reflected by patents.

Patent counts can be used to measure innovation in environmentally relevant plastics technologies. To do so, textual information in patent abstracts were searched in the PATSTAT database using various combinations of keywords. For example, inventions on mechanical recycling can be identified by a search string such as "shred plastic waste" or "recover polymer scrap", while patents for plastic-to-plastic chemical recycling can be identified by words such as "hydrolysis" and "glycolysis".

Following the database sweep, the identified inventions were scrutinised to extract the patent families related to innovation in environmentally relevant plastics technologies and were classified into three main groups (Figure 5.1):

1. Innovations for plastics prevention and recycling: "plastics prevention" is a broad term capturing not only plastic waste prevention innovations, but also the innovations for technologies or processes that will use fewer plastics in the first place – they will also be referred to as innovations for plastics circularity.
2. Innovations for converting or disposing of waste and removing leakages of plastic from the environment.
3. Innovations in biobased feedstock.

When conducting cross-country comparison, only patent families that have been granted by multiple national patent offices were counted in order to avoid the inflating the number of low-value patents.[1] The analysis includes patent data from 1990 and goes up to 2017 since databases for more recent years may be incomplete due to the delay in patent registrations. Moreover, when focusing on international/regional patent families, the available years are pushed back further – from 2017 to 2014 – due to the time lag between the first patent application in a given country and the subsequent patent applications in other countries.

Figure 5.1. Classification of innovation in environmentally relevant plastics technologies

PREVENTION & RECYCLING TECHNOLOGIES	CONVERSION OR DISPOSAL OF WASTE & LEAKAGE REMOVAL	BIOBASED FEEDSTOCK
Prevention Design for longer lifespans, light weighting or recycling Reuse and repair **Recycling** Sorting plastic waste Mechanical recycling Plastic-to-plastic chemical recycling Enabling digital technologies	**Conversion or disposal of waste** Biodegradable plastics Plastic-to-fuel conversion Waste to energy Sanitary landfill **Leakage removal** Mitigating release at the source Removing from wastewater Monitoring and removing from nature	**Feedstock** Crop-based feedstock Algae-based feedstock Fungi-based feedstock Other biomass

Source: Dussaux and Agrawala (forthcoming[2]).

Innovation in some technologies is not necessarily captured well by patent data.[2] This is the case for inventions for reusing plastics, which contain low-tech innovation and so are generally not patented; and for inventions for repairing plastics, which are more commercialised. The number of registered trademarks is a more appropriate indicator to capture innovation trends in these technologies. For example, trademarks are used to protect innovation in reusable plastic transport containers (e.g. cups); reusable plastic water bottles and distribution services for reusable plastic packing material. While reusable products may seem relatively low-tech, the logistics behind shared transport systems and containers involve innovation.

5.1.1. Environmentally relevant plastics innovation is growing but is still small scale

Innovation in environmentally relevant plastics technologies has increased rapidly over the last 30 years (Figure 5.2). The total number of patents rose by a factor of 3.4 between 1990 and 2017. Patented technologies for plastics prevention and recycling form the largest group and increased the most – by a factor four. In comparison, new technologies for biobased feedstock and for converting, disposing of or removing leakage of plastic waste rose by a factor of three.

Figure 5.2. Innovation in plastics prevention and recycling have grown the most

Worldwide patented inventions in environmentally relevant plastics technologies, 1990-2017

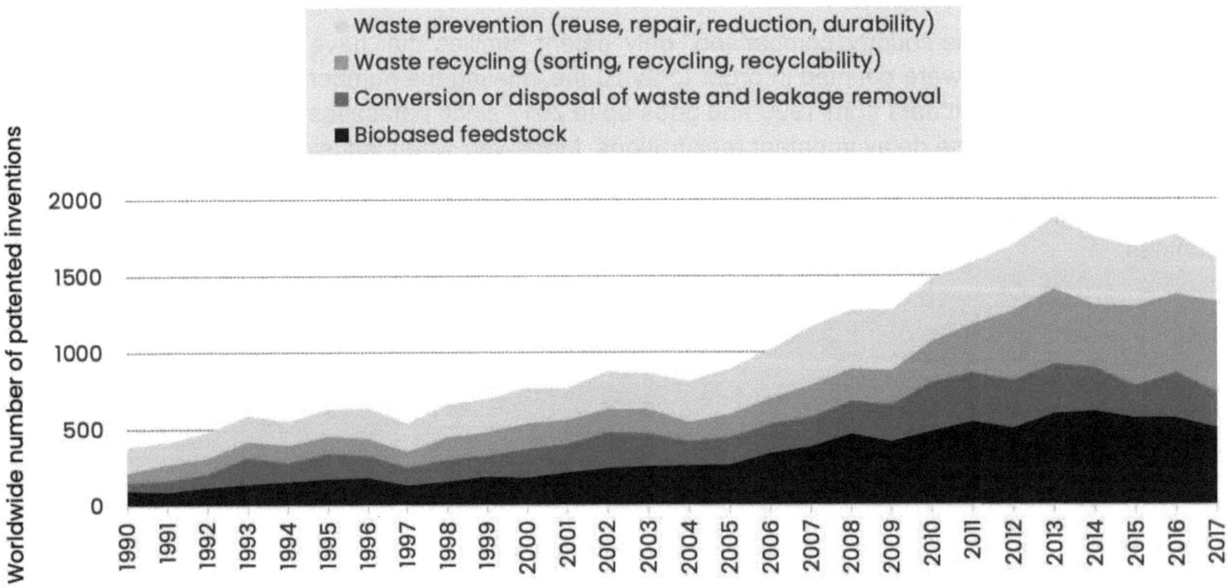

Source: Calculation based on textual analysis of data from the OECD, STI Micro-data Lab: Intellectual Property Database, http://oe.cd/ipstats, June 2020.

StatLink https://stat.link/ae8tnl

Between 2012 and 2017, the growth in patents for environmentally relevant plastics technologies levelled off. Since 2012, the number of new patents for prevention and recycling technologies has remained constant, while it has slightly declined for biobased feedstock technologies as well as for technologies converting or disposing of waste and removing leakages of plastics from the environment. However, public awareness of plastic waste leakage and political action to address the issue have increased following the 2015 launch of the G7 Action Plan against marine litter. Therefore, it is likely that patents will have increased since then, but the data are not yet available.

Trademarks data provide additional insights into low-tech plastics innovation. Every year between 2013 and 2017 there were on average 65 new registered trademarks related to plastics reuse technologies and 2 700 for plastics repair technologies. The number of trademarks related to plastics reuse increased by

23% every year between 1995 and 2017, while the number of trademarks related to plastics repair rose by 12% every year.

Since 2012, innovation in recycling technologies has outpaced plastic waste prevention technologies; they saw almost twice as many patents in 2017 (Figure 5.2). The shift towards recycling is probably driven by increased environmental awareness by consumers, who are willing to pay more for recycled content, and by policies such as extended producer responsibility (EPR) which make producers financially responsible for recycling waste, including packaging (Chapter 6).

Although innovation in plastic waste prevention and recycling has increased since 1990, its share in overall plastics innovation at the global level remains small. Innovation in preventing and recycling plastic waste accounted for only 1.1% of all plastics innovation in 1991 and only 1.2% in 2017. Therefore, the large-scale adoption of much stronger policies is needed to redirect innovation towards the circular use of plastics.

The remainder of this section focuses on prevention and recycling technologies, since biobased feedstock (Chapter 2) and technologies for converting or disposing of waste have been covered comprehensively in previous chapters (see Box 2.2 and Box 2.3, among others).

5.1.2. Plastics prevention and recycling innovation is concentrated in a few countries

Innovation in plastics prevention and recycling (innovation for plastics circularity) is not evenly distributed around the globe (Figure 5.3). The vast majority is concentrated in OECD countries and China. For instance, only ten countries accounted for 92% of plastic prevention and recycling patents between 2010 and 2014, with Japan, the United States, China, Korea, Germany and France alone accounting for 85%.

Figure 5.3. OECD countries and China lead on innovation in plastics circularity

Regional distribution of patented inventions for plastic prevention and recycling, 2010-14

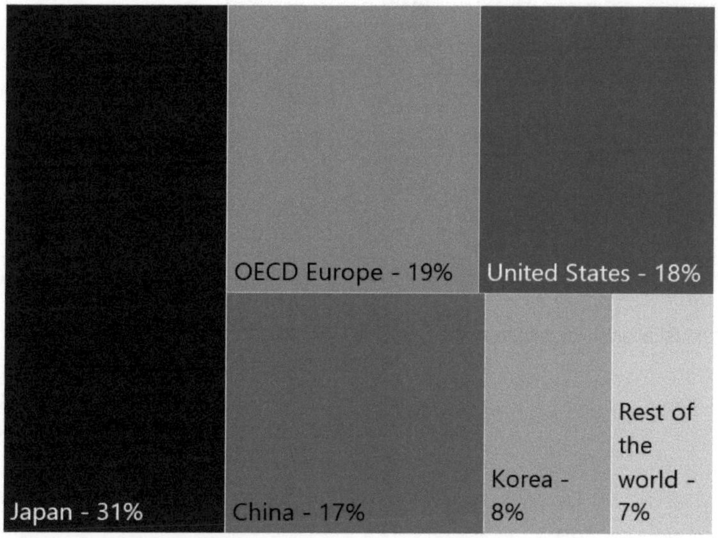

Source: Calculation based on textual analysis of data from the OECD, STI Micro-data Lab: Intellectual Property Database, http://oe.cd/ipstats, June 2020.

Figure 5.4 looks at the top ten innovating countries and compares their global share in patented inventions for plastics prevention and recycling with their global share in all plastics-related patents, environmental or otherwise. Unsurprisingly, countries that innovate in plastics in general also tend to innovate in plastics circularity technologies. Nevertheless, some countries invest relatively greater effort in plastics prevention and recycling technologies. For instance, France, Japan, Korea, the United Kingdom and United States invested a relative large share of their innovation efforts in plastics circularity between 2010 and 2014. In contrast, Germany, China and Australia were relatively less focused on plastics circularity during the same period. Nonetheless, due to their high number of plastic-related innovations, these three countries are leaders when considering the absolute number of circular plastics patents filed. In addition, the focus on circular plastics technologies is likely to increase in several countries. For example, a full waste export ban will come into effect in Australia by mid-2024 and will significantly increase the domestic demand for plastic recycling. The growing Australian market, also supported by a public investment of AUD 190 million in recycling modernisation, will likely spur innovation in plastic waste recycling.

This large concentration of plastics prevention and recycling innovations highlights the need to accelerate the international transfer of these technologies towards developing countries where plastics use and problems of plastic leakage are growing rapidly.

Figure 5.4. Some countries specialise in circular plastics innovation

Top ten inventing countries in plastics prevention and recycling innovations, global share 2010-14

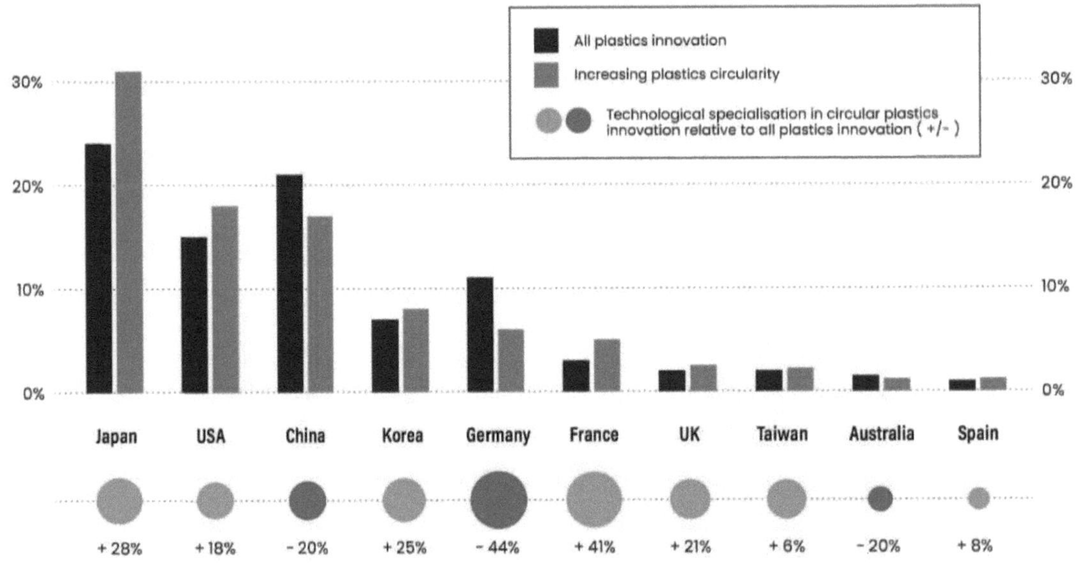

Note: All plastics innovation includes plastics innovation that is environmentally relevant and not environmentally relevant

Source: Calculation based on textual analysis of data from the OECD, STI Micro-data Lab: Intellectual Property Database, http://oe.cd/ipstats, June 2020.

StatLink https://stat.link/ax0bg4

5.2. What role for policies in driving circular plastics innovation?

The previous section showed that there are significant differences across countries in circular plastic innovation. This section explores how circular economy policies contribute to these differences, using the case study of the German packaging ordinance – the first EPR system for the recycling and recovery of sales packaging in the world.

The 1991 packaging ordinance, replaced by the German Packaging Act (Verpackungsgesetz) in 2019, required retailers and producers to take back and recycle a fixed but annually increasing percentage of packaging materials. The take-back system was deemed to be effective as the volume of packaging materials declined by 500 000 tonnes between 1992 and 1993.

Three years after the introduction of the Packaging Ordinance, plastic recycling capacities had increased by a factor of four (OECD, 1998[3]). Qualitative evidence suggests that this significant increase in plastic recycling capacity was due to the sizeable positive impact of the ordinance on plastic recycling innovation. To meet the quotas set by the take-back system, producers had to find new processes to convert plastic waste and create new markets for secondary materials. Among the new technologies developed at the time were new recycling processes, such as those using hydrocyclones and centrifuges to separate individual plastics (OECD, 1998[3]).

To provide some quantitative evidence of the effect of the German packaging ordinance on plastic recycling innovation and go further than correlation, a synthetic control method that builds a counterfactual or control group for Germany is employed.[3] This control group is composed of Canada, Japan, the Netherlands, Korea and the United States. These are all similar to Germany in terms of recycling patents but none had introduced a similar recycling policy around 1991.[4] Using several predictors, patent filing in recycling technologies in Germany before the regulation is introduced is successfully replicated in the control group (Figure 5.5).[5] It is found that five years after its introduction in Germany, the packaging ordinance increased the stock of recycling innovation by 190% compared to the control group for Germany in which the regulation is not introduced.[6]

Figure 5.5 also shows that there had already been a spurt in plastic recycling innovation between 1989 and 1991 in Germany. This cannot be fully explained by strategic patenting prior to the ordinance taking effect, since it was introduced within a very short timeframe making it difficult to anticipate for most stakeholders to anticipate. However, it could be explained by the first German Ministry of the Environment issuing a regulation in 1988 for the take back of plastic drinks packaging in reaction to the massive use of single-use polyethylene terephthalate (PET) bottles. This might explain the observed difference between Germany and the control group.

Figure 5.5. The German packaging ordinance prompted innovation in plastic recycling

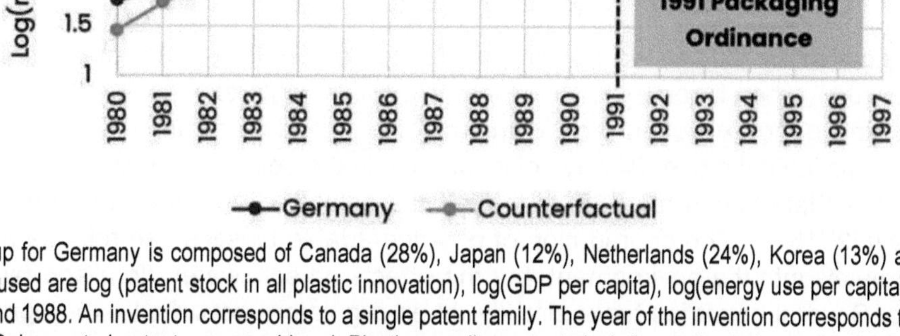

Note: The control group for Germany is composed of Canada (28%), Japan (12%), Netherlands (24%), Korea (13%) and the United States (23%). The predictors used are log (patent stock in all plastic innovation), log(GDP per capita), log(energy use per capita), log(recycling patent stock) in 1982, 1984 and 1988. An invention corresponds to a single patent family. The year of the invention corresponds to the application date of the priority patent. Only granted patents are considered. Plastic recycling patents include mechanical recycling, plastic-to-plastic chemical recycling, sorting and other pre-treatments. Data before 1990 includes only the Federal Republic of Germany (FRG).

Source: Calculation based on textual analysis of data from the OECD, STI Micro-data Lab: Intellectual Property Database, http://oe.cd/ipstats, June 2020.

StatLink https://stat.link/7sjehm

This case study suggests that plastic recycling policies successfully triggered innovation in plastic recycling. However, the effect of current and future circular economy policies on the emergence of new technologies has yet to be fully explored. The next sections take a step back from these aggregated analyses to present recent trends in specific environmentally relevant plastics innovation and derive policy implications.

5.3. What are the latest innovation challenges?

5.3.1. Biodegradable plastics innovation is slowing after decades of sustained growth

Biodegradable plastics gained some popularity with the idea they would degrade in the natural environment into carbon dioxide, water and biomass.[7] They are currently used for packaging, agriculture, horticulture, textiles and consumer goods. Global production capacities of biodegradable plastics was 1.2 Mt in 2019 or less than 0.3% of total plastics (Crevel, 2016[4]; European Bioplastics, 2019[5]).

Innovation in biodegradable plastics, measured by the number of patented inventions, doubled between 1995 and 2017. Between 2013 and 2017, 228 patent families for biodegradable plastics were granted every year (Dussaux and Agrawala, forthcoming[2]). However, since 2013, the speed of innovation has slowed down, probably because the environmental impact of compostable plastics has become controversial due to the issues related to biodegradation in natural environments (Box 5.1).

Box 5.1. "Biodegradable" plastics have become controversial

Microbial degradation of biodegradable polymers is not easily achieved in a natural environment (Wierckx et al., 2018[6]). For example, to biodegrade in a reasonable time, some polymers such as polylactic acid (PLA) require the temperature used in industrial composting to be above 60°C (Farah, Anderson and Langer, 2016[7]). Biodegradation also requires optimal conditions, such as the concentration of enzymes, strains of microorganisms, temperature, pH value, humidity, oxygen supply and light. These optimal conditions are rarely present in natural environments (Laycock et al., 2017[8]; Haider et al., 2019[9]).

Napper and Thompson (2019[10]) compared the deterioration of conventional polyethylene bags with bags that claimed biodegradable, oxo-degradable or compostable properties. The study included various environments, including open air, buried in soil and submersed in the marine environment. Apart from the compostable bag in the marine environment, fragments of all bags were present in all environments after 27 months. Moreover, some bags were still functional as grocery bags after three years in the soil or a marine environment. Strikingly, the "biodegradable" bags used in this experiment did not deteriorate faster than conventional polyethylene.

Although most ecotoxicity studies do not find evidence of harmful effects of degradation products (Haider et al., 2019[9]), when it comes to PLA there are two notable exceptions. Souza et al. (2013[11]) found cytotoxic and genotoxic effects on common onions and Adhikari et al. (2016[12]) found that microbial activity was inhibited after 84 days of incubation in the soil. Another concern is the use of oxo-degradable plastics that contain metal salts that act as catalysers to speed up degradation (OECD, 2013[13]; Kershaw, 2015[14]). The degradation of oxo-degradable plastics can release micro fragments of plastics and metals into the environment, but the effects on soil, water, flora and fauna are still not well understood. Several countries have already taken regulatory action on oxo-degradable plastics. For example, since 2015, France has banned bags and packaging made of oxo-degradable plastics and the European Union has prohibited products made from oxo-degradable plastic since 2019.

In addition to biodegradation issues, there are other concerns. First, some biodegradable plastics are produced from biobased polymers, which whose have mixed environmental impacts are mixed. Second, if collection and recycling conditions are not suitable, biodegradable plastics may compromise the quality of the recycled resources (Hornitschek, 2012[15]; Hann et al., 2015[16]). In addition, consumers may become confused, and put non-compostable plastics in the kitchen waste to be collected for composting. Furthermore, labelling plastics as biodegradable may suggest that littering is acceptable (Kershaw and Rochman, 2015[17]).

Despite these drawbacks, making plastics compostable can be an advantage for specific applications. For example, plastics in a restaurant can be directly composted together with all kitchen waste without further processing. Also, many different compostable plastics exist, so more innovation in this field could lead to better polymers and new applications.

5.3.2. Chemical recycling is only emerging but is facing significant challenges

Chemical recycling involves chemical processes that break down the waste polymers into feedstock for the production of fuels or into new polymers (Thiounn and Smith, 2020[18]). Chemical recycling is different from incineration, which essentially recovers heat from the combustion of plastic waste. As with mechanical recycling, sorting and pre-treatment are essential to optimise chemical recycling.

Chemical recycling can be divided in two categories (Figure 5.6). The first category is the transformation of plastic waste mainly into fuels via thermolysis, also referred to as "plastic-to-fuels" technologies. Examples of thermolysis processes include thermal cracking, pyrolysis, gasification, hydrothermal liquefaction and catalytic pressureless depolymerisation (Rahimi and García, 2017[19]).[8]

Figure 5.6. Chemical recycling covers a wide range of chemical processes

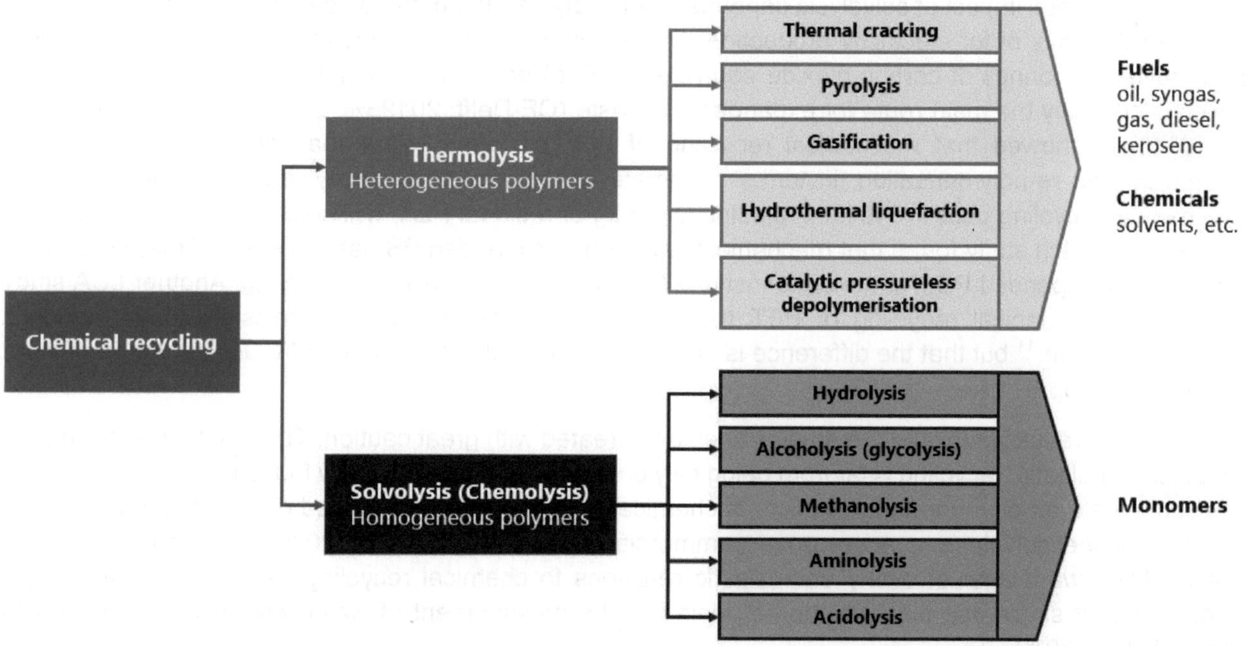

Thermolysis of plastic waste operates at high temperatures that consume a large part of the energy embodied in the plastics. For instance, pyrolysis typically occurs at 550°C and theoretically requires 1 328 megajoules (MJ) per kg of polyethylene (PE) waste to generate fuels with a calorific value of around 40 MJ per kg of waste (Gao, 2010[20]; Ripley, 2014[21]; Rollinson and Oladejo, 2019[22]). These relatively high internal energy needs and the focus on the production of fuels, instead of materials, make the term recycling controversial for most thermolysis processes.

Each thermolysis method has different environmental impacts. For example, Khoo (2019[23]) argues that gasification of mixed plastic waste requires ten times more energy but emits less nitrogen oxides (NOx), sulphur dioxide (SO_2) and particulate matter (PM) than pyrolysis. However, this result is based on old references and would benefit from further research. Using life cycle analysis (LCA), Demetrious and Crossin (2019[24]) find that pyrolysis and gasification have lower environmental impacts than landfilling, but comparable environmental impacts to incineration with energy recovery. Khoo (2019[23]) shows that pyrolysis and gasification have lower impacts on climate change than incineration with energy recovery, but significantly higher impacts in terms of terrestrial acidification and particulate matter formation. In the same study, mechanical recycling is found to vastly outperform these thermolysis processes in terms of environmental impacts.

The second category of chemical recycling technologies is called solvolysis or "plastic-to-plastic" chemical recycling. In this process, plastic waste is converted to monomers as feedstock for new polymers (Figure 5.6). These chemical depolymerisation technologies include hydrolysis, alcoholysis, methanolysis, glycolysis and aminolysis (BCG, 2019[25]; Das and Pandey, 2007[26]). Plastic-to-plastic chemical recycling is less controversial than thermolysis because it can potentially reduce the demand for new virgin polymers. Solvolysis or plastic-to-plastic chemical recycling aims to overcome the principal obstacle faced by mechanical recycling (downcycling[9]) by yielding polymers that are identical to the originals.

Plastic-to-plastic technologies are only just emerging and are less mature than the "plastic-to-fuels" conversion techniques. Between 1995 and 2017, innovation in plastic-to-plastic chemical recycling as measured by patents only increased by 5.2% every year (Dussaux and Agrawala, forthcoming[2]). This is not surprising given that plastic-to-plastic chemical recycling has only attracted interest recently, so the patent data are not yet fully available. In interviews for this study, market actors indicated that they expect the global capacity of pilot and demonstration plants for "plastic-to-plastic" to grow to at least 140 kilotonnes of waste per year in 2022.[10]

The environmental impact of solvolysis depends on the polymer, the method used and local elements such as the energy mix of for electricity production. One study found that solvolysis of expanded polystyrene (PS) saves 3.3 tonnes of carbon dioxide equivalent (CO_2e) per tonne of input compared to incineration, which is currently the main route for expanded PS waste (CE Delft, 2019[27]). Conversely, De Andrade et al. (2016[28]) showed that mechanical recycling of PLA performs better than chemical recycling via hydrolysis and re-polymerisation, in terms of climate change, human toxicity and fossil fuel depletion. Mechanical recycling uses 2 649 kJ of electricity per kg of residual PLA, while solvolysis uses 11 211 kJ. However, a Dutch study found that mechanical recycling of expanded PS has the same climate impact as solvolysis of expanded PS (Netherlands Institute for Sustainable Packaging, 2018[29]). Another LCA study found that mechanical recycling of PET trays has lower greenhouse gas emissions than magnetic depolymerisation,[11] but that the difference is not high and limited to 0.7 tonnes of CO_2e per tonne of input (CE Delft, 2019[27]).

However, the results of these LCA studies should be treated with great caution. The environmental impact of "plastic-to-plastic" recycling is far from being fully understood. A recent review found that it is complicated to acquire data on environmental impacts of chemical recycling that are of good quality due to the limited maturity of the solvolysis concept on a commercial scale (Tabrizi et al., 2020[30]). In addition, some stakeholders warn against overly enthusiastic reactions to chemical recycling as it could reinforce the acceptance of single-use plastics, thereby delaying the development of waste prevention technologies (Tabrizi et al., 2020[30]).

5.3.3. Myriad innovations along the value chain of plastics are emerging

In addition to plastic-to-plastic chemical recycling, there are many other emerging innovations that aim to address the environmental issues associated with plastics. Some notable examples include:

- *Machine learning to sort plastic waste*: To achieve a high level of purity, advanced techniques for sorting plastic waste now involve "deep learning", in which a machine is trained to recognise different types of plastics and other materials. For example, machine learning is currently applied to sort plastic waste from electrical and electronic equipment, such as acrylonitrile butadiene styrene (ABS), high impact polystyrene (HIPS), polypropylene and crystal polystyrene. It is especially useful for sorting dark plastics that are difficult to identify using near infrared techniques due to the absorption of radiation. As computation power keeps increasing, many new algorithms and applications will be unlocked in the future (Tarun, Sreelakshmi and Peeyush, 2019[31]).
- *Blockchain tools to foster recycling*: The uncertainty about the quality of sorted plastics is a barrier for plastics manufacturers (Chidepatil et al., 2020[32]). Blockchain is a digital technology that allows detailed tracking and the verification of information. Blockchain can make the information required by plastics manufacturers accessible when sorting is combined with multi-sensor-driven artificial intelligence and when a large share of actors in the supply chain are willing to collaborate. For example, Radical Innovations Group has developed a blockchain platform with smart contracts that contain validated data on the waste source, type, colour, quantity, origin and sorting process.
- *Filter washing bags to reduce microplastics release at source*: Plastics or other textiles can be put into the Guppyfriend Washing Bag to reduce microfibre shedding during washing.[12] After washing, the microfibres captured in the bag can be removed and disposed of in the residual waste bin. The laundry bag is produced from a plastic woven polyamide and is designed to maximise user-friendliness.
- *Autonomous leakage removal systems in rivers and oceans*: the Ocean Cleanup Interceptor 2.0 contains barriers that guide floating plastic waste to a vessel that collects the waste. The aim is to capture leaked plastics in rivers before they enter the ocean.[13] The vessel is solar-powered, works autonomously and can store up to 50 cubic metres of trash.
- *New delivery models*: Innovation is about more than new technologies. Loop is an example of an organisational innovation in which the business model of a delivery service is changed to avoid single-use packaging and to reduce the overall environmental footprint.[14] Loop delivers online orders to households in reusable containers that will afterwards be collected, cleaned and refilled.

5.4. How to transition from innovation to scalability?

With so many technologies to choose from, the question arises as to which ones should be developed and deployed more widely to address the environmental problems caused by the production and use of plastics. The usefulness of a technology depends strongly on the context of a country. For instance, massive deployment of proprietary filtration systems might not be cost effective for countries that have centralised wastewater treatment plants (WWTP) capable of capturing microplastics from wastewater installed all over the country.[15] They may, however, be effective for other countries. In addition, capturing plastic debris from rivers makes more sense in countries where mismanaged waste is a major issue.

Innovation in products, processes and business models is essential, but is only part of what is needed. In order to prioritise technologies for a more circular use of plastics and to give compelling incentives to consumers and entrepreneurs, a comprehensive set of policies is required, including regulations, education and information campaigns to drive behavioural changes. Innovations will only be scaled up if there is strong market demand. Using regulatory obligations and financial incentives, policy makers can set market conditions that enhance the uptake of circular technologies in consumption and production patterns. Moreover, upstream policies will be needed to restrain the overall consumption of materials. These policy issues are the topic of the next chapter.

References

Adhikari, D. et al. (2016), "Degradation of bioplastics in soil and their degradation effects on environmental microorganisms", *Journal of Agricultural Chemistry and Environment*, Vol. 5/1, p. 23. [12]

Aguiar, A. et al. (2019), "The GTAP Data Base: Version 10", *Journal of Global Economic Analysis*, Vol. 4/1, pp. 1-27, http://dx.doi.org/10.21642/jgea.040101af. [34]

BCG (2019), *A Circular SOlution to Plastic Waste.* [25]

Benavides, P. et al. (2018), "Exploring Comparative Energy and Environmental Benefits of Virgin, Recycled, and Bio-Derived PET Bottles", *ACS Sustainable Chemistry & Engineering*, Vol. 6/8, pp. 9725-9733, http://dx.doi.org/10.1021/acssuschemeng.8b00750. [36]

Bown, C. (2020), *COVID-19: China's exports of medical supplies provide a ray of hope*, Peterson Institute for International Economics, https://www.piie.com/blogs/trade-and-investment-policy-watch/covid-19-chinas-exports-medical-supplies-provide-ray-hope. [41]

CE Delft (2019), "Exploratory study on chemical recycling. Update 2019. What are the opportunities for climate policy, now in the future?". [27]

Chateau, J., R. Dellink and E. Lanzi (2014), "An Overview of the OECD ENV-Linkages Model: Version 3", *OECD Environment Working Papers*, No. 65, OECD Publishing, Paris, http://dx.doi.org/10.1787/5jz2qck2b2vd-en. [33]

Chidepatil, A. et al. (2020), "From Trash to Cash: How Blockchain and Multi-Sensor-Driven Artificial Intelligence Can Transform Circular Economy of Plastic Waste?", *Administrative Sciences*, Vol. 10/2. [32]

Crevel, R. (2016), "Bio-based food packaging in Sustainable Development: Challenges and opportunities to utilize biomassresidues from agriculture and forestry as a feedstock for bio-based food packaging", *FAO.* [4]

Das, S. and S. Pandey (2007), "Pyrolysis and catalytic cracking of municipal plastic waste for recovery of gasoline range hydrocarbons", *Doctoral dissertation, National Institute of Technology Rourkela.* [26]

De Andrade, M. et al. (2016), "Life cycle assessment of poly (lactic acid)(PLA): comparison between chemical recycling, mechanical recycling and composting.", *Journal of Polymers and the Environment*, Vol. 24/4, pp. 372-384. [28]

Demetrious, A. and E. Crossin (2019), "Life cycle assessment of paper and plastic packaging waste in landfill, incineration, and gasification-pyrolysis", *Journal of Material Cycles and Waste Management*, Vol. 21/4, pp. 850-860. [24]

Dussaux, D. and S. Agrawala (forthcoming), "Quantifying innovation for a circular plastic economy", *Forthcoming OECD ENV Working Paper.* [2]

European Bioplastics (2019), *Bioplastics market data 2019 - Global production capacities of bioplastics 2019-2024.* [5]

Farah, S., D. Anderson and R. Langer (2016), "Physical and mechanical properties of PLA, and their functions in widespread applications—A comprehensive review.", *Advanced drug delivery reviews*, Vol. 107, pp. 367-392. [7]

Gao, F. (2010), "Pyrolysis of Waste Plastics into Fuels", *A Thesis, University of Canterbury.*. [20]

Haider, T. et al. (2019), "Plastics of the future? The impact of biodegradable polymers on the environment and on society", *Angewandte Chemie International Edition*, Vol. 58/1, pp. 50-62. [9]

Hann, S. et al. (2015), "The Impact of the Use of "Oxo-degradable" Plastic on the Environment", *Final Report for the European Commission DG Environment. Project conducted under Framework Contract No ENV.A.2/FRA/2015/0008and 07.0201/2016/748104/ETU/ENV.B.3.* [16]

Hornitschek, B. (2012), "Impact of degradable and oxydegradable plastics carrier bags on mechanical recycling", *Report by the Transfer Center for Polymer Technology (TCKT) on behalf of the European Plastic Converters (EuPC)*, p. 22. [15]

Kershaw, P. (2015), "Biodegradable Plastics & Marine Litter: Misconceptions, Concerns and Impacts on Marine Environments", *UNEP GPA.* [14]

Kershaw, P. and C. Rochman (2015), "Sources, fate and effects of microplastics in the marine environment: a global assessment.", *Joint Group of Experts on the Scientific Aspects of Marine Environmental Protection (GESAMP)*, Vol. 93. [17]

Khoo, H. (2019), "LCA of plastic waste recovery into recycled materials, energy and fuels in Singapore", *Resources, Conservation and Recycling*, Vol. 145, pp. 67-77. [23]

Law, K. et al. (2020), "The United States' contribution of plastic waste to land and ocean", *Science Advances*, Vol. 6/44, http://dx.doi.org/10.1126/sciadv.abd0288. [45]

Laycock, B. et al. (2017), "Lifetime prediction of biodegradable polymers", *Progress in Polymer Science*, Vol. 71, pp. 144-189. [8]

Merrington, A. (2017), "Recycling of Plastics", in *Applied Plastics Engineering Handbook: Processing, Materials, and Applications: Second Edition*, Elsevier Inc., http://dx.doi.org/10.1016/B978-0-323-39040-8.00009-2. [44]

Napper, I. and R. Thompson (2019), "Environmental deterioration of biodegradable, oxo-biodegradable, compostable, and conventional plastic carrier bags in the sea, soil, and open-air over a 3-year period", *Environmental science & technology*, Vol. 53/9, p. 47. [10]

Narin, F. (1995), "Patents as indicators for the evaluation of industrial research output", *Scientometrics*, Vol. 34/3, pp. 489-496. [1]

Netherlands Institute for Sustainable Packaging (2018), "Chemical recycling of plastic packaging materials. Analysis and opportunities for upscaling". [29]

OECD (2021), *Trends of ODA for a sustainable ocean economy*, OECD, Paris, https://oecd-main.shinyapps.io/ocean/. [38]

OECD (2018), *Improving Markets for Recycled Plastics: Trends, Prospects and Policy Responses*, OECD Publishing, Paris, https://dx.doi.org/10.1787/9789264301016-en. [37]

OECD (2013), "Policies for Bioplastics in the Context of a Bioeconomy", *OECD Science, Technology and Industry Policy Papers*, No. 10, OECD Publishing, Paris, https://dx.doi.org/10.1787/5k3xpf9rrw6d-en. [13]

OECD (1998), "Extended Producer Responsibility Phase 2: Case study on the German packaging ordinance". [3]

OECD (n.d.), *Intellectual Property Database*, https://www.oecd.org/sti/intellectual-property-statistics-and-analysis.htm (accessed on 1 June 2020). [46]

Rahimi, A. and J. García (2017), "Chemical recycling of waste plastics for new materials production", *Nature Reviews Chemistry*, Vol. 1/6, pp. 1-11. [19]

Ren, D. (2020), *China boosts face mask production capacity by 450 per cent in a month, threatening a glut scenario*, South China Morning Post, https://www.scmp.com/business/companies/article/3075289/china-boosts-face-mask-production-capacity-450-cent-month. [39]

Ripley, J. (2014), "Routine Caol and Coke Analysis: Collection, Interpretation, and Use of Analytical Data MNL57-2ND (2nd Edn), Chapter 5: Proximate Analysis", *ASTM International, West Conshohocken*, pp. 29-48. [21]

Rollinson, A. and J. Oladejo (2019), "'Patented blunderings', efficiency awareness, and self-sustainability claims in the pyrolysis energy from waste sector", *Resources, Conservation and Recycling*, Vol. 141, pp. 233-242. [22]

SCIO (2020), *Fighting COVID-19: China in Action*, The State Council, The People's Republic of China, http://english.scio.gov.cn/whitepapers/2020-06/07/content_76135269.htm. [40]

Souza, P. et al. (2013), "PLA and organoclays nanocomposites: degradation process and evaluation of ecotoxicity using Allium cepa as test organism", *Journal of Polymers and the Environment*, Vol. 21/4, pp. 1052-1063. [11]

Stefanini, R. et al. (2020), "Plastic or glass: a new environmental assessment with a marine litter indicator for the comparison of pasteurized milk bottles", *The International Journal of Life Cycle Assessment*, Vol. 26/4, pp. 767-784, http://dx.doi.org/10.1007/s11367-020-01804-x. [35]

Subramanian, S. (2020), *How the face mask became the world's most coveted commodity*, The Guardian, https://www.theguardian.com/world/2020/apr/28/face-masks-coveted-commodity-coronavirus-pandemic. [42]

Tabrizi, A. et al. (2020), "Understanding the Environmental Impacts of Chemical Recycling – ten concerns with existing life cycle assessments", *Zero Waste Europe, Brussels*. [30]

Tarun, K., K. Sreelakshmi and K. Peeyush (2019), "Segregation of Plastic and Non-plastic Waste using Convolutional Neural Network", *IOP Conference Series: Materials Science and Engineering*, Vol. 561/1, p. 012113. [31]

Thiounn, T. and R. Smith (2020), "Advances and approaches for chemical recycling of plastic waste", *Journal of Polymer Science*, Vol. 58/10, pp. 1347-1364. [18]

Wang, C. et al. (2020), "Structure of the global plastic waste trade network and the impact of China's import Ban", *Resources, Conservation and Recycling*, Vol. 153, http://dx.doi.org/10.1016/j.resconrec.2019.104591. [43]

Wierckx, N. et al. (2018), "Plastic biodegradation: Challenges and opportunities", *Consequences of Microbial Interactions with Hydrocarbons, Oils, and Lipids Biodegradation and Bioremediation*, pp. 1-29. [6]

Notes

[1] A patent family is a collection of patent applications covering the same or similar technical content. See Dussaux and Agrawala (forthcoming[2]) for more information on the methodology and on the advantages and drawbacks of patent data.

[2] However, use of patent data remains the favoured option since it captures all categories of innovation; trademark data can only recover innovation in a limited number of fields.

[3] See Dussaux and Agrawala (forthcoming[2]) for more details on the methodology.

[4] We exclude Austria and France because they introduced an EPR scheme for packaging in 1993, and we exclude Sweden as it introduced one in 1994.

[5] The predictors used are log (patent stock in all plastic innovation), log (GDP per capita), log (energy use per capita), log (recycling patent stock) in 1982, 1984 and 1988.

[6] The predictors are well balanced between Germany and the control group. The result is robust when backdating the treatment five years in advance. Permutation distribution of the placebo indicates that the increase is significantly different to zero. The result is also robust when excluding all donor countries separately (leave-one-out) except Canada. A similar analysis shows that the packaging ordinance had no statistically significant effect on all plastic innovation. See Dussaux and Agrawala (forthcoming[2]) for more details.

[7] A European standard, EN 13432, defines biodegradability as a biodegradation level of at least 90% that must be reached in less than six months. For disintegrability, the mass of test material residues greater than 2 mm must be less than 10% of the initial mass.

[8]Catalytic pressureless depolymerisation is also known as the Katalytische Drucklose Verölung (KDV) process.

[9] Downcycling occurs during mechanical recycling when contaminated plastic waste is melted into a new raw material the properties of which are poorer than the original plastic products. For example, the plastic waste from a jug of milk is not used again for the production of a new jug of milk but can only be used for less demanding applications such as a layer of a detergent packaging.

[10] As not all actors were interviewed, this estimate should be taken with caution.

[11] Magnetic depolymerisation is a technology developed by the Dutch start-up Ioniqa, and consists of chemically depolymerising PET under the influence of a magnetic liquid. Magnetic depolymerisation of

PET removes various dyes and contaminants from PET waste and produces virgin equivalent BHET that can used as raw material for PET production (https://ioniqa.com/).

[12] Guppyfriend was registered as a EUIPO trademark in December 2018 and as a USPTO trademark in May 2020. An EPO patent was granted in November 2019. Patents were also filed in Japan and in the United States.

[13] The Interceptor was registered as a EUIPO trademark in April 2019.

[14] For details see https://loopstore.com/how-it-works.

[15] Nevertheless, the management of microplastics captured in WWTP sludges that are mostly used for agricultural land is still problematic (see Chapter 2).

6. The policy landscape

Policy makers around the world are looking for effective instruments to tackle the environmental pressures from the production, consumption and end-of-life management of plastics. This chapter describes the policy approaches and key instruments available to address these issues. It takes stock of the current global policy landscape and lays out a policy roadmap to reduce the leakage of land-based macroplastics and to make the lifecycle of plastics more circular

KEY MESSAGES

- Plastics have a wide range of environmental impacts, with leakage of macroplastics into the environment as a top priority to governments. Reducing these impacts requires a comprehensive set of complementary policy instruments, grouped into restraining demand, designing for circularity, enhancing recycling, closing leakage pathways and cleaning up.
- An inventory of economic and regulatory measures across 50 countries, representing 69% of the global population and 84% of global gross domestic product (GDP), suggests that the current policy landscape for plastics is fragmented and can be strengthened significantly.
- Restraining demand can bring the largest environmental gains: fewer plastics in use mean less embodied energy, fewer health risks and less plastic waste to deal with. Plastics taxes, recycled content targets and extended producer responsibility (EPR) with fee modulation schemes can all create financial incentives to reduce use and foster circularity. Only a few countries are experimenting with these innovative economic instruments and targets – their adoption needs to be extended to more products and more countries.
- Recycling can be encouraged through financial incentives. EPR, landfill taxes and incineration taxes work well for enterprises and municipalities. However, only 33 out of the 50 analysed countries (representing 18% of the population covered by the inventory) have national regulations and operational schemes for EPR in place, while 25 countries (representing 11% of the covered population) have effectively implemented national landfill and incineration taxes. Households can be encouraged to sort plastic waste at source through deposit-refund and Pay-as-You-Throw schemes. Yet only 13 countries (representing 4% of the covered population) are subject to such schemes.
- While bans and taxes on single-use plastics are a popular approach to reducing litter – having been implemented globally by more than 120 countries – they only target a small share of plastics by volume and may not always have positive environmental outcomes. Enlarging the scope of anti-littering policies and enhancing implementation of legislation on the ground is needed to structurally reduce plastics littering.
- Leakage pathways can be closed by investing in basic waste management infrastructure. With mismanaged waste a widespread problem, especially in developing economies, major investments in infrastructure are needed, combined with support for effective legal frameworks to enforce disposal obligations for all economic actors.
- Our analysis concludes with a roadmap which can be adopted by all countries. It involves three increasingly ambitious phases: 1) close leakage pathways: build sanitary waste management infrastructure, organise waste collection and ban or tax frequently littered items; 2) create incentives for recycling and enhance sorting at source; and 3) restrain demand and optimise design to make plastic value chains more circular and recycled plastics more price competitive.

6.1. A broad array of policy instruments is needed to address the negative impacts of plastics use

The production, consumption and end-of-life management of plastics generate a wide range of environmental impacts, including greenhouse gas emissions, water and air pollution, and the release of hazardous chemicals. The most notorious negative effect of plastics is the increased mortality of marine species, due to entanglement in floating plastic debris or ingestion of plastic particles. But plastic litter in the marine environment also has substantial economic costs due to negative impacts on tourism and fishing (Krelling, Williams and Turra, 2017[1]). Human health concerns have also emerged over certain plastic additives and substances being inhaled, or ingested in food.

Of the many of impacts of plastics use, the release of plastic waste and litter into the environment is one of the issues currently of most concern to governments. To address this issue, there are essentially five policy approaches that can be used (Figure 6.1):

- Restrain demand: reduce the excessive amount of plastics and other materials in use by promoting longer product lifespans, reuse, a demand shift to services and other upstream measures.
- Design for circularity: make the plastic production process more circular by avoiding hazardous materials in the lifecycle, maximising recycled content and adopting other design measures.
- Enhance recycling: close material loops by sorting and recycling plastic waste.
- Close leakage pathways: decrease losses into the environment through, among others, effective waste plastic collection and disposal (e.g. disposal in sanitary landfills) and effective waste water treatment plants (WWTP).
- Clean up: remove plastic from the environment, e.g. via beach clean-up activities or installing river litter booms that capture plastics before they flow into oceans.

Policies to address microplastics are much less well evolved than policies for macroplastics. There remains significant uncertainty about the effectiveness of measures that can be used to mitigate unintentionally released microplastics (e.g. those that occur during production and use, such as releases of microfibres when garments are washed) (OECD, 2021[2]). As a consequence, there is also uncertainty about which policy approaches are best suited to address microplastic leakage. This chapter therefore focuses on land-based macroplastics and only includes microbeads incorporated into cosmetics and detergents because these microplastics can easily be replaced with more environmentally friendly materials. Voluntary and regulatory approaches to phase out and substitute intentionally added microbeads are already becoming widespread.

Figure 6.1. Policy approaches to reduce plastic leakage

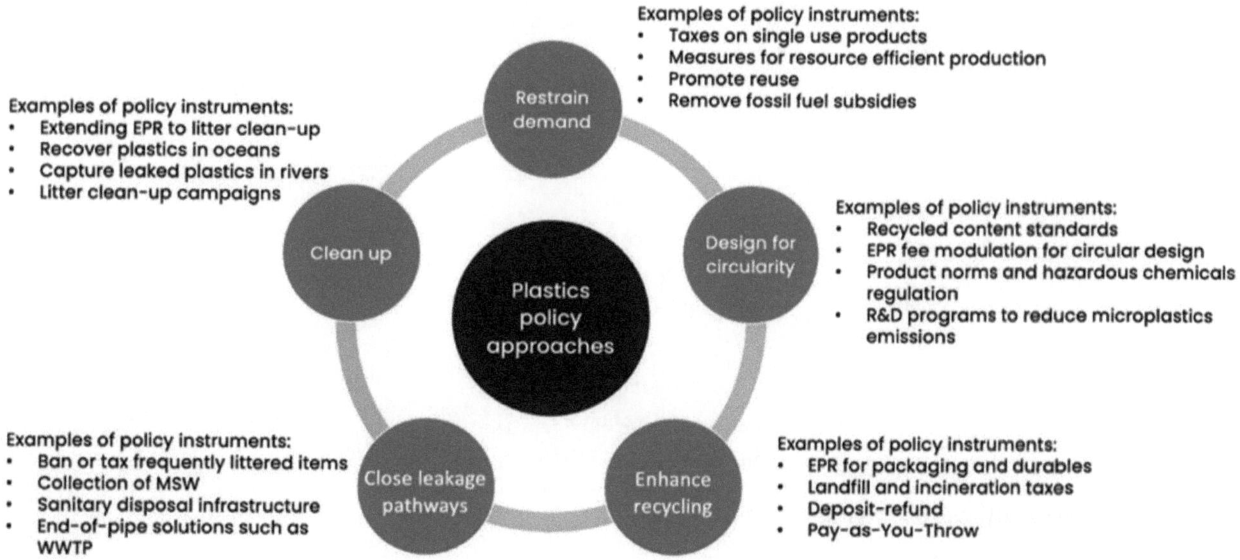

Note: EPR = Extended Producer Responsibility; MSW = municipal solid waste; WWTP = waste water treatment plant.

Reducing the negative impacts of macroplastics requires intervention through a broad array of policy instruments (Figure 6.2). Some of these instruments specifically target plastics, whereas others have a broader scope and address a wider range of waste or material types. For instance, bans and taxes on single-use plastics are very targeted and aim to diminish the use of items such as plastic bags, while landfill taxes usually address solid waste more generally with the aim to discourage disposal and encourage recycling or energy recovery.

Sectoral policies, such as for chemicals, waste management, agriculture or construction, can also be useful, as can policies that address specific externalities, such as a carbon tax aiming to reduce greenhouse gas (GHG) emissions. Some policies are more relevant at local or national levels (e.g. waste management legislation), whereas others are implemented at the international level (e.g. trade rules for plastic waste).

Figure 6.2. The scope of policies that affect plastics management is large

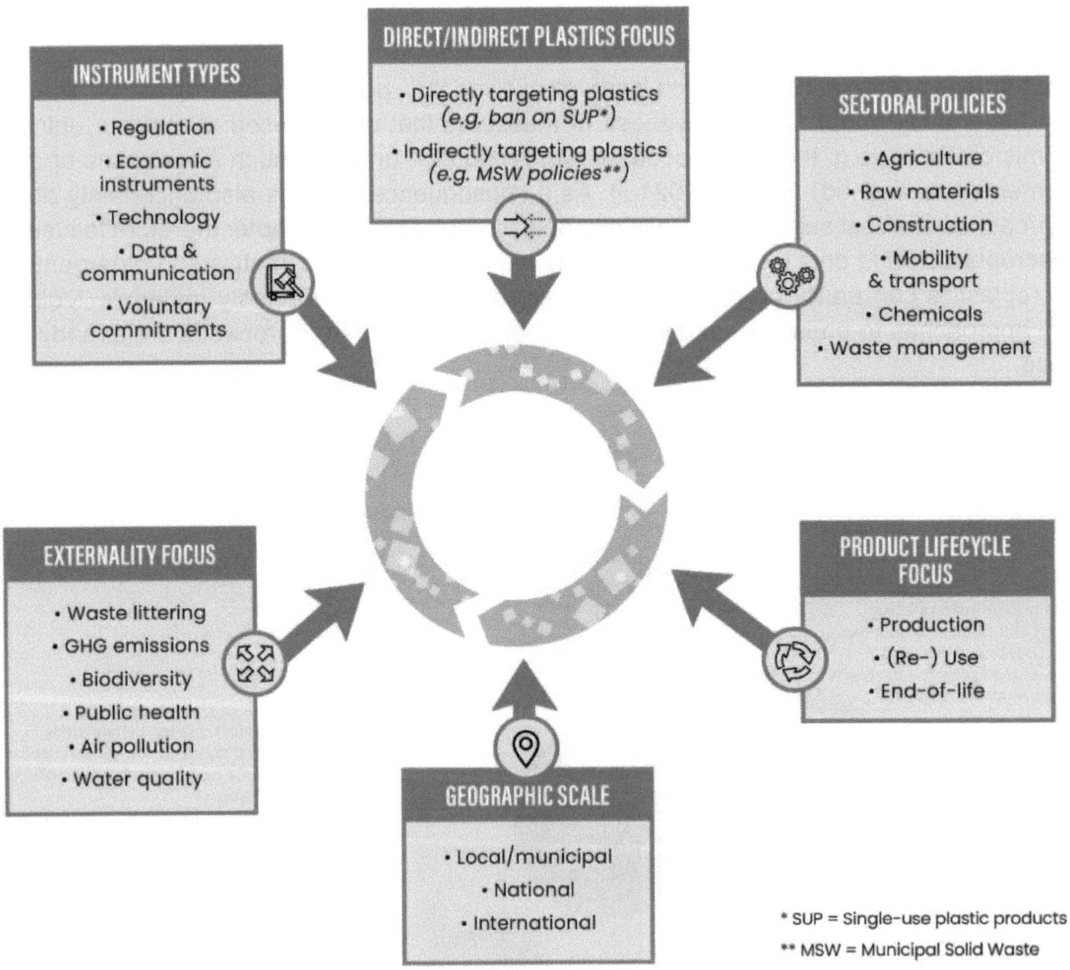

Note: MSW = municipal solid waste, SUP = single-use plastic products.

None of the policy instruments that have been selected for this review of the plastics policy landscape will be highly effective on their own – they need to be embedded in a broader policy mix which combines a number of mutually supportive and complementary instruments. In addition to steering policy instruments (such as legally binding regulatory interventions, mandatory standards and economic instruments), a range of enabling and soft policies – such as research and development (R&D) investment, communication, nudging and education measures, voluntary approaches and stakeholder alliances – are also needed (Figure 6.3).

Figure 6.3. A comprehensive policy package requires a mix of steering and enabling policies

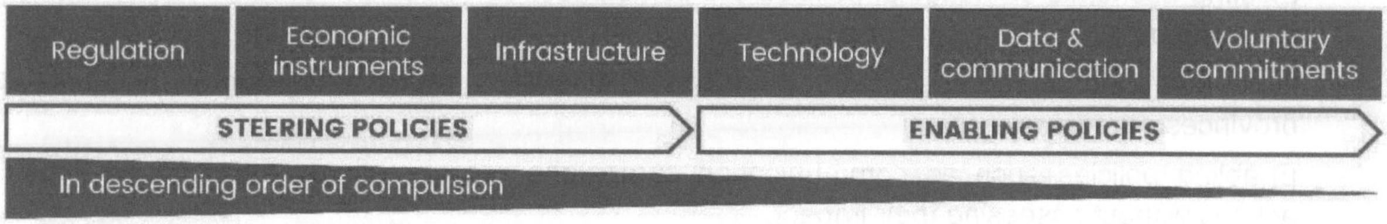

The review and assessment of a limited set of policy instruments in this report (predominantly regulatory and economic instruments) is a substantial simplification. Nevertheless, regulatory and economic instruments are essential to provide the right incentive structure for an environmentally sound plastics economy and the presence of these instruments usually correlates with reduced mismanaged plastic waste and greater plastics recycling rates, amongst others (Watkins et al., 2012[3]).

6.2. The fragmented use of economic and regulatory instruments leaves room for improvement

The OECD has recently developed a Plastics Policy Inventory to analyse steering policy instruments. The inventory contains key economic and regulatory policy instruments that are exclusively focused on plastics, as well as broader instruments that target products and waste streams, such as municipal solid waste (MSW), that contain important fractions of plastics. It covers policy in 50 countries: the 38 OECD member countries, as well as 12 non-OECD countries selected for the size of their populations and their geographic coverage (Brazil, the People's Republic of China, India, Indonesia, Russia and South Africa, as well as several countries with large populations in South-East Asia and Africa) (Table 6.1). Overall, the inventory covers 69% of the world's population and 84% of global GDP. The policy inventory relies on an extensive literature review, including the OECD Policy Instruments for the Environment (PINE) database (OECD, 2021[4]), UNEP (2018[5]), Cornago et al. (2021[6]), OECD (forthcoming[7]), Ecoprog (2020[8]) and Karasik et al. (2020[9]). Moreover, for the non-OECD countries, local experts provided individual country case studies to validate and expand the information in the inventory. The inventory includes policies that came into force before December 2020. Despite the extensive research, gaps in the inventory or issues with classification are still possible, so all results need to be interpreted with care (Box 6.1).

This section draws on the analysis of the inventory to assess the global plastics policy landscape and highlight gaps that need to be addressed, based on the five key policy areas shown in Figure 6.1.

Box 6.1. Mapping and benchmarking international policy instruments is challenging

Mapping and comparing the use of policy instruments in different countries can yield valuable insights and best practices. However, global inventories of polices encounter a range of difficulties:

- Not all policies stated in policy documents are operational in practice.
- Existing economic or industrial policies are sometimes rebranded as “circular” without actually including new circular obligations.
- In countries with a federal structure, there can be diversity in regulations adopted by the states, provinces or regions.
- Enabling policies such as communication campaigns are sometimes heralded as flagship actions without assessing their impact.
- The benefits of upstream measures to restrain demand and promote eco-design are often intangible.
- Definitions, available data, measurement methodologies and framework conditions relating to materials and waste management differ structurally between countries.

Consequently, international policy inventories can highlight key circular economy trends, but should be interpreted with care.

6.2.1. Current bans and taxes on single-use items are insufficient to restrain demand

The largest environmental gains can be achieved by reducing excessive use of plastics. Fewer plastics in use mean less embodied energy, fewer health risks and less plastic waste to deal with. However, steering production and consumption patterns requires sophisticated policies that take into account international trade and potentially undesirable side-effects.

Many countries have taken measures to curb the use of microbeads in rinse-off applications, and single-use items such as straws or polystyrene food packaging. However, most attention has been paid to single-use plastic shopping bags. According to UNEP (2020[10]), 127 countries have already issued legislation to either ban, tax or regulate the use of plastic shopping bags. This includes emerging markets such as Botswana, Mongolia and Yemen. However, not all of these regulations are fully implemented or enforced (OECD, 2021[11]). Moreover, an exclusive focus on plastics can lead to other materials being used instead, rather than to a reduction overall (Box 6.2). Most importantly, these measures focus on small product streams, which means that while they may reduce littering, they have less impact on total volumes in use.

There are plenty of soft measures used to restrain demand and use resources more efficiently. For example, communication and nudging strategies are being used to promote reuse and product sharing services (PBM, 2020[12]). However, despite frequent calls for “plastics taxes”, there are no economy-wide taxes or obligations that steer consumption structurally away from plastics. This is partly due to the complexity of introducing taxes in an international market and the potential disadvantages of material substitution (Box 6.2). On the other hand, there are still many examples of fossil fuel subsidies that incentivise overconsumption by keeping the prices of plastics feedstock low (OECD/IEA, 2021[13]).

Box 6.2. Targeting plastic shopping bags is only part of the picture

The case of plastic shopping bags highlights how an exclusive focus on plastic products can induce substitution without reducing the overall footprint of consumption. In recent years, taxes on single-use plastic shopping bags have been successfully implemented in many parts of the world (IEEP, 2017[14]). However, in some cases the exclusive focus on plastics has induced a shift to other materials, rather than reducing materials consumption overall. For example, a 2009 litter study found that the introduction of a partial ban on polystyrene cups in San Francisco reduced littered polystyrene cups, but also prompted a sharp increase in the littering of paper cups instead (HDR, 2009[15]; Cornago, Börkey and Brown, 2021[6]).

The use of plastics is often perceived by consumers as the least favourable alternative for packaging, but there are many cases where this intuition is contradicted by life cycle analyses (LCAs) (Boesen, Bey and Niero, 2019[16]; Stefanini et al., 2020[17]). For example, a recent meta-analysis of seven LCAs concludes that single-use polyethylene (PE) bags have lower climate impact and cause less acidification, eutrophication and ozone-related impacts than non-plastic single-use alternatives such as paper bags, mainly because of their much lighter weight (UNEP, 2020[18]). Therefore, legislation that targets products such as shopping bags should take into account possible substitution effects and aim to incentivise reuse (Cornago, Börkey and Brown, 2021[6]).

6.2.2. Innovative policies are needed to encourage design for circularity

Design is deeply entrenched in both production and sales processes, and affects the environmental footprint of plastics throughout their lifecycle. Product norms, regulatory risk assessment schemes and bans on hazardous substances are in place in many countries. Although these regulatory instruments are critical to detoxify materials' lifecycles (Box 6.3), they are only able to affect a tiny share of the substances that generate health risks (Wiesinger, Wang and Hellweg, 2021[19]). Moreover, the multitude of products and the speed of innovation make it challenging for regulatory instruments to steer design processes. Therefore, several countries are exploring how to apply innovative economic instruments and binding targets to foster the design of more circular products. For instance:

- France uses EPR (Box 6.4) to incentivise eco-design. By modulating EPR fees, i.e. recycling contributions paid by producers, circular product designs receive a bonus or penalty depending on their design criteria (Laubinger et al., 2021[20]). Similar eco-modulation measures are in place or envisioned in Canada (Quebec), Chile, Estonia, Italy and Portugal (Box 6.4). However, more research is needed to substantiate the effectiveness of the measure for instigating design changes.
- In 2022, the United Kingdom will apply a GBP 200 per tonne tax on packaging plastics that contain less than 30% recycled content.
- The European Union has launched several new regulations:
    - A directive[1] which obliges Member States to introduce modulated EPR fees that take into account, where possible, a product's durability, reparability, re-usability and recyclability, as well as the presence of hazardous substances. Guidance on how to implement modulated EPR fees is currently being drafted (Laubinger et al., 2021[20]).

      A mandatory 25% recycled content target for polyethylene terephthalate (PET) bottles by 2025 and 30% for all beverage bottles by 2030.[2]
- California is the first US state to impose a recycled content target for plastics in beverage containers. The target will start at 15% in 2022 and climb to 50% in 2050.

Box 6.3. Aligning regulation of chemical substances and design approaches across countries can reduce health risks and improve circularity

The selection of chemicals at the design stage determines health and environmental impacts along the entire lifecycle of a product (OECD, 2021[21]). For example, orthophthalates or phthalates are a large group of chemicals that can, among other things, be used as a plasticiser for PVC to make the rigid material flexible. Applications include electrical wires, gloves, toys and flexible flooring tiles as well as cosmetics and personal care products. Phthalate use is widespread and biomonitoring of urine samples shows that we take up significant volumes via ingestion and other routes of exposure (Holland, 2018[22]; CDC, 2021[23]; 2021[24]). Some phthalates, such as DEHP, BBP and DBP, have proven adverse health effects (e.g. reduced long-term fertility), with high frequency of exposure, high concentrations and cumulative exposure to different phthalates increasing the risks (Benjamin et al., 2017[25]; Engel et al., 2021[26]; Silano et al., 2019[27]). Clearly, the use of such hazardous substances in plastics and plastic products raises concerns at the production, use and waste stages. Risk assessments to better understand potential impacts, government regulations to restrict their use and industry commitments to phase out such hazardous substances, are critical to achieving safer and more circular materials.

Regulatory and industrial efforts to detoxify material loops are, however, hampered by several problems. The first issue is the international disparity of policies, as illustrated by the example of phthalates. For example, Australia restricts the use of DEHP in plastics applications for children to a maximum weight-based level of 1% (Australian Competition & Consumer Commission, 2021[28]; Commonwealth of Australia, 2011[29]). This regulation is complemented by a voluntary commitment by the Australian PVC industry to phase out phthalates in food contact packaging, and to phase out the more mobile and potentially more hazardous low-weight phthalates[3] from all applications by 2023 (Vinyl Council Australia, 2018[30]). The United Kingdom and European Union also have legal restrictions in place for several phthalates.[4] In the EU the maximum weight-based level for DEHP, in combination with other targeted phthalates, is 0.1% for toys and childcare applications, as well as for some other consumer applications. In addition, the European PVC industry has succeeded in almost phasing out low molecular phthalates by substituting them with high molecular weight phthalates and non-phthalate plasticisers (Vinyl Plus, 2021[31]; INERIS, 2021[32]). In contrast, in most non-OECD countries there are no restrictions in place and low molecular phthalates are still widely used in consumer applications. In 2016, DEHP was not only the largest plasticiser, with global consumption estimated at 3 million tonnes, but sales volumes were still growing (Polymers, 2017[33]). Such disparate regulatory frameworks incur compliance costs but leave health risks unaddressed on a global level. For example, in 2017, inspectors contributing to an EU-wide project co-ordinated by the European Chemical Agency (ECHA), analysed almost 5 000 imported articles and found that 18% contained non-compliant chemical substances. The most frequent breach concerned high concentrations of phthalates in toys (ECHA, 2018[34]). International co-operation to align regulations and market conditions is needed to prevent health hazards while generating efficiency gains by removing obstacles to trade (Chapter 7).

A second important barrier to the detoxification of material loops is the presence of historical hazardous substances in the economy. For example, at the end-of-life stage, the presence of DEHP in recycled plastics has created controversy regarding trade-offs between the benefits of removing hazardous substances from materials loops, and the need to increase recycling rates. The granting of authorisations for use of recycled soft PVC containing DEHP in the EU has led to public debate and even legal disputes (Chemical Watch, 2021[35]; European Parliament, 2015[36]). Proactively designing plastics with a sustainable chemistry perspective will reduce misalignment and lessen the need to deal with legacy chemical issues in the future.

Box 6.4. Extended Producer Responsibility has proven its worth, but challenges remain

The OECD defines EPR as an environmental policy approach that gives producers financial or physical responsibility for a product's entire lifecycle, including the treatment or disposal of post-consumer products (OECD, 2001[37]) (Figure 6.4). EPR has been successfully implemented to increase recycling rates in a range of countries and across a diversity of products, such as packaging, batteries, cars, electronics and tyres (Kaffine and O'Reilly, 2015[38]).

Figure 6.4. Extended producer responsibility

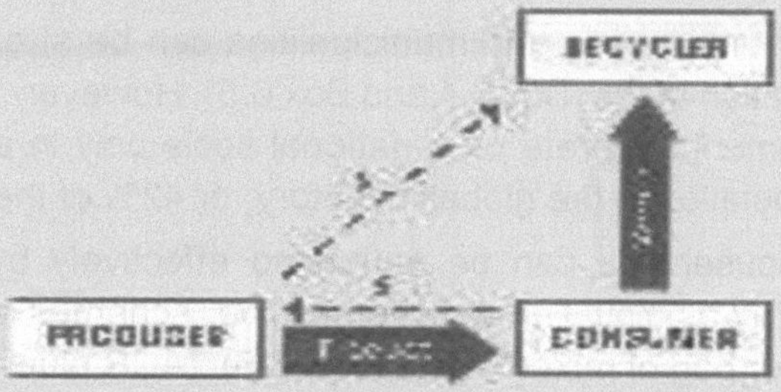

Note: The block arrows represent physical flows of products, packaging or waste. The dotted lines represent financial flows.

The most common type of EPR works by imposing recycling targets or other obligations on producers to internalise external costs and create a stable financing framework for recycling. Consumers pay for waste management at the moment of procurement, rather than at the moment of disposal, which is difficult to monitor.

Despite its success in many high-income countries, several announced EPR regulations have been abandoned in emerging economies, due to, among other reasons, weak institutions and resistance by stakeholders (OECD, 2016[39]). Following the public call to action on plastics, several organisations representing international companies have taken bold positions in favour of EPR, including the Consumer Goods Forum (2020[40]) and the Ellen MacArthur Foundation (2021[41]). The support of such stakeholders stresses the potential of EPR to foster the circular use of plastics and may give the impetus to promote EPR implementation across the world.

In pursuing economies of scale, most EPR schemes are organised industry-wide, which severs the link between product design and recycling liabilities for individual producers. Consequently, without further intervention, producers have few financial incentives to invest in eco-design (OECD, 2016[39]). Modulating EPR fees (i.e. recycling contribution) is one way forward, allowing producers with a more circular design to pay a lower EPR fee. Several countries are experimenting with modulated EPR fees, but their implementation needs to be scaled up to have substantial impact (Laubinger et al., 2021[20]):

- Quebec, Canada (packaging): fee reduced by 20% for packaging that is entirely manufactured with recycled content.
- Estonia (packaging): Reusable packaging does not need to be declared as long as it is reused effectively.
- France (packaging): 100% fee increase for non-recyclable material (per national guidelines) and opaque PET with >4% mineral filler.
- France (textiles): 50% fee reduction for textiles and shoes with 15% recycled fibres/materials.
- France (electronics): 20% fee reduction for a washing machine or dish washer with spare parts available up to 11 years, or post-consumer recycled content > 10%.
- Portugal (packaging): 10% penalty applied to PET bottles with PVC label or metal cap, and glass bottles with stopper made of ceramic or steel.
- Chile (packaging): bonus/malus based on recyclability and recycled content of packaging.

6.2.3. Recycling and sorting can be enhanced by making them profitable

Plastics are only recycled on a large scale if it is profitable to do so. Economic and regulatory policy instruments can ensure a business case for collecting and recycling plastic waste. Moreover, incentivising sorting at source is a critical lever because the quality of sorting determines the purity and value of recycled materials, and therefore the profitability of recycling operations.

Table 6.1 combines data from the OECD Plastics Policy Inventory with the fraction of municipal solid waste that is mismanaged per country (Kaza et al., 2018[42]). It suggests that there is significant scope for countries to further strengthen their policy frameworks for recycling:

- *Recycling incentives* for enterprises and municipalities can be strengthened effectively by EPR, landfill taxes and incineration taxes (Box 6.4 and Box 6.5). However, Table 6.1 highlights that these well-known policy instruments operate on a national scale only in a limited number of countries, covering 11% of the population in the global inventory, or 42% of the OECD population.
- *Sorting at source* by households can be enhanced effectively by deposit-refund systems for beverage bottles and Pay-as-You-Throw schemes, i.e. schemes where citizens have to pay a variable cost per kg or per bag of mixed waste (Box 6.5). (ACR plus, 2019[43]; Zhou et al., 2020[44]). For example, deposit-refund systems for beverage bottles can increase collection rates beyond 90% and reduce litter rates substantially (Reloop Platform, 2020[45]). However, Table 6.1 shows that only 4% of the population covered in the global inventory have at least one of these instruments in place on a national scale.

Box 6.5. Taxes can be powerful levers to change behaviour, as seen in several OECD countries

Pay-as-You-Throw encourages sorting at source in Belgium

In Belgium, Pay-as-You-Throw is a central pillar of the policy portfolio to encourage citizens to sort their waste. Flanders, one of Belgium's three regions, mandates municipalities to set a variable price for mixed waste collection of between EUR 0.11 and 0.33 per kg. Therefore, for a single 10kg bag of mixed waste, the cost could reach EUR 3.3 (Government of Flanders, 2021[46]). These financial incentives, combined with other measures, have led to one of the highest sorting and material recovery rates in Europe and the world (Eurostat, 2021[47]; OECD, 2021[48]). A crucial success factor is combining Pay-as-You-Throw with sustained awareness campaigns and enforcement measures to avoid mixed waste being disposed of in recycling receptacles or dumped in the street to avoid paying the variable fee. A fixed annual fee to finance waste management does not qualify as Pay-as-You-Throw because it does not give financial incentives to sort waste.

The landfill tax discourages landfilling in the United Kingdom

The UK introduced a landfill tax in 1996 and has gradually increased the rates over time. The standard rate for 2021 reached GBP 96.7 per tonne. This landfill "ladder" is considered a key driver of the reduction of the share of MSW landfilled from 86% (440 kg per inhabitant) in 1996 to 15% (69 kg per inhabitant) in 2018 (UK Government, 2021[49]).

Landfill taxes can only be successful when illegal dumping can be countered by effective regulation and operational control mechanisms.

The plastic bag tax as a game-changer for plastic bag littering in Ireland

In 2002, Ireland introduced a tax of EUR 0.15 on single-use plastic bags. This acted as a direct incentive to consumers to reduce the amount of shopping bags consumed and littering fell sharply. Discarded plastic bags amounted to about 5% of litter pollution in 2001 but dropped to less than 0.5% after 2003 (OECD, 2021[50]).

Table 6.1. The use of key policy instruments to enhance recycling is disparate across the world

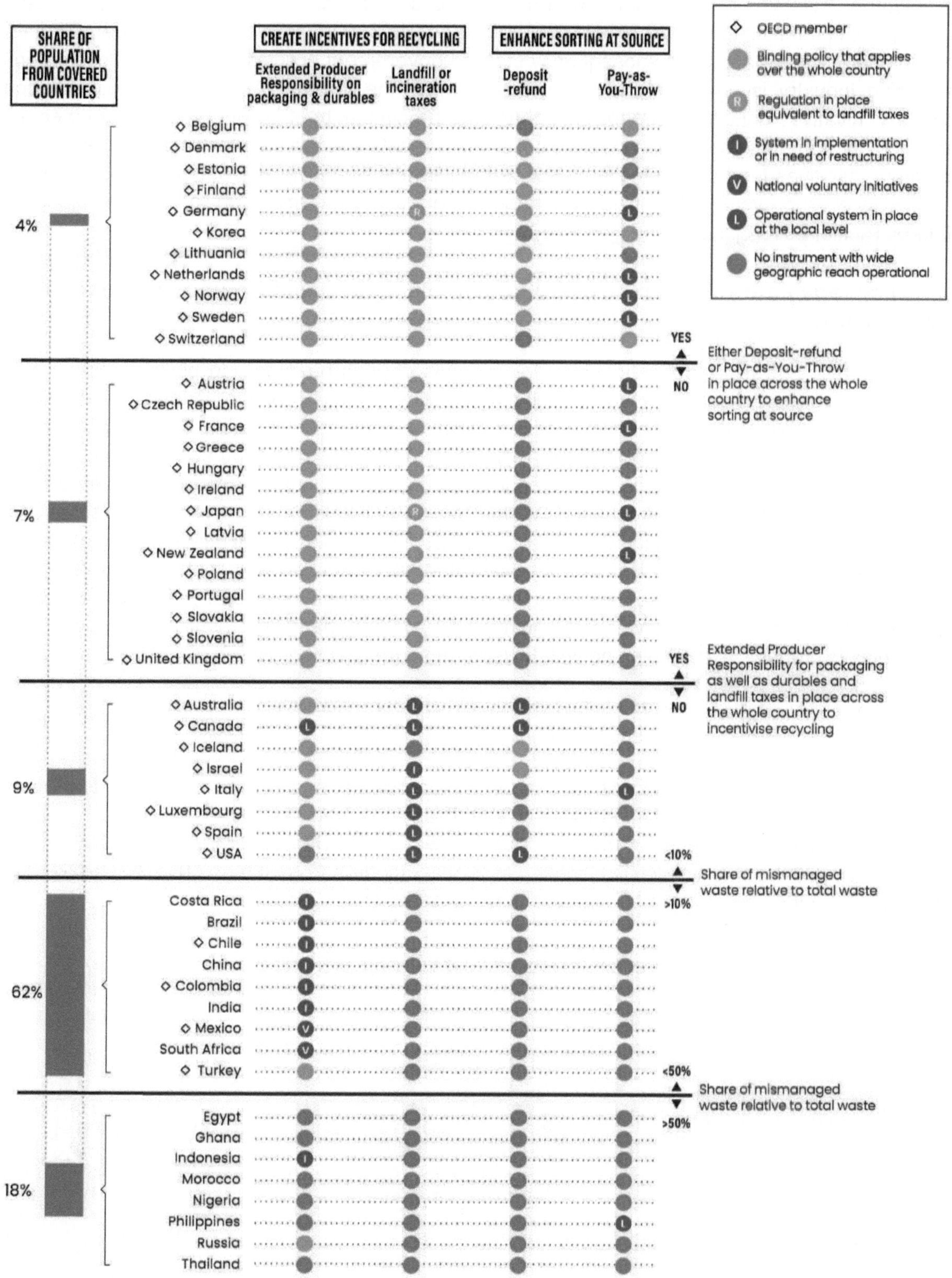

Source: OECD Plastics Policy Inventory and (Kaza et al., 2018[42]).

In addition to the economic and regulatory instruments showcased in Table 6.1, several countries also rely on voluntary initiatives or agreements with the private sector. For example, in Australia the packaging industry has committed to recycle 70% of packaging and use 50% recycled content by 2025. These targets are nationally agreed and have subsequently steered government policies, actions and investments. The packaging industry is proactively engaged in achieving the targets (APCO, 2022[51]). Although such voluntary initiatives contribute strongly to enhancing the circularity of products, they are categorised as "enabling" instruments, rather than steering policy instruments and are therefore not captured in Table 6.1. Voluntary initiatives tend to be smaller in scope than schemes driven by legal obligations and follow, or sometimes even prevent, policy initiatives, rather than leading the transition to more circularity (OECD, 2003[52]; Hickle, 2013[53]; Nash and Bosso, 2013[54]).

6.2.4. Leakage pathways can be closed by investing in basic waste management infrastructure

The most basic but also most critical step for mitigating health hazards and plastic leakage is to build infrastructure for safe disposal of waste, including plastics (typically sanitary landfills), and ensuring that mixed waste is collected for transport to these facilities. As shown in Table 6.1, Kaza et al. (2018[42]) estimate that more than 10% of MSW is mismanaged in countries representing 80% of the global population covered in the inventory. Moreover, in countries accounting for 18% of the covered population, more than 50% of MSW is mismanaged. Within the OECD, mismanaged waste is also an important challenge, with countries that account for 21% of the OECD's population still mismanaging more than 10% of their waste. As highlighted in Box 6.6, an integrated set of policies and sustained effort is needed to address this issue. Chapter 7 also discusses the role of international co-operation to enhance basic waste management infrastructure in developing countries. In addition, banning or limiting the use of frequently littered plastic products is a simple and widely used measure (Section 6.2.1).

Box 6.6. Brazil's fight against dumping waste

Dumpsites and uncontrolled landfills used to be the most common places for disposing of mixed waste in Brazil. Although there still is a long road ahead, Brazil has made significant progress in dealing with mismanaged waste, especially in the first decade of the 2000s (Figure 6.5). Between 2000 and 2019, Brazil increased the share of waste disposed in sanitary landfills from 38% to 60% (ABRELPE, 2003[55]; ABRELPE, 2020[56]).

Figure 6.5. Solid waste management in Brazil has improved significantly between 2000 and 2010

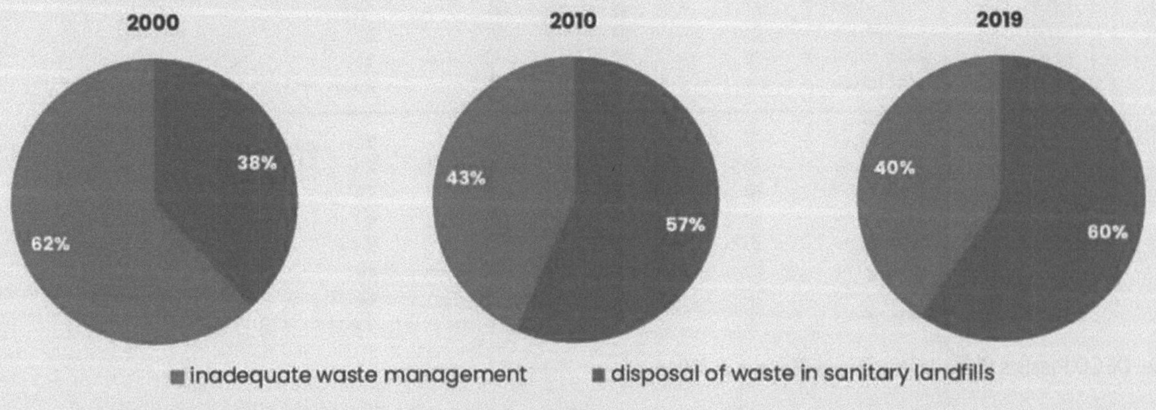

Source: (ABRELPE, 2003[55]; ABRELPE, 2020[56]).

The significant progress between 2000 and 2010 was achieved via a combination of policies and stakeholder actions. In 1998, a Federal Law made the inappropriate disposal of solid waste an environmental crime (Presidência da República, 1998[57]). A wider coverage of legislation and political attention resulted in inspections of municipal bodies, closures of open-air dumps and increased financial support for new sanitary landfills from the federal government (Neto, Petter and Cortina, 2009[58]). Another important piece of legislation, the National Sanitation Policy, was enacted in 2007 and defined basic sanitary conditions including provision of adequate solid waste management (Presidência da República, 2007[59]).

After 2010, it seemed difficult to sustain the momentum although some new policies were initiated. In 2010, the National Policy on Solid Waste (NPSW) was launched (Presidência da República, 2010[60]), but implementation of this progressive piece of legislation fell short of expectations (Alfaia, Costa and Campos, 2017[61]; Pereira et al., 2020[62]). Two major obstacles were local authorities' lack of expertise and financial means. In order to provide more incentives for circular (plastic) waste management in Brazil, the regulatory framework, enforcement of obligations on the ground and implementation of economic instruments need to be strengthened (World Bank, 2018[63]).

6.2.5. Cleaning up leaked plastics is expensive and only a policy of last resort

Beach clean-up campaigns and litter removal are often organised by stakeholders and NGOs. Few steering policy measures have focused on cleaning up leaked plastics as it is expensive (Table 6.2) and preventing pollution in the first place is more structural. Nonetheless several EPR regulations for packaging and EPR oblige producers to organise and finance the cleaning up of litter (Box 6.7).

Table 6.2. The high costs of cleaning up beach litter highlight the cost effectiveness of prevention

Source	Country scope	Clean-up scope	Clean-up cost
Mouat, Lozano and Bateson (2010[64])	United Kingdom	Beach litter	EUR 121/t
	Netherlands and Belgium	Beach litter	EUR 1 877/t
Hwang and Ko (2017[65])	Korea	Shoreline cleaning, marine debris	USD 1 300/t
McIlgorm, Campbell and Rule (2008[66])	France	Shoreline cleaning, marine debris	Mechanical: USD 1 100-11 400/t Manual: USD 2 200-22 800/t
Raaymakers (2007[67])	North-West Hawaiian Islands	Derelict fishing gear	USD 25 000/t
McIlgorm, Campbell and Rule (2008[66])	Southeast Alaska	Shoreline cleaning, marine debris	USD 2 339/t (Direct costs only: USD 1 766/t)
Burt et al. (2020[68])	Aldabra Atoll (a remote small island)	Shoreline cleaning, marine debris	USD 8 900/t

Box 6.7. The EU Single-Use Plastics Directive discourages the use of frequently littered items

EU Directive 2019/904[5] focuses on the ten most commonly found plastic items on beaches plus fishing gear. From the second half of 2021, it gradually started to phase in bans (among other measures) for plastic cotton bud sticks, cutlery, plates, straws, stirrers, balloon sticks, expanded polystyrene for food and beverage containers and cups. It will also impose a 25% recycled content target for beverage bottles and the development of EPR systems for balloons, tobacco products with filters and wet wipes to discourage pollution and finance the clean-up of litter.

6.3. Getting the policy mix right is crucial for structural change

The regulatory and economic instruments discussed in Section 6.2 can affect recycling and littering, but the depth of their impact on both aspects differs strongly for each instrument. If it is to increase the overall recycling rate of plastics substantially, a policy instrument must target a large share of plastic waste. For example, policies that target all plastics in MSW have a high potential to increase recycling. In contrast, policies to discourage littering must target items that are frequently littered, though these often only represent a small share of overall plastic waste. A good example is cigarette butts.

Figure 6.6. plots a selection of steering policy instruments against these two dimensions to highlight their differences. The size of the bubbles illustrates how often a policy is used in countries covered in the Plastics Policy Inventory. Only regulatory country-wide systems or systems operating at state, region or province level are taken into account (Table 6.1). The most recurring policy measure is to ban or tax single-use shopping bags (applied in 45 out of the 50 countries in the inventory), followed by EPR regulations (34 out of 50) for packaging and durables (e.g. electronics, cars, batteries or tyres), bans or taxes on other single use items (31 out of 50) and landfill or incineration taxes (31 out of 50).

Since the size of the bubble is driven by the number of countries that have the policy instrument in place, the bubble size should be interpreted as the instrument's popularity with policy makers, rather than its coverage of global plastics. Most steering instruments taken up in the inventory apply across the whole country, but some only apply to part of the country. For example, the 34 countries with EPR in place, include one country with provincial schemes, and the 31 countries with landfill and incineration taxes include 6 countries that only have waste taxes in place in some provinces or regions (Table 6.1).

Figure 6.6. Policy instruments vary in their potential impact on littering and recycling

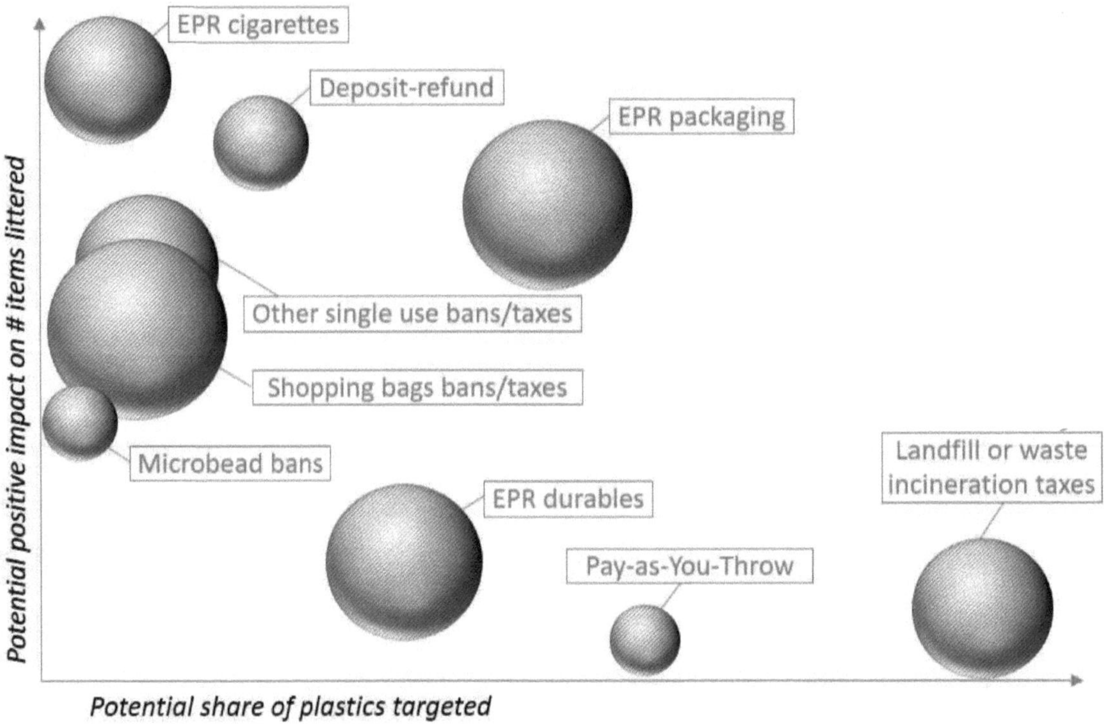

Note: the size of the bubble illustrates the number of countries that use the instrument at national, regional or provincial level (the inventory contains 50 countries).
Source: OECD Plastics Policy Inventory.

The horizontal axis in Figure 6.6. shows the share of global plastics that can be targeted by these policy instruments. Regulatory and economic instruments that target a large share of plastics can have a strong positive impact on overall recycling rates:

- **Landfill and incineration taxes** are effective at fostering recycling and target a large share of total plastic waste because they can affect both MSW and industrial waste streams. The rates of taxes applied vary significantly across countries and waste streams – for example, from a couple of USD per tonne for landfilling inert materials to over EUR 100 per tonne for mixed waste fractions in some countries (Box 6.5). Waste incineration taxes are implemented less often, but can internalise the environmental impacts of incineration in an efficient way (Dubois, 2013[69]). Tax rates on waste incineration are often lower than for landfilling. Typical rates are around EUR 10 per tonne of waste incinerated, though higher rates exist. The new EU tax on non-recycled plastics of EUR 800 per tonne is essentially also a tax on landfilling and waste incineration, as they are the most direct alternatives to recycling. However, this tax is imposed on the EU Member States and it is up to them to decide whether they cascade this cost down to the waste generators.
- **Pay-as-You-Throw** can be a highly effective measure to encourage sorting of plastic waste by households. Many plastics are directly or indirectly managed by households and Pay-as-You-Throw gives them a strong financial signal to minimise and sort waste streams (Box 6.5). The small size of the bubble (only 13 countries out of 50, have a national, regional or provincial regulation in place) highlights that this instrument is vastly underused to enhance recycling.
- **EPR for packaging** can target a substantial share of plastic waste because packaging accounts for almost one-third of plastics use and its lifecycle is short. Since the recycling rates of plastic packaging are substantially lower than for other packaging materials such as glass, metals or paper, substantial progress in recycling and circular design can be made by leveraging EPR (Box 6.4).
- **EPR** is applied on a range of **durable products,** such as electronic equipment or cars. However, plastics are often only a small part of the material composition in durable products and current EPR systems mainly focus on the recovery of other materials such as metals. Integrating recycled content targets and recycling targets specific to plastics in EPR regulations would foster plastics recycling markets.

The vertical axis of Figure 6.6. focuses on the potential impact of regulatory and economic instruments on littering. The instruments are ranked in the figure by their potential impact on reducing the amount of litter, taking into account the occurrence of litter on beaches as counted during the Ocean Conservancy (2017[70]) coastal clean-up. The figure highlights that most instruments that target littering or other direct leakage to the environment focus on minor shares of total plastic waste:

- **Single-use shopping bags** are highly visible but constitute only a small part of total plastic waste. For example, in the United States and Europe carrier bags accounted for less than 1% of total plastic waste in 2019 (EPA, 2020[71]; OECD, 2022[72]; Plastics Recyclers Europe, 2020[73]). Moreover, **bans and taxes** often only target bags with certain specifications (e.g. less than 35µm thick), which substantially limits the volumes of plastics concerned.
- **Bans and taxes on other frequently littered single-use items,** such as polystyrene food boxes, plates, cups, straws and cigarettes, have the potential to prevent littering, but they target a limited fraction of total plastic waste. For example, in the United States plastic plates and cups accounted for less than 2% of total plastics in 2017 (EPA, 2020[71]; OECD, 2022[72]). Moreover, the policies often only target a small part of these product streams, thus the impact of bans on single-use items are more limited than often suggested.
- The recent EU Single-Use Plastics Directive 2019/904 will impose **EPR for tobacco products with filters** from January 2023 (Box 6.7). The aim is to internalise the costs of cigarette butt

littering. In all EU Member States, producers will have to cover at least the costs of raising awareness, cleaning up litter and monitoring results. The national regulation and operational start-up of the various EPR schemes in the Member States are currently underway. This measure will have an important impact on managing littered cigarette butts, but will have no impact on recycling.

- Microbeads in rinse-off applications for personal care are designed to be removed with water and so enter the waste-water system. If WWTP are in place, most of these plastics are retained in the sludge,[6] but if not they will end up in nature. A growing number of countries have introduced **microbead bans,** including Canada, China, France, Italy, New Zealand, Sweden, the United Kingdom and United States (Anagnosti et al., 2021[74]). Moreover, the European Chemical Agency made a proposal in 2020 for an EU-wide ban on intentionally added microplastics in a range of products (ECHA, 2020[75]). In most countries, the scope up to now is limited to rinse-off personal care and cosmetics, while cleaning products, which sometimes also contain microbeads, have been left untouched. Importantly, the bans have had global resonance, with leading international companies committing to phasing out microbeads throughout their global product portfolio. The effectiveness of the international policy measures is high, but the total volume concerned is tiny (representing less than 0.01% of all plastics). As a consequence, these measures succeed in reducing health and environmental risks, but do not contribute much to restraining overall plastics demand.

Some economic instruments can affect recycling and littering simultaneously, but they also have their limitations:

- As discussed earlier, **EPR for packaging** is typically focused on increasing recycling rates, but increasingly the instrument is also used to shift the responsibility for littering towards producers. For example, packaging producers in Belgium have to finance anti-littering actions.[7] However, the scope of this obligation is limited to packaging waste and does not contain binding measurable targets that have to be achieved.
- **Deposit-refund systems** can induce high quality recycling or even reuse of beverage packaging while reducing littering. However, the scope is typically limited to beverage bottles, which only make up a limited share of total plastic waste. For example, in the United States PET bottles and jars accounted for less than 5% of total plastic waste in 2019 (EPA, 2020[71]; OECD, 2022[72]).

Measures that target highly visible streams such as single-use plastic bags attract ample policy attention. Many countries implement such measures and refer to them as flagship measures in the transition to a circular economy. These policy instruments indeed help to close leakage pathways by discouraging littering, but their impact on recycling or prevention is often limited because they target only a minor share of overall plastics use. To close material loops and enhance recycling structurally, wider implementation of landfill taxes, incineration taxes, Pay-as-You-Throw, deposit-refund schemes and EPR for packaging as well as for durables is needed. Moreover, the effects of these instruments can be further complemented by recycled content targets and other measures that encourage recycling by fostering the circular design of products.

6.4. A policy roadmap for a more circular use of plastics

The analysis allowed to develop a high-level roadmap to combat plastic pollution and increase the circularity of plastics along their entire lifecycle that policy makers can adapt to national conditions (Figure 6.7). It involves a phased approach that can be implemented over time to achieve increasingly ambitious policy objectives.

Figure 6.7. A policy roadmap for more circular use of plastics

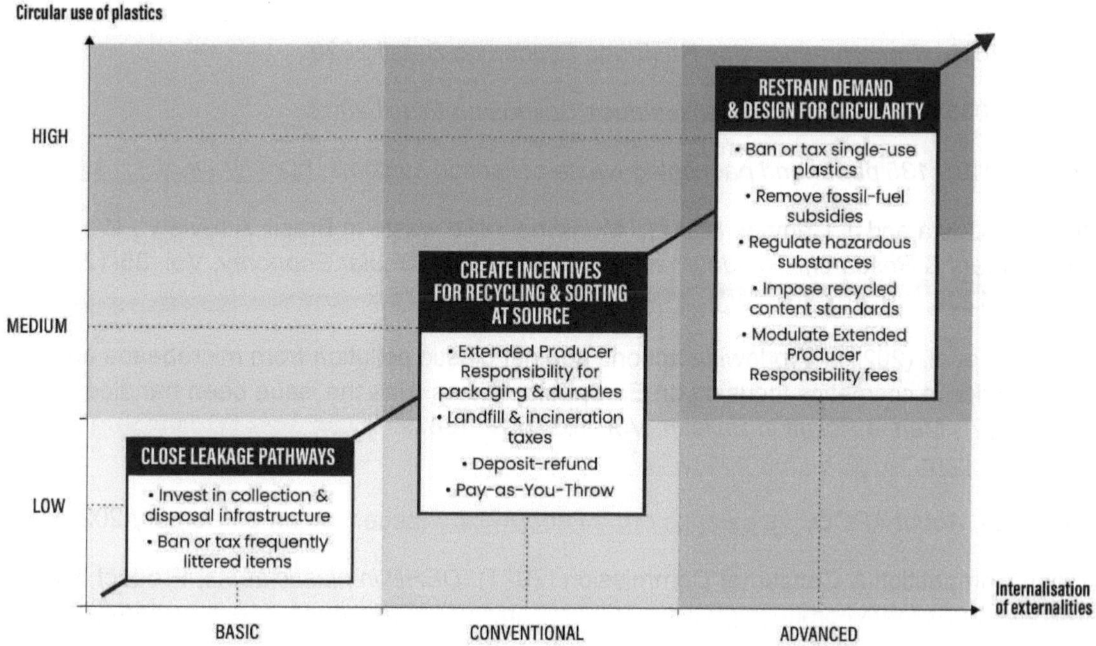

The roadmap emphasises the need for regulatory and economic policy instruments that can induce economy-wide behavioural changes. For successful implementation, these steering instruments need to be accompanied with enabling policies, such as investments in innovation, communication and collaboration with stakeholders. The roadmap clusters the key actions into three phases:

- *Close leakage pathways:* the most basic step for mitigating health hazards and plastics pollution is to build sanitary waste management infrastructure, typically landfills, and organise waste collection (Watkins et al., 2019[76]). Moreover, by banning or taxing items that are frequently littered, leakage to the environment can be significantly reduced.
- *Create incentives for recycling and enhance sorting at source:* recycling plastics only occurs on a large scale if it is profitable. Policy makers can apply taxes to landfill and incineration to make recycling more cost competitive. By also imposing EPR, policy makers can make producers responsible for recycling packaging and durable products such as cars, batteries, tyres and electronics. As the quality of collected waste streams drives the feasibility and profitability of recycling, countries can achieve much greater circularity by sharpening the financial incentives to sort waste at source. Deposit-refund systems give a strong financial incentive to return beverage bottles, while Pay-as-You-Throw makes mixed waste disposal by households expensive. If combined with policies to avoid dumping and contaminating other waste streams, making householders pay per bag or kilo of mixed waste is an effective way to incentivise sorting at source.
- *Restrain demand and optimise design:* the largest environmental gains can be achieved by reducing the use of virgin materials and by improving product design (Watkins et al., 2019[76]). Removing support schemes for fossil-based plastics, such as shale gas subsidies (OECD, 2016[77]), will make plastic value chains more circular by restraining consumption and by making recycled plastics more price competitive. By removing hazardous substances and recycling inhibitors from plastics at the design stage, chemical hazards can be avoided and recycling rates can be increased. Several countries have launched advanced policies such as (single-use) plastic taxes, reuse incentives, recycled content targets and fee modulation in EPR systems, but their impact could be improved considerably by extending coverage to more product types, and more countries.

References

ABRELPE (2020), *Panoramados dos Resíduos Sólidos no Brasil 2020.* [56]

ABRELPE (2003), *Panoramados dos Resíduos Sólidos no Brasil 2003.* [55]

ACR plus (2019), *135 paper and packaging waste collection systems*, http://www.acrplus.org. [43]

Alfaia, R., A. Costa and J. Campos (2017), "Municipal solid waste in Brazil: A review", *Waste Management & Research: The Journal for a Sustainable Circular Economy*, Vol. 35/12, pp. 1195-1209, http://dx.doi.org/10.1177/0734242x17735375. [61]

Anagnosti, L. et al. (2021), "Worldwide actions against plastic pollution from microbeads and microplastics in cosmetics focusing on European policies. Has the issue been handled effectively?", *Marine Pollution Bulletin*, Vol. 162, p. 111883, http://dx.doi.org/10.1016/j.marpolbul.2020.111883. [74]

APCO (2022), *About APCO*, https://apco.org.au/about-apco (accessed on 8 February 2022). [51]

Australian Competition & Consumer Commission (2021), *DEHP in plastic items*, Product Safety Australia, https://www.productsafety.gov.au/products/chemicals/dehp-in-plastic-items. [28]

Benjamin, S. et al. (2017), "Phthalates impact human health: Epidemiological evidences and plausible mechanism of action", *Journal of Hazardous Materials*, Vol. 340, http://dx.doi.org/10.1016/j.jhazmat.2017.06.036. [25]

Boesen, S., N. Bey and M. Niero (2019), "Environmental sustainability of liquid food packaging: Is there a gap between Danish consumers' perception and learnings from life cycle assessment?", *Journal of Cleaner Production*, Vol. 210, pp. 1193-1206, http://dx.doi.org/10.1016/j.jclepro.2018.11.055. [16]

Burt, A. et al. (2020), "The costs of removing the unsanctioned import of marine plastic litter to small island states", *Scientific Reports*, Vol. 10/1, http://dx.doi.org/10.1038/s41598-020-71444-6. [68]

CDC (2021), *Fourth National Report on Human Exposure to Environmental Chemicals Update*, https://www.cdc.gov/nchs/nhanes/. (accessed on 21 May 2021). [23]

CDC (2021), *Phthalates Factsheet | National Biomonitoring Program*, https://www.cdc.gov/biomonitoring/Phthalates_FactSheet.html (accessed on 21 May 2021). [24]

Chemical Watch (2021), *European Commission wins NGO appeal case on DEHP authorisation: ClientEarth says reforms are needed to tackle SVHC use in recycled material*, Chemical Watch, https://chemicalwatch.com/347913/european-commission-wins-ngo-appeal-case-on-dehp-authorisation. [35]

Commonwealth of Australia (2011), *Consumer Protection Notice No. 11 Of 2011: Permanent Ban On Children's Products Containing More Than 1% Diethylhexyl Phthalate (DEHP)*, Commonwealth of Australia, https://www.legislation.gov.au/Details/F2011L00192. [29]

Cornago, E., P. Börkey and A. Brown (2021), "Preventing single-use plastic waste: Implications of different policy approaches", *OECD Environment Working Papers*, No. 182, OECD Publishing, Paris, https://dx.doi.org/10.1787/c62069e7-en. [6]

Dubois, M. (2013), “Towards a coherent European approach for taxation of combustible waste”, *Waste Management*, Vol. 33/8, pp. 1776-1783, http://dx.doi.org/10.1016/j.wasman.2013.03.015. [69]

ECHA (2020), *Microplastics*, European Chemicals Agency, https://echa.europa.eu/hot-topics/microplastics#:~:text=In%20January%202019%2C%20ECHA%20proposed,their%20release%20to%20the%20environment.&text=ECHA%27s%20Committee%20for%20Risk%20Assessment,its%20opinion%20in%20June%202020. [75]

ECHA (2018), *Inspectors find phthalates in toys and asbestos in second-hand products*, https://echa.europa.eu/nl/-/inspectors-find-phthalates-in-toys-and-asbestos-in-second-hand-products (accessed on 21 May 2021). [34]

ECHA (2013), *Evaluation of new scientific evidence concerning DINP and DIDP In relation to entry 52 of Annex XVII to REACH Regulation (EC) No 1907/2006*, http://echa.europa.eu/ (accessed on 26 May 2021). [79]

Ecoprog (2020), *Waste to Energy 2020/2021*, https://www.ecoprog.com/fileadmin/user_upload/extract_market_report_WtE_2020-2021_ecoprog.pdf (accessed on 26 May 2021). [8]

Ellen MacArthur Foundation (2021), *Extended Producer Responsibility: a necessary part of the solution to packaging waste and pollution.* [41]

Engel, S. et al. (2021), “Neurotoxicity of Ortho-Phthalates: Recommendations for Critical Policy Reforms to Protect Brain Development in Children”, *American journal of public health*, Vol. 111/4, pp. 687-695, http://dx.doi.org/10.2105/AJPH.2020.306014. [26]

EPA (2020), *Advancing Sustainable Materials Management: 2018 Tables and Figures*, United States Environment Protection Agency, https://www.epa.gov/sites/default/files/2021-01/documents/2018_tables_and_figures_dec_2020_fnl_508.pdf. [71]

European Parliament (2015), *Don’t allow recycling of plastics that contain toxic phthalate DEHP, warn MEPs*, European Parliament News, https://www.europarl.europa.eu/news/en/press-room/20151120IPR03616/don-t-allow-recycling-of-plastics-that-contain-toxic-phthalate-dehp-warn-meps. [36]

Eurostat (2021), *Waste statistics*, https://ec.europa.eu/eurostat/statistics-explained/index.php?title=Waste_statistics#Waste_treatment. [47]

Government of Flanders (2021), *Afvalinzameling en sorteren*, https://www.vlaanderen.be/afvalinzameling-en-sorteren. [46]

HDR (2009), *The city of San Francisco, Streets litter Re-audit*, San Francisco Environment Department. [15]

Hickle, G. (2013), “Comparative Analysis of Extended Producer Responsibility Policy in the United States and Canada”, *Journal of Industrial Ecology*, Vol. 17/2, pp. 249-261, http://dx.doi.org/10.1111/jiec.12020. [53]

Holland, M. (2018), “Socio-economic assessment of phthalates”, *OECD Environment Working Papers*, No. 133, OECD Publishing, Paris, https://dx.doi.org/10.1787/a38a0e34-en. [22]

Hwang, S. and J. Ko (2017), *Achievement and progress of marine litter retrieval project in near coast of Korea - based on activities of Korea Fisheries Infrastructure Promotion Association*. [65]

IEEP (2017), *EPR in the EU Plastics Strategy and the Circular Economy: A focus on plastic packaging*, Institute for European Environmental Policy. [14]

INERIS (2021), *Phthalates substitution*, https://substitution-phtalates.ineris.fr/en (accessed on 21 May 2021). [32]

Kaffine, D. and P. O'Reilly (2015), *What Have We Learned About Extended Producer Responsibility in the Past Decade? A Survey of the recent EPR Economic Literature*, OECD Publishing, Paris. [38]

Karasik, R. et al. (2020), *20 Years of Government Responses to the Global Plastic Pollution Problem: The Plastics Policy Inventory*, Duke University, Durham, https://nicholasinstitute.duke.edu/sites/default/files/publications/20-Years-of-Government-Responses-to-the-Global-Plastic-Pollution-Problem-New_1.pdf. [9]

Kaza, S. et al. (2018), *What a Waste 2.0: A Global Snapshot of Solid Waste Management to 2050*, The World Bank, http://dx.doi.org/10.1596/978-1-4648-1329-0. [42]

Krelling, A., A. Williams and A. Turra (2017), "Differences in perception and reaction of tourist groups to beach marine debris that can influence a loss of tourism revenue in coastal areas", *Marine Policy*, Vol. 85, pp. 87-99, http://dx.doi.org/10.1016/j.marpol.2017.08.021. [1]

Laubinger, F. et al. (2021), "Modulated fees for Extended Producer Responsibility schemes (EPR)", *OECD Environment Working Papers*, No. 184, OECD Publishing, Paris, https://dx.doi.org/10.1787/2a42f54b-en. [20]

McIlgorm, A., H. Campbell and M. Rule (2008), *Understanding the economic benefits and costs of controlling marine debris in the APEC region (MRC 02/2007)*, A report to the Asia-Pacific Economic Cooperation Marine Resource Conservation Working Group by the National Marine Science Centre (University of New England and Southern Cross University),Coffs Harbour, https://d3n8a8pro7vhmx.cloudfront.net/boomerangalliance/pages/510/attachments/original/1481158813/Understanding_the_Economic_Benefits_and_Costs_of_Controlling_Marine_Debris_in_the_APEC_Region.pdf?1481158813. [66]

Mouat, J., R. Lozano and H. Bateson (2010), *Economic Impacts of Marine Litter*, Kommunernes Internationale Miljøorganisation (KIMO), https://www.kimointernational.org/wp/wp-content/uploads/2017/09/KIMO_Economic-Impacts-of-Marine-Litter.pdf. [64]

Nash, J. and C. Bosso (2013), "Extended Producer Responsibility in the United States", *Journal of Industrial Ecology*, Vol. 17/2, pp. 175-185, http://dx.doi.org/10.1111/j.1530-9290.2012.00572.x. [54]

Neto, R., C. Petter and J. Cortina (2009), "Report: The current situation of sanitary landfills in Brazil and the importance of the application of economic models", *Waste Management & Research: The Journal for a Sustainable Circular Economy*, Vol. 27/10, pp. 1002-1005, http://dx.doi.org/10.1177/0734242x09104583. [58]

Ocean conservancy (2017), *International coastal cleanup report*. [70]

OECD (2022), *Global Outlook Plastics Database*, https://doi.org/10.1787/c0821f81-en. [72]

OECD (2021), *A Chemicals Perspective on Designing with Sustainable Plastics : Goals, Considerations and Trade-offs*, OECD Publishing, Paris, https://dx.doi.org/10.1787/f2ba8ff3-en. [21]

OECD (2021), *OECD Environmental Performance Reviews: Belgium 2021*, OECD Environmental Performance Reviews, OECD Publishing, Paris, https://dx.doi.org/10.1787/738553c5-en. [48]

OECD (2021), *OECD Environmental Performance Reviews: Ireland 2021*, OECD Environmental Performance Reviews, OECD Publishing, Paris, https://dx.doi.org/10.1787/9ef10b4f-en. [50]

OECD (2021), *Policies to Reduce Microplastics Pollution in Water: Focus on Textiles and Tyres*, OECD Publishing, Paris, https://dx.doi.org/10.1787/7ec7e5ef-en. [2]

OECD (2021), *Policy Instruments for the Environment (PINE) Database*, http://oe.cd/pine. [4]

OECD (2021), *Progress report on the implementation of the Recommendation of the Council on Resource Productivity*, https://one.oecd.org/document/C(2021)62/REV1/en/pdf. [11]

OECD (2016), *Extended Producer Responsibility: Updated Guidance for Efficient Waste Management*, OECD Publishing, Paris, https://dx.doi.org/10.1787/9789264256385-en. [39]

OECD (2016), *Policy Guidance on Resource Efficiency*, OECD Publishing, Paris, https://dx.doi.org/10.1787/9789264257344-en. [77]

OECD (2003), *Voluntary approaches for environmental policy: effectiveness, efficiency and usage in policy mixes*. [52]

OECD (2001), *Extended Producer Responsibility: A Guidance Manual for Governments*, OECD Publishing, Paris, https://dx.doi.org/10.1787/9789264189867-en. [37]

OECD (forthcoming), *The cost of preventing ocean plastic pollution*. [7]

OECD/IEA (2021), *Update on recent progress in reform of inefficient fossil-fuel subsidies that encourage wasteful consumption*. [13]

PBM (2020), *(2020) Tackling plastic litter: a nudging strategy for reducing consumption of single-use disposable cups*. [12]

Pereira, A. et al. (2020), "Waste policy reforms in developing countries: A comparative study of India and Brazil", *Waste Management & Research: The Journal for a Sustainable Circular Economy*, Vol. 38/9, pp. 987-994, http://dx.doi.org/10.1177/0734242x20938435. [62]

Plastics Recyclers Europe (2020), *Flexible films market in Europe*. [73]

Polymers, A. (2017), "Global demand for plasticizers continues to rise", *Additives for Polymers*, Vol. 2017/10, pp. 10-11, http://dx.doi.org/10.1016/s0306-3747(17)30137-9. [33]

Presidência da República (2010), *Federal Law n. 12.305*, http://www.planalto.gov.br/ccivil_03/_ato2007-2010/2010/lei/l12305.htm. [60]

Presidência da República (2007), *Federal Law n. 11.445*, http://www.planalto.gov.br/ccivil_03/_ato2007-2010/2007/lei/L11445compilado.htm. [59]

Presidência da República (1998), *Federal Law n. 9.605*, http://www.planalto.gov.br/ccivil_03/leis/L9605.htm. [57]

Raaymakers, S. (2007), *The problem of derelict fishing gear: Global review and proposals for action*, Food and Agricultural Organisation on the United Nations United Nations Environment Programme. [67]

Reloop Platform (2020), *Global Deposit Book 2020: An Overview of Deposit Systems for one-way Beverage Containers*, https://www.reloopplatform.org/wp-content/uploads/2020/12/2020-Global-Deposit-Book-WEB-version-1DEC2020.pdf (accessed on 19 March 2021). [45]

Silano, V. et al. (2019), “Update of the risk assessment of di-butylphthalate (DBP), butyl-benzyl-phthalate (BBP), bis(2-ethylhexyl)phthalate (DEHP), di-isononylphthalate (DINP) and di-isodecylphthalate (DIDP) for use in food contact materials”, *EFSA Journal*, Vol. 17/12, http://dx.doi.org/10.2903/j.efsa.2019.5838. [27]

Stefanini, R. et al. (2020), “Plastic or glass: a new environmental assessment with a marine litter indicator for the comparison of pasteurized milk bottles”, *The International Journal of Life Cycle Assessment*, Vol. 26/4, pp. 767-784, http://dx.doi.org/10.1007/s11367-020-01804-x. [17]

The Consumer Goods Forum (2020), *Driving Positive Change*, https://www.theconsumergoodsforum.com/. [40]

UK Government (2021), *Policy paper: Changes to Landfill Tax rates from 1 April 2021*, https://www.gov.uk/government/publications/changes-to-landfill-tax-rates-from-1-april-2021/changes-to-landfill-tax-rates-from-1-april-2021. [49]

UNEP (2020), *Single-use plastic bags and their alternatives: Recommendations from Life Cycle Assessments*, https://www.lifecycleinitiative.org/single-use-plastic-bags-and-their-alternatives-recommendations-from-life-cycle-assessments/. [18]

UNEP (2020), *Tackling Plastic Pollution: Legislative Guide for the Regulation of Single-Use Plastic Products*, United Nations Environment Programme, https://wedocs.unep.org/bitstream/handle/20.500.11822/34570/PlastPoll.pdf.pdf?sequence=3&isAllowed=y. [10]

UNEP (2018), *Legal Limits on Single-Use Plastics and Microplastics: A Global Review of National Laws and Regulations*, UN Environment Programme, https://www.unep.org/resources/publication/legal-limits-single-use-plastics-and-microplastics-global-review-national. [5]

van den Driesche, S. et al. (2020), “Systematic comparison of the male reproductive tract in fetal and adult Wistar rats exposed to DBP and DINP in utero during the masculinisation programming window”, *Toxicology Letters*, Vol. 335, pp. 37-50, http://dx.doi.org/10.1016/j.toxlet.2020.10.006. [78]

Vinyl Council Australia (2018), *PVC Stewardship Program: Progress Report 2018*, Vinyl Council Australia, https://vinyl.org.au/images/vinyl/Sustainability/PSP/VCAPSPReport2018-FINAL_VERSION.pdf. [30]

Vinyl Plus (2021), *REPORTING ON 2020 ACTIVITIES and summarising the key achievements of the past 10 years*, https://vinylplus.eu/uploads/Progress%20Report%202021/VinylPlus%20Progress%20Report%202021_WEB_sp.pdf (accessed on 21 May 2021). [31]

Watkins, E. et al. (2012), *Use of Economic Instruments and Waste Management Performances. Final report prepared for the European Commission.*, European Commission (DG ENV), https://www.ecologic.eu/sites/default/files/publication/2021/2670-04-Economic-instruments-waste-management-performance-web.pdf. [3]

Watkins, E. et al. (2019), "Policy approaches to incentivise sustainable plastic design", *OECD Environment Working Papers*, No. 149, OECD Publishing, Paris, https://dx.doi.org/10.1787/233ac351-en. [76]

Wiesinger, H., Z. Wang and S. Hellweg (2021), "Deep Dive into Plastic Monomers, Additives, and Processing Aids", *Environmental Science & Technology*, Vol. 55/13, pp. 9339-9351, http://dx.doi.org/10.1021/acs.est.1c00976. [19]

World Bank (2018), *Brazil: Integrated Solid Waste Management.* [63]

Zhou, G. et al. (2020), "A systematic review of the deposit-refund system for beverage packaging: Operating mode, key parameter and development trend", *Journal of Cleaner Production*, Vol. 251, p. 119660, http://dx.doi.org/10.1016/j.jclepro.2019.119660. [44]

Notes

[1] Waste Framework Directive 2008/98/EC, amended by Directive 2018/851, Article 8a, 4b

[2] Single-Use Plastics Directive, Article 6.5. For details see https://ec.europa.eu/environment/topics/plastics/single-use-plastics_en.

[3] High weight molecular phthalates that have longer chemical chains such as DINP and DIDP have more limited health hazards (ECHA, 2013[79]) and are less mobile within the plastic which reduces potential exposure (van den Driesche et al., 2020[78]).

[4] Including EU Regulation 2018/2005 and the US Toxic Substances Control Act.

[5] https://ec.europa.eu/environment/topics/plastics/single-use-plastics_en.

[6] Although microplastics captured in sludge may eventually leak into the environment via land spreading.

[7] For more information on the anti-litter campaigns in Belgium: https://www.fostplus.be/en, https://mooimakers.be/, https://www.bewapp.be/.

7. International co-operation to make plastics value chains more circular

This chapter reviews the current landscape of international agreements and initiatives, as well as the status of efforts to improve it. It then zooms in on the financial resources that would be needed to stop plastic leakage linked to poor waste management practices in developing countries, which has been recognised as an important priority for international co-operation. Finally, the chapter assesses the current contribution of ODA towards this goal

KEY MESSAGES

- The environmental damages generated by the current use and disposal of plastics, are global problems that require international co-operation to resolve. The international community has voiced strong ambitions to limit the pollution of the environment by plastics and momentum is building for a binding global agreement on plastic pollution.
- Improving waste management to reduce land-based sources of marine plastic is one of the main priorities for action, alongside upstream preventative measures. Since the bulk of macroplastic waste mismanagement occurs in low and middle-income countries, the investments needed in these countries are particularly large.
- Building the basic waste management infrastructure is estimated to cost more than EUR 25 billion per year in low and middle-income countries.
- Analysis of official development assistance (ODA) highlights that although the financial support to address plastic leakage in developing countries is increasing, it is only a fraction of what's needed.
- Additional sources of funding will need to be tapped into and enabling policy frameworks established to ensure that the resources are used effectively. Without international support and local political leadership, the required investment and governance for high-quality infrastructure will not materialise.

7.1. Addressing the environmental consequences of global plastics value chains requires international co-operation

National efforts to address the challenges linked to the use of plastics, described in the previous chapter, need to be supplemented with international co-operation for several reasons:

- Plastics are shipped across the world as materials, products and waste streams, and supply chains are spread across the globe – policy responses would be more effective if co-ordinated internationally.
- The environmental consequences of plastics polluting water bodies are often transboundary and threaten the ocean – a global commons.
- Tackling both the upstream and downstream environmental challenges posed by plastics requires innovation and investment on a significant scale, as well as a steep policy learning curve all of which can be accelerated through international co-operation.

7.2. A more comprehensive global approach to plastic pollution is needed

Even before the rise of plastics up the political agenda, a series of international agreements had put forward binding requirements and non-binding recommendations for managing plastics and preventing pollution (Figure 7.1). However, this patchwork of agreements has gaps and there is no international governance instrument that comprehensively addresses the challenges at the different stages of the plastics lifecycle. For example, there are few policy instruments dedicated to marine plastic litter,[1] national legislation on ocean affairs is fragmented, requirements are incompletely implemented and multilateral monitoring systems are not functional (UN Report of the Secretary-General, 2018[1]).

Table 7.1. The fragmented nature of global agreements on plastics is hindering environmental protection

Key international agreements that cover pollution and impacts of plastics

	Agreement	Description	Signatories
Binding agreements			
Pollution	United Nations Convention on the Law of the Seas (UNCLOS)	Sets the legal framework for marine activities. Includes general obligation to take all necessary measures to prevent, reduce, and control (plastic) pollution. UNCLOS came into force in 1994.	167 countries (+EU)
	The Convention on the Prevention of Marine Pollution by Dumping of Wastes and Other Matter 1972 (London Convention) and its 1996 Protocol (the London Protocol)	Prohibits the direct dumping or discharge of plastic waste into the ocean.	87 states
	Annex V of the International Convention for the Prevention of Pollution from Ships (MARPOL)	MARPOL is the only global international treaty to address marine debris (Parker, 2019[2]). Annex V bans dumping of plastic waste by ships into the ocean. The annex entered into force in 1988.	156 states
Biodiversity	The Convention on Biological Diversity (CBD)	Aichi Biodiversity Target 8 aimed to reduce (plastic) pollution to levels not detrimental to ecosystem function by 2020. Adopted at CBD COP 10 (2010). The draft[1] Post-2020 Global Biodiversity Framework includes target 7 to eliminate the discharge of plastic waste.	195 states (+EU), U.S. signed but not ratified
	The United Nations Fish Stocks Agreement of 10 December 1982	Obliges states to minimise (plastic) pollution, waste, discards, and catch by ghost fishing gear.	59 states
Chemicals	The Stockholm Convention on Persistent Organic Pollutants (Stockholm Convention)	Regulates the production, use and disposal of additives used with plastics that are listed as persistent organic pollutants Entered into force in 2004.	184 parties
Waste trade	The Basel Convention on the Control of Transboundary Movements of Hazardous Wastes and Their Disposal (Basel Convention)	Sets requirements and prohibitions for trade of hazardous and other (plastic) wastes. Entered into force in 1992, with amendments to plastic waste trade in 2020.	188 parties
Non-binding agreements			
Pollution	FAO Code of Conduct for Responsible Fisheries	Provides legal principles for responsible fishing, including measures to address ghost fishing gear. Adopted in 1995.	
	Global Programme of Action for the Protection of the Marine Environment from Land-based Activities (GPA)	An inter-governmental forum for guidelines on how to address land-based sources of marine (plastic) pollution. Adopted in 1995.	108 states (+EU)
	Global Partnership on Marine Litter (GPML)	Platform for co-operation and sharing of best practices on instruments to address marine plastic pollution (GPML, 2018[3]). It was launched at the UN Conference on Sustainable Development (Rio+20) in June 2012.	412 members
	Clean Seas Pact	Countries pledged to reduce pollution from single-use plastics, protect national waters and encourage recycling (UNEP, 2019[4]). The Clean Seas Pact was endorsed in 2017.	63 countries joined
	Honolulu Strategy, following the Fifth International Marine Debris Conference in 2011	The strategy set a global framework, recommended strategies and potential actions to reduce the amount and impacts of plastic litter (NOAA and UNEP, 2012[5]). The strategy does not prescribe specific targets or actions.	
Waste trade	The Plastic Waste Partnership (PWP) of the Basel Convention	A forum to promote environmentally sound management of plastic waste. The PWP was launched in 2019.	50 parties (+EU)

Note: 1. The draft CBD framework is currently being negotiated and is expected to be adopted during the second phase of the UN Biodiversity Conference in May 2022, in Kunming, People's Republic of China (Convention on Biological Diversity, 2021[6]).
Source: Adapted from UNEP (2017[7]), *Combating Marine Plastic Litter and Microplastics: An assessment of the effectiveness of relevant international, regional and subregional governance strategies and approaches*, https://www.gpmarinelitter.org/resources/information-documents/combating-marine-plastic-litter-and-microplastics-assessment.

The Sustainable Development Goals (SDGs), adopted by the United Nations in 2015, also contain targets that are relevant for plastic waste management and leakage (see Table 7.2 for a selection of relevant targets). Importantly, the SDGs are aspirational and non-binding.

Table 7.2. The SDGs highlight international ambitions to reduce the environment and health impacts of waste

Most relevant Sustainable Development Goals	11 SUSTAINABLE CITIES AND COMMUNITIES	12 RESPONSIBLE CONSUMPTION AND PRODUCTION	14 LIFE BELOW WATER
Targets directly related to plastic waste and leakage	11.6: by 2030 reduce the adverse per capita environmental impact of cities, through municipal and other waste management	12.4: environmentally sound management of waste throughout the lifecycle, reduce release to air, water, and soil 12.5: by 2030 substantially reduce waste generation	14.1: by 2025 prevent and reduce marine pollution, in particular from land-based activities

Source: Adapted from (United Nations, 2021[8]).

Recent years have seen a ramping up of international attention on plastic pollution, and specifically marine litter. As a result, a number of high-profile initiatives on plastic leakage (see Glossary) have been launched by the G7 and subsequently by the G20 (Figure 7.1). Communiqués and commitments have primarily focused on land-based sources of marine plastic litter. One of the flagship initiatives at the G20 level is the Osaka Blue Ocean Vision, which was announced in 2019 and sets the strategic target of reducing plastic leakage to the ocean to net zero by 2050. The Convention on Biological Diversity[2] and the European Union have also set additional targets;[3] but, they remain voluntary.

Figure 7.1. The G7 and G20 have hosted several initiatives to tackle plastic pollution

Timeline of key G7 (top) and G20 (bottom) communiqués and commitments

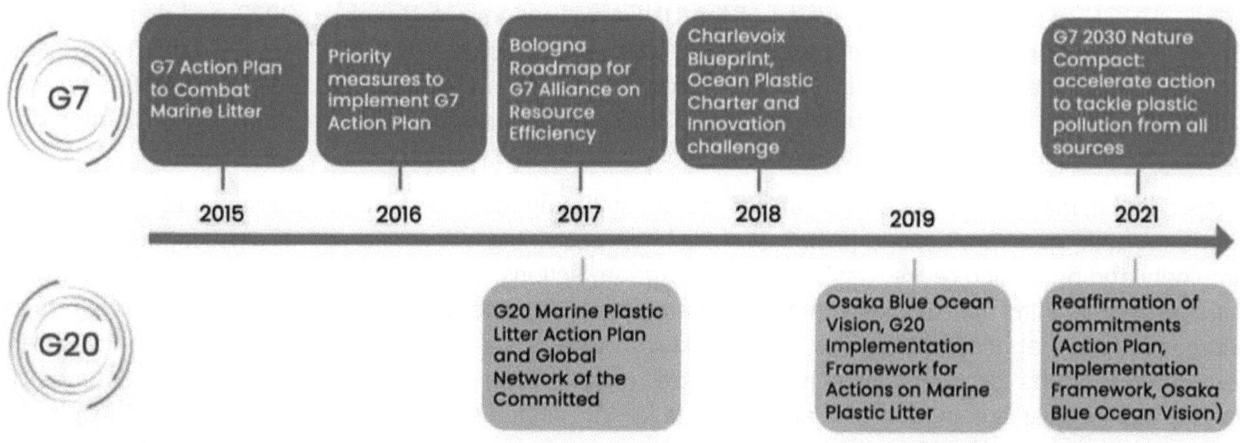

Note: The G7 Oceans Plastic Charter was endorsed by Canada, France, Germany, Italy, the United Kingdom and the European Union.

In the absence of a global agreement, some regional organisations have co-ordinated their members' policies to address particular plastic-related issues, such as marine plastic pollution (Table 7.3). However, gaps remain in the coverage of regions and issues (UN Report of the Secretary-General, 2018[11]).

Table 7.3. Regional organisations help to co-ordinate members' policies and actions

Regional organisation	Description	Example(s)
Regional sea conventions and action plans (RSCAP)	To date, 18 regional sea conventions have been established around the world. They adopt regional action plans and protocols, provide monitoring and regional environmental assessments related to marine litter and prevention of pollution from land-based sources.	• The Convention for the Protection of the Marine Environment of the North-East Atlantic (OSPAR convention) adopted a Regional Action Plan for Prevention and Management of Marine Litter in the North-East Atlantic (OSPAR Commission, 2014[9]). • The Protocol Concerning Pollution from Land-Based Sources and Activities (LBS Protocol) adopted by the Cartagena Convention (UNEP, 1999[10]), and the Regional Action Plan for Marine Litter Management (RAPMaLi), address marine litter in the wider Caribbean region (UNEP, 2014[11]).
Regional fisheries bodies	Co-ordinate measures to address marine-based sources of plastic litter (e.g. ghost gear)	The Indian Ocean Tuna Commission (IOTC) has banned high seas large-scale driftnets in its area of competence and also requires gear marking of flags and buoys (Gilman et al., 2016[12]).
Large marine ecosystem (LME) projects	Globally there are 66 LMEs that have Strategic Action Plans or co-ordinate activities.	11 of the 66 LME projects have implemented Strategic Action Plans that identify marine litter or debris as a concern and identify measures and activities for their members to combat marine litter (Wienrich, Weiand and Unger, 2021[13]).
Regional economic unions	Co-ordinate policy direction through policy advice, capacity building, regulations and legally binding directives.	• In the European Union, several directives, such as the Single-Use Plastics Directive, set requirements for Member States, including collection targets and bans on certain single-use plastic items. • The Association of Southeast Asian Nations (ASEAN) has adopted several measures to address marine plastic litter, including the Bangkok Declaration on Combating Marine Debris and the ASEAN Framework of Action on Marine Debris. ASEAN members have also launched a Regional Action Plan on Combating Marine Debris that sets forth 14 regional actions for plastics reduction, enhanced collection and value from waste (Ministry of the Environment Japan, 2020[14]). • The Polythene Materials Control bill of the East African Community, passed in 2016, sets a series of restrictions for manufacture, trade and use of polyethylene.

A number of governments and civil society actors have been calling for an international treaty to improve this fragmented and incomplete policy landscape (Simon et al., 2021[15]; Duncan et al., 2020[16]; EIA, 2020[17]). Discussions on a global agreement are being held under the auspices of the UN Environment Assembly (UNEA).[4,5] An Ad Hoc Open Ended Expert Group was established in 2017 and has held four high-level events to consider the international governance needs, completing its mandate in 2020 (AHEG, 2020[18]; IUCN, n.d.[19]). The fifth session of the UNEA will resume in Nairobi in 2022 and aims to make further progress on resolutions on marine litter and microplastics (UNEA, 2021[20]). So far, 81 countries have endorsed the Oceans Plastic Pollution Declaration, which calls for the development of a binding global agreement on plastic pollution (AOISIS, 2022[21]). This support signals the likely willingness of dozens of countries to adopt a global measure.

In this context, many countries and organisations are stressing the need to focus international co-operation efforts on both upstream actions (Box 6.3) – such as restraining excessive use of plastics, designing for circularity and promoting reuse – as well as downstream actions, such as enhancing recycling, minimising leakage and cleaning up.[6] On the former, the international trade community has been gearing up efforts to address issues that occur across the global plastics value chain (see Box 7.1 for details). On the latter, co-operation efforts focus on strengthening waste management in places where land-based sources of marine plastic litter are particularly large. The following sections discuss the costs of reducing plastic leakage in low- and middle-income countries and the role of official development assistance (ODA).

Box 7.1. Addressing issues that occur across global plastics value chains requires international co-operation

The plastics value chain is becoming increasingly interconnected and globalised, requiring co-ordinated action between countries to effectively address plastic pollution and to promote the circular use of plastics. Acknowledging the global acceleration of plastics production and consumption and their associated environmental impacts due to fossil fuel inputs and leakage into the environment, the international trade community has begun to take action to seek co-operation on trade-related aspects.

One conventional aspect in trade related dimensions of the global plastic pollution issue is the prevalence of trade in plastic waste and the related environmental risks (Chapter 4). Another important aspect is plastic embodied in traded products, including primary, intermediate, and final forms of plastics. There are not only apparent trade flows such as virgin plastics, plastic based commodities, and plastic waste and scrap, but also hidden trade flows, such as plastic casings for electronic components, plastic composites used in bumpers and dashboards in vehicles, and fruit juice sold in plastic containers. While these fractions are not captured in official trade statistics (as they are recorded by customs as electronics, vehicles or fruit juice), the magnitude of these fractions can be huge. Recent estimates from the United Nations Conference on Trade and Development (UNCTAD) suggest that exports of primary, intermediate and final forms of plastics can reach over USD 1 trillion, representing 5% of global trade in value in 2018 (Barrowclough, Deere Birkbeck and Christen, 2020[22]). This finding implies that international co-operation efforts to combat plastic pollution should not only focus on end-of-pipe solutions for recycling and waste management, but also need to look upstream in the plastics value chain. In particular, product policies that aim to foster the uptake of innovative and more circular solutions, and deter the use of hazardous additives are important (Box 6.3).

In this context, product policies, such as eco-design, eco-labelling, and green public procurement, can play an important role (OECD, 2020[23]). For example, eco-labelling programmes are increasingly used to stimulate demand for circular products (Laubinger and Börkey, 2021[24]). Hazardous content and recycled content of products can be used as a basis for calculating modulated fees in extended producer responsibility schemes (Laubinger et al., 2021[25]) (Chapter 6). Product-based standards are also emerging in various jurisdictions setting forth material content standards (recycled content, hazardous content), recyclability standards, reparability standards, standards on sustainable production, material quality standards (e.g. waste and scrap, secondary materials), product quality standards (e.g. second-hand goods, remanufactured goods) (Yamaguchi, 2021[26]).

At the same time, the fragmentation of product policies related to the circular use of plastics can potentially act as trade impediments for businesses to pursue circular economy business models (Yamaguchi, 2021[26]). In particular, the costs to comply with different regulations and standards, can act as barriers for market access for businesses (Yada et al., 2017[27]). While many product policies related to the circular use of plastics are still under consideration, international co-operation across the plastics value chain can be essential to address these potential trade-related challenges.

In this context, a number of international co-operation initiatives are already underway. In December 2021, 68 members to the World Trade Organization (WTO) issued a joint ministerial statement on the Informal Dialogue on Plastics Pollution and Environmentally Sustainable Plastics Trade (IDP) (WTO, 2021[28]). The initiative explores how improved trade co-operation can contribute to domestic, regional, and global efforts to reduce plastic pollution.

International harmonisation of product policies related to circular economy and plastics is also taking place. In 2020, the International Organization of Standardization (ISO) developed standards on eco-design and circularity of materials (ISO, 2020[29]). Between 2019 and 2020, the EU's standardisation body CEN-CENELEC developed nine standards related to "material efficiency aspects for products in scope of eco-design legislation" (CEN-CENELEC, 2021[30]). Both initiatives may contribute to aligning plastics policies and trade policies towards mutually supportive and coherent outcomes.

Continued dialogues appear to be critical to make the plastics value chains more circular by tackling illegal trade in plastics, harmonising efforts on product policies, removing subsidies to fossil fuel inputs, and harnessing trade policies including tariffs and non-tariff measures towards more sustainable outcomes. Exploring further synergies between on-going global initiatives such as those of the WTO and ISO, as well as forthcoming global initiatives under the UNEA process, may provide promising avenues for addressing the trade dimensions of global plastic pollution.

7.3. Eliminating plastic pollution will be costly for low and middle-income countries

As shown in Chapter 2, mismanaged waste is by far the largest source of plastic leakage. Macroplastics account for almost 90% of total leakage, with land-based leakage from improper waste management practices accounting for 95% of all macroplastics. Since the bulk of mismanaged macroplastic waste occurs in low and middle-income countries, the investments needed in these countries are particularly large.

An OECD report developed in conjunction with this *Global Plastics Outlook* (OECD, 2022 forthcoming[31]) estimates the per-capita capital (i.e. initial investment in facilities, equipment and installation) and annualised costs (i.e. ten-year annualised capital investment costs, operating and maintenance costs). Countries were grouped based on the stringency of their current policies (high, moderate, and low) and the capacity of their current waste management infrastructure (high and moderate). The report makes estimates for a moderate ambition and a high ambition investment scenario. Both scenarios target full waste collection, recovery and disposal, but the high ambition scenario includes circular economy solutions such as prevention measures and recycling targets, while the moderate ambition scenario included mixed waste collection, landfilling and energy recovery.[7]

For countries with a moderate to low policy stringency and a low level of existing infrastructure, the estimated initial investment required to implement the moderately ambitious investment profile is EUR 20.2 per capita, with annualised current costs of EUR 6.5 per capita (Figure 7.2). When applied to the population of low and lower middle-income countries (using World Bank data for 2019 (World Bank, 2021[32])), this represents an initial investment of EUR 80 billion and an annualised cost of more than EUR 25 billion.

Figure 7.2. The cost of preventing plastic pollution varies by ambition, policy stringency and needs

Per-capita investment and annualised costs by country profile and level of investment ambition

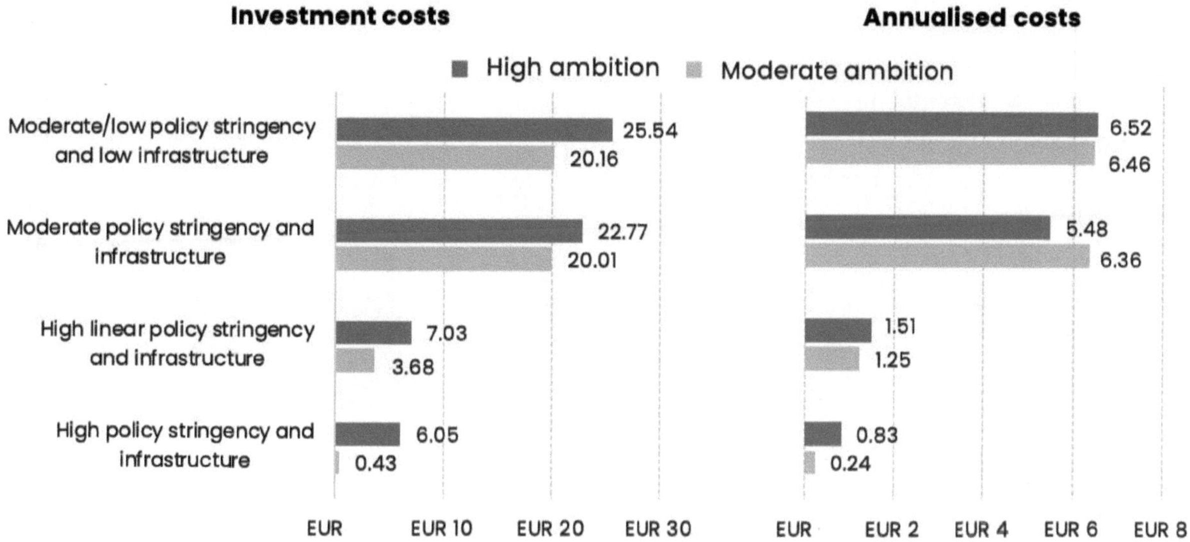

Source: (OECD, 2022 forthcoming[31]), *The Cost of Preventing Ocean Plastic Pollution.*

The annual cost represents 0.3% of total GDP of the concerned low and lower middle-income countries and would be an important financial burden, especially for the group of least developed countries. International support will be instrumental in accelerating the investments required in infrastructure and changes to waste management practices, policies and governance.

7.4. Official Development Assistance (ODA) dedicated to plastic waste management is increasing, but insufficient

There are numerous international initiatives in place to help countries address marine plastic litter and other plastics-related issues. For example, UNEP has identified 138 relevant initiatives for technical support and 74 for financial support to countries (UNEP, 2020[33]). These initiatives differ substantially in scope, focus, size and operations. Comparing and analysing them in a consistent way is challenging. In contrast, international co-operation in the form of ODA is one type of support to developing countries that can be tracked across years and regions. Therefore, this section will analyse trends in ODA and compare the available budgets with the required investments.

Whilst ODA to address plastic pollution has increased significantly in recent years, it started from a low base and volumes remain small relative to overall ODA finance (Figure 7.3). ODA targeting plastics specifically increased from around USD 27 million in 2014 to USD 149 million in 2019. ODA targeting solid waste management more generally increased from USD 224 million to USD 327 million over the same period.

While absolute ODA finance has increased, the share of plastic-related ODA (i.e. ODA targeting plastics specifically and ODA targeting solid waste management) compared to total ODA spending remains marginal. In the period 2017-19, it accounted for only 0.2% of ODA gross commitments, compared to 18.6% for climate mitigation and adaptation and 4.6% for biodiversity. Currently annual ODA accounts for less than 2% of the financial needs to set up basic waste management in developing countries (Section 7.3).

Figure 7.3. Plastic-related gross commitments for ODA have increased steadily but remain small

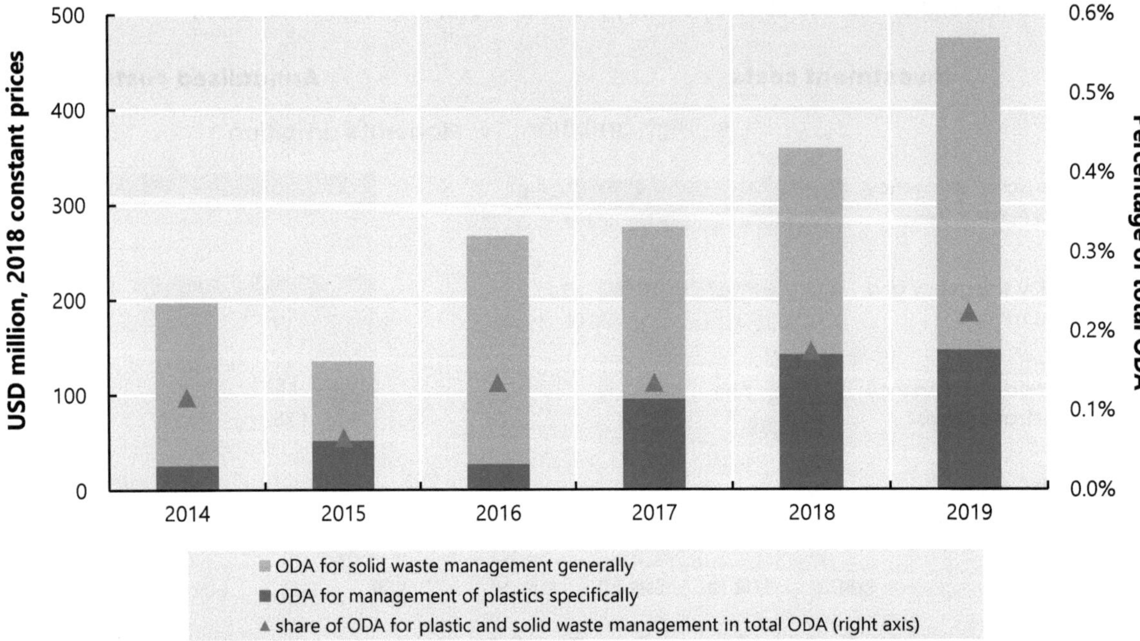

Source: Own calculations based on (OECD, 2021[34]), *OECD Data Platform on Development Finance for the Sustainable Ocean Economy* and the OECD's Creditor Reporting System, https://stats.oecd.org/Index.aspx?DataSetCode=crs1.

StatLink https://stat.link/fzvote

Prior to 2017, development co-operation largely focused on improving general solid waste disposal and management systems, which received an annual average of USD 206 million between 2008 and 2016. While ODA to enhance solid waste management has continued to increase, and reached USD 327 million in 2019, a growing number of emerging projects also specifically focus on plastic pollution. These projects, for instance, support public awareness raising and the development of national strategies for plastics management in developing countries, finance recycling and clean-up, or research into the sources and impacts of plastic pollution. ODA targeting plastics specifically has increased significantly in recent years, from an average of USD 34 million annually in the 2008-16 period (0.02% of global ODA) to USD 147 million in 2019 (0.07% of global ODA in the same year).

Asian countries are the largest beneficiaries of plastic-related ODA, attracting one-third of these funds over 2017-19 (Figure 7.4). This reflects the fact that Asia is one of the worst-affected regions in the world, with coastal populations, environments and economic sectors such as fisheries, tourism and shipping being increasingly harmed by plastic waste leakage (Schmidt, Krauth and Wagner, 2017[35]). Countries in the south-east of Europe that are not members of the EU were the second-largest recipients, receiving one-quarter of plastic-related ODA in 2017-19, mostly from EU institutions and other EU countries. One-third of plastic-related ODA is provided through regional or cross-regional allocations that target transboundary issues and multi-country solutions for marine pollution and ocean plastics.

Figure 7.4. Asian countries attract the most plastic-related ODA

Plastic-related ODA flows, 2017-19. The top ten providers of ODA are depicted on the left axis while the beneficiaries are grouped by global region on the right axis

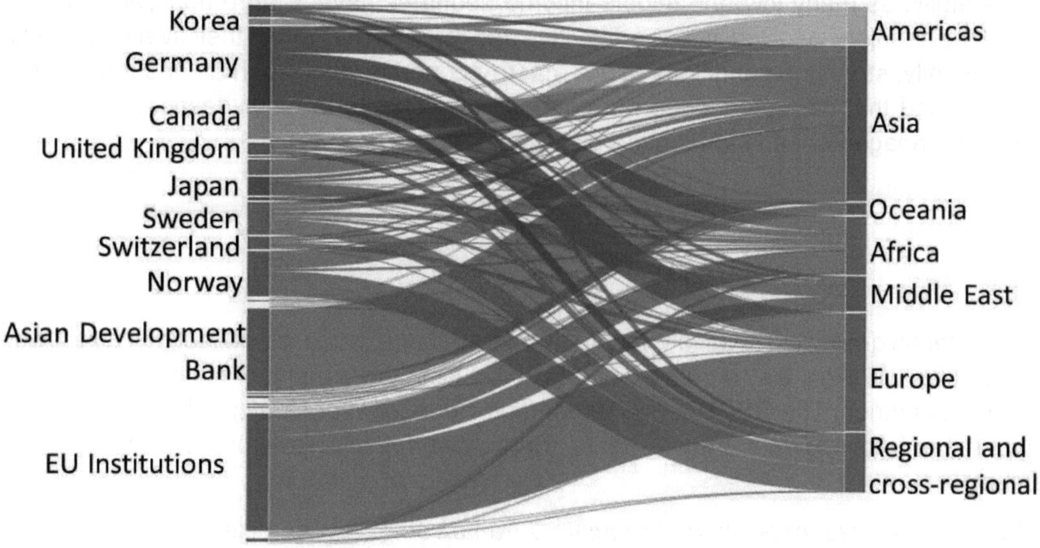

Note: Plastic-related ODA flows include those for solid waste management generally and those for management of plastics specifically.
Source: Own calculations based on (OECD, 2021[34]), *OECD Data Platform on Development Finance for the Sustainable Ocean Economy* and the OECD's Creditor Reporting System, https://stats.oecd.org/Index.aspx?DataSetCode=crs1.

The bulk of plastic-related ODA is extended through bilateral development co-operation, which accounted for 79% of the 2017-19 total. The top five bilateral providers were the European Union, Germany, Norway, Sweden and Canada, collectively accounting for 64% of ODA to tackle plastic pollution. Plastic-related ODA from multilateral providers accounts for a smaller share of the total, but has increased significantly, from an annual average of USD 45 million over 2008-15 period to an annual average of USD 79 million over 2016-19 (+76%). The second largest provider overall was the Asian Development Bank, which provided 17% of ODA during the 2017-2019 period.

Recent initiatives by development banks signal increasing involvement by multilateral providers in this area in the years to come. For example, the Asian Development Bank has issued an Action Plan for Healthy Oceans and Sustainable Blue Economies for the Asia and Pacific region; the World Bank has established the ProBlue trust fund; and the European Investment Bank has launched the Clean Ocean Initiative together with France and Germany. Multilateral co-operation and international organisations can help donors to align goals and prevent duplicative or competing bilateral aid.

In summary, while ODA targeting solid waste management and plastics has increased substantially in recent years, it represents a very small share of the total finance needed to effectively address plastic pollution in low and middle-income countries (as discussed in Section 7.3). Additional sources of funding need to be tapped to provide adequate and sustainable levels of funding. These sources include revenue from the households and firms benefiting from public waste management services, as well as domestic government subsidies and private sector investment. For instance, one of the world's largest consumer goods companies, Unilever, has announced that it will help collect and process more plastic packaging than it sells by 2025 by investing in waste management infrastructure and partnering with relevant stakeholders (Global Plastic Action Partnership, 2021[36]; Unilever, 2021[37]).[8] ODA can be instrumental for leveraging such initiatives.

In addition to investments in waste-management hardware, improvements to the software – i.e. the regulatory framework, governance mechanisms and the capacity of key actors – will also be needed. The OECD provides some recent guidance through its *Implementation Handbook for Quality Infrastructure Investment* (Box 7.2). Moreover, the social implications of waste management reforms will need to be considered carefully, as many low and middle-income countries have a large number of informal waste pickers and waste handlers involved in these activities and reforms may affect their livelihoods (see Box 4.1 in Chapter 4). Finally, structural conditions at the macro-economic level, such as ensuring that the rule of law is respected and that corruption does not channel investments to other destinations, are critical for improving waste management and preventing plastic leakage.

Box 7.2. Successful waste management investment requires strong regulatory frameworks and governance mechanisms

Cost-effective techniques and relatively low-tech infrastructure, such as collecting mixed waste and sanitary landfilling, will likely play a primordial role in reducing the amount of plastic leakage in low and middle-income countries. The OECD's *Implementation Handbook for Quality Infrastructure Investment* puts forward the following four requirements for successful infrastructure investments for waste management:

- *Adopt the necessary policy and regulatory frameworks*: set up a clear institutional framework with well-specified responsibilities for each public actor, issue legal waste management obligations as well as standards, and develop monitoring schemes to verify compliance.
- *Set up strong governance mechanisms*: take into account stakeholder opinions and develop a long-term vision that determines the waste management infrastructure needed, procure infrastructure in a competitive way that leverages the expertise inside and outside of the country, organise infrastructure management in line with the *OECD Recommendation of the Council on the Governance of Infrastructure*[1] and foresee a mechanism to incorporate informal waste pickers in the system.
- *Ensure adequate and stable financing*: do not only focus on investments, but also ensure the financing of recurring costs for operations and maintenance; provide sufficient investor protection and warrant payments by the national treasury to support procurement at sub-national level; and consider using economic instruments such as taxes that generate revenues and incentives for waste prevention or sorting.
- *Enhance the capacity of sub-national governments*: local authorities are typically responsible for organising the collection and disposal of waste from households and small companies. They need sufficient technical expertise to oversee the operations, legal tools to enforce local rules, adequate financing, the authority to impose local taxes, and communication skills to inform as well as motivate the population.

Note: [1]available at https://legalinstruments.oecd.org/en/instruments/OECD-LEGAL-0460
Source: OECD Implementation Handbook for Quality Infrastructure Investment, https://www.oecd.org/finance/oecd-implementation-handbook-for-quality-infrastructure-investment.htm

References

AHEG (2020), *Chair's Summary for the Ad Hoc Open-Ended Expert Group on Marine Litter and Microplastics*, http://www.env.go.jp/press/files/en/871.pdf. [18]

AOISIS (2022), *Oceans Day Plastic Pollution Declaration*, https://plasticdeclaration.aosis.org/ (accessed on 20 July 2021). [21]

Barrowclough, D., C. Deere Birkbeck and J. Christen (2020), *Global trade in plastics: insights from the first life-cycle trade database*, UNCTAD Research Paper No. 53, UNCTAD/SER.RP/2020/12, United Nations Conference on Trade and Development, DECEMBER 2020, https://unctad.org/system/files/official-document/ser-rp-2020d12_en.pdf. [22]

CEN-CENELEC (2021), *Material efficiency aspects for products in scope of Ecodesign legislation*, CEN/CLC/JTC 10, https://standards.cencenelec.eu/dyn/www/f?p=205:32:0::::FSP_ORG_ID,FSP_LANG_ID:2240017,25&cs=10B7B067CC7107748A52C1C034BB4CFD3 (accessed on 31 January 2022). [30]

Convention on Biological Diversity (2021), *Preparations for the Post-2020 Biodiversity Framework*, https://www.cbd.int/conferences/post2020 (accessed on 14 December 2021). [6]

Duncan, J. et al. (2020), *The Business Case for a UN Treaty on Plastic Pollution*, https://www.ellenmacarthurfoundation.org/our-work/activities/new-plastics-economy/projects/un-treaty (accessed on 1 March 2021). [16]

EIA (2020), *Convention on Plastic Pollution – Toward a new global agreement to address plastic pollution*, https://eia-international.org/report/convention-on-plastic-pollution-toward-a-new-global-agreement-to-address-plastic-pollution/ (accessed on 12 October 2021). [17]

EU Commission (2021), "EU Action Plan: 'Towards Zero Pollution for Air, Water and Soil'", https://eur-lex.europa.eu/resource.html?uri=cellar:a1c34a56-b314-11eb-8aca-01aa75ed71a1.0001.02/DOC_1&format=PDF (accessed on 12 October 2021). [38]

Gilman, E. et al. (2016), *Abandoned, lost and discarded gillnets and trammel nets*, FAO, Rome. [12]

Global Plastic Action Partnership (2021), *Trade and the circular economy: a deep dive into plastics action in Ghana*, https://globalplasticaction.org/blog/trade-and-the-circular-economy-a-deep-dive-into-plastics-action-in-ghana/#:~:text=Plastic%20Action%20Partnership-,Trade%20and%20the%20Circular%20Economy%3A%20A%20deep,into%20plastics%20action%20in%20Ghana&text=The%20ca. [36]

GPML (2018), *Global Partnership on Marine Litter Purpose, Function and Organization*, https://www.gpmarinelitter.org/who-we-are/objectives (accessed on 25 February 2021). [3]

ISO (2020), *Environmental management systems — Guidelines for incorporating ecodesign*, ISO 14006:2020, International Organization for Standardization. [29]

IUCN (n.d.), "Geneva meeting deliberates on global convention to address plastic pollution _ IUCN". [19]

Laubinger, F. and P. Börkey (2021), "Labelling and Information Schemes for the Circular Economy", *OECD Environment Working Papers*, No. 183, OECD Publishing, Paris, https://dx.doi.org/10.1787/abb32a06-en. [24]

Laubinger, F. et al. (2021), “Modulated fees for Extended Producer Responsibility schemes (EPR)”, *OECD Environment Working Papers*, No. 184, OECD Publishing, Paris, https://dx.doi.org/10.1787/2a42f54b-en. [25]

Ministry of the Environment Japan (2020), *G20 Report on Actions against Marine Plastic Litter*, https://g20mpl.org/wp-content/uploads/2020/11/G20mpl_20201130_IGES_second-edition.pdf (accessed on 19 February 2021). [14]

NOAA and UNEP (2012), *The Honolulu Strategy: A Global Framework for Prevention and Management of Marine Debris*, https://wedocs.unep.org/bitstream/handle/20.500.11822/10670/Honolulu%20strategy.pdf?sequence=1&isAllowed=y (accessed on 25 February 2021). [5]

OECD (2021), *Trends of ODA for a sustainable ocean economy*, OECD, Paris, https://oecd-main.shinyapps.io/ocean/. [34]

OECD (2020), “Improving resource efficiency and the circularity of economies for a greener world”, *OECD Environment Policy Papers*, No. 20, OECD Publishing, Paris, https://dx.doi.org/10.1787/1b38a38f-en. [23]

OECD (2022 forthcoming), *The Cost of Preventing Ocean Plastic Pollution*, OECD, Paris. [31]

OSPAR Commission (2014), *Marine Litter Regional Action Plan*, OSPAR, London, https://www.ospar.org/documents?v=34422 (accessed on 25 October 2021). [9]

Parker, L. (2019), *The world agrees there’s a plastic waste crisis—can it agree on a solution?*, National Geographic. [2]

Schmidt, C., T. Krauth and S. Wagner (2017), “Export of Plastic Debris by Rivers into the Sea”, *Environmental Science & Technology*, Vol. 51/21, pp. 12246-12253, http://dx.doi.org/10.1021/acs.est.7b02368. [35]

Simon, N. et al. (2021), “A binding global agreement to address the life cycle of plastics”, *Science*, Vol. 373/6550, pp. 43-47, http://dx.doi.org/10.1126/science.abi9010. [15]

UN Report of the Secretary-General (2018), *Gaps in international environmental law and environment-related instruments: towards a global pact for the environment*, https://globalpact.informea.org/sites/default/files/documents/Gap-Report-Final.pdf (accessed on 25 February 2021). [1]

UNEA (2021), *Looking ahead to the resumed UN Environment Assembly in 2022 - Message from online UNEA-5,Nairobit22-23 February 2021*, https://papersmart.unon.org/resolution/uploads/k2100514-e.pdf#overlay-context=node/315 (accessed on 1 March 2021). [20]

UNEP (2020), *Report on the inventory of technical and financial resources or mechanisms for supporting countries in addressing marine plastic litter and microplastics*, https://wedocs.unep.org/bitstream/handle/20.500.11822/35934/UNEP%20AHEG%204%20INF%207%20English%2028%20Oct%202020.pdf?sequence=7&isAllowed=y (accessed on 7 February 2022). [33]

UNEP (2019), “Surfing a wave of change: Clean Seas campaign celebrates two years of action”, https://www.unep.org/news-and-stories/story/surfing-wave-change-clean-seas-campaign-celebrates-two-years-action (accessed on 25 February 2021). [4]

UNEP (2017), *Combating marine plastic litter and microplastics:An assessment of the effectiveness of relevant international, regional and subregional governance strategies and approaches*. [7]

UNEP (2014), *Regional Action Plan for Marine Litter Management in the wider Caribbean region (RAPMaLi)*, http://gefcrew.org/carrcu/CEP_TR_72-en.pdf (accessed on 27 October 2021). [11]

UNEP (1999), *LBS Protocol Text*, https://www.unep.org/cep/resources/policy-and-strategy/lbs-protocol-text (accessed on 27 October 2021). [10]

Unilever (2021), *Rethinking plastic packaging*, https://www.unilever.com/planet-and-society/waste-free-world/rethinking-plastic-packaging/. [37]

United Nations (2021), *THE 17 GOALS | Sustainable Development*, https://sdgs.un.org/goals (accessed on 30 July 2021). [8]

Wienrich, N., L. Weiand and S. Unger (2021), *Stronger together: The role of regional instruments in strengthening global governance of marine plastic pollution*, Institute for Advanced Sustainability Studies (IASS), Potsdam, http://dx.doi.org/10.48440/iass.2021.008. [13]

World Bank (2021), *Population, total - Low Income, Middle Income*, The World Bank, https://data.worldbank.org/indicator/SP.POP.TOTL?locations=XM-XP. [32]

WTO (2021), *MINISTERIAL STATEMENT ON PLASTIC POLLUTION AND ENVIRONMENTALLY SUSTAINABLE PLASTICS TRADE, Revision*, INFORMAL DIALOGUE ON PLASTIC POLLUTION AND ENVIRONMENTALLY SUSTAINABLE PLASTICS TRADE (IDP), WT/MIN(21)/8/Rev.2, World Trade Organization, 10 December 2021, https://docs.wto.org/dol2fe/Pages/SS/directdoc.aspx?filename=q:/WT/MIN21/8R2.pdf. [28]

Yada, J. et al. (2017), *Harmonization of product energy efficiency standards and free trade agreements: the role of international cooperation*, International Partnership for Energy Efficiency Cooperation (IPEEC), https://www.eceee.org/library/conference_proceedings/eceee_Summer_Studies/2017/2-policy-governance-design-implementation-and-evaluation-challenges/harmonization-of-product-energy-efficiency-standards-and-free-trade-agreements-the-role-of-international-coo. [27]

Yamaguchi, S. (2021), "International trade and circular economy - Policy alignment", *OECD Trade and Environment Working Papers*, No. 2021/02, OECD Publishing, Paris, https://dx.doi.org/10.1787/ae4a2176-en. [26]

Notes

[1] With the exception of some regional action plans on marine litter.

[2] The New Global Framework for Managing Nature through 2030 includes a target to reduce pollution from all sources to levels that are not harmful to biodiversity and ecosystem functions and human health, including by eliminating the discharge of plastic waste.

[3] The EU action plan *Towards a Zero Pollution for Air, Water and Soil* includes a target for EU Member States to reduce plastic litter at sea (by 50%) and microplastics released into the environment (by 30%) (EU Commission, 2021[38]).

[4] The UNEA has previously adopted resolutions on marine plastic pollution that acknowledged the emerging threat (UNEA Resolution 1/6), requested an assessment of current governance gaps (UNEA Resolution 2/11), set a vision for ending plastic pollution entering oceans (UNEA Resolution 3/7), and, most recently, acknowledged a need for greater co-ordination and knowledge sharing (UNEA Resolution 4/6).

[5] The first draft of the Post-2020 Global Biodiversity Framework, produced by UNEP for the Convention on Biological Diversity, includes target 7, which aims to eliminate the discharge of plastic waste. The draft text of the Post-2020 Biodiversity Framework is currently being negotiated and is expected to be adopted during the second phase of the UN Biodiversity Conference in May 2022, in Kunming, People's Republic of China (Convention on Biological Diversity, 2021[6]).

[6] See for example the interventions at the Ministerial Conference on Marine Litter and Plastic Pollution under the auspices of the UN Environment Programme, held in Geneva and online on 1-2 September 2021, available at https://enb.iisd.org/ocean/conference-marine-litter-and-plastic-pollution/summary

[7] The report estimates investment costs and annualised costs. It is not a cost-benefit analysis because the model does not include the benefits, such as the revenues generated from recycling in the high-ambition scenario. The estimates in the study were for end-of-life plastic pollution and did not include marine-based sources, primary microplastics or leakage from production (abrasion) or consumption (littering).

[8] For other private sector initiatives, see the Ellen MacArthur Foundation's reports at https://archive.ellenmacarthurfoundation.org/resources/apply/global-commitment-progress-report/organisation-reports

Annex A. Modelling approaches used to compose the OECD Global Plastics Outlook Database

The Annex presents the methodologies applied to provide the estimates contained in this report and in the OECD Global Plastics Outlook Database.[1] These estimates include, plastics use, plastic waste generation, plastic waste management and the environmental impacts of plastics, i.e. 1) leakage to the environment, detailing the macroplastics and microplastics fractions; 2) leakage to aquatic environments; 3) particulate matter emissions from tyre and brake abrasion; and 4) greenhouse gas (GHG) emissions.

The Annex contains the following sections:

- Overview of the modelling framework
- Modelling plastics use in ENV-Linkages
- Modelling plastic waste and end-of-life fates in ENV-Linkages
- Modelling plastic leakage to the environment (Technical University of Denmark)
- Modelling plastic leakage to aquatic environments (Laurent Lebreton)
- Modelling plastic leakage to terrestrial and aquatic environments (University of Leeds)
- Modelling plastic leakage to the terrestrial and aquatic environments (OECD Global Plastics Outlook Database)
- Modelling particulate matter emissions to air from tyre and brake wear (Norwegian Institute for Air Research)
- Modelling greenhouse gas emissions from plastics in ENV-Linkages.

1.1. Overview of the modelling framework

This section explains in more detail the methodologies employed to obtain the estimates of plastics use, waste and environmental impacts presented in the Outlook and included in the OECD Global Plastics Outlook Database. Estimates have been generated by building on output from the OECD computable general equilibrium (CGE) model ENV-Linkages (Chateau, Dellink and Lanzi, 2014[1]), by filling existing data gaps and by generating projections on the environmental impacts.

The modelling of economic flows, plastics use, plastic waste and environmental impacts involves different steps, as illustrated in Figure A A.1. Sectoral and regional economic estimates drive the evolution of plastics use over time. Volumes of plastics are then used to calculate generated waste, based on product lifespans of different applications. The waste generated is further broken down by waste treatment, i.e. recycled (collected for recycling), incinerated, landfilled, mismanaged and littered waste (Chapter 2), taking into account differences across regions. Finally, estimates for a subset of environmental impacts are calculated: leakage of microplastics and macroplastics to the environment, leakage to aquatic environments, particulate matter linked to tyre and brake wear and GHG emissions.

The analysis relies on a suite of modelling tools. More specifically, estimates of the economic flows, plastics use, plastic waste (Steps 1-4), and greenhouse gas emissions (within Step 5) rely on the OECD in-house modelling tools, while other environmental impacts (also in Step 5) rely on external models. Some of the information provided by external models in Step 5 have been used to calibrate the ENV-Linkages models in Steps 1-4.

Figure A A.1. Methodological steps

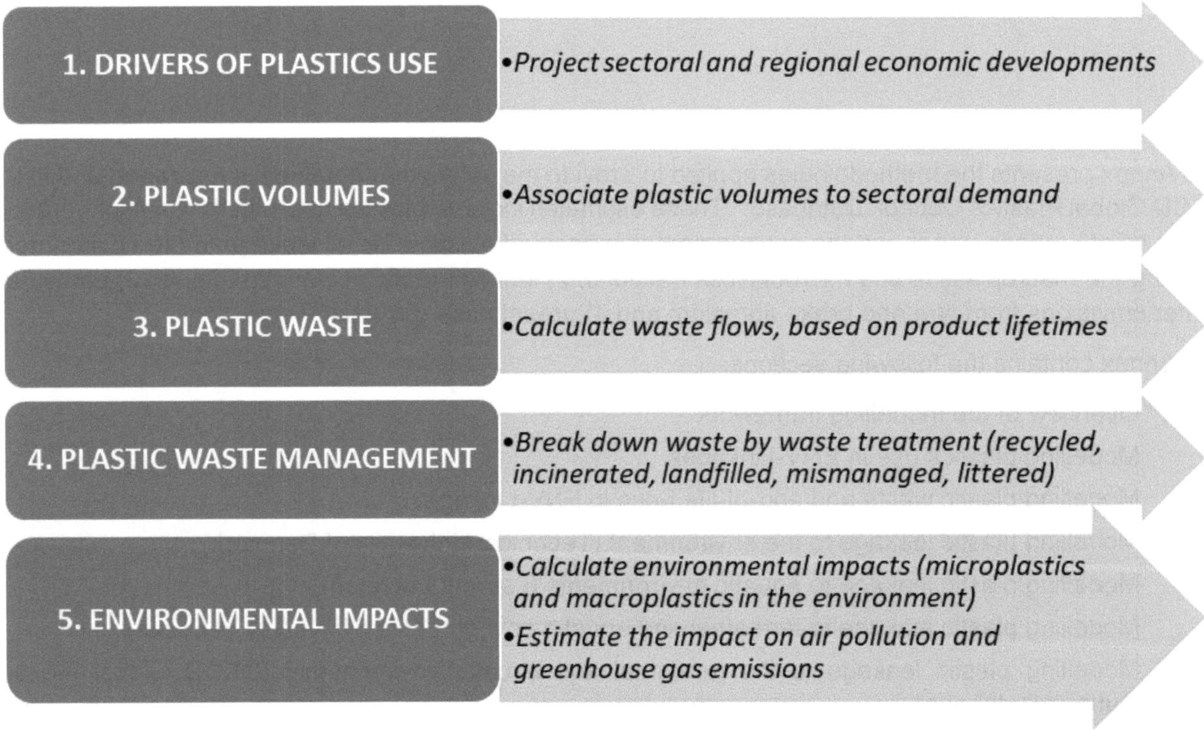

The OECD's in-house dynamic CGE model ENV-Linkages is used as the basis to estimate the economic activities that drive plastics use in 2019. ENV-Linkages is a multi-sectoral, multi-regional model that links economic activities to energy and environmental issues. A more comprehensive model description is given in Chateau, Dellink and Lanzi (2014[1]). A description of the baseline scenario construction procedure is given in Chateau, Rebolledo and Dellink (2011[2]), while recent baseline results are illustrated in OECD (2019[3]).

The model is based on the Social Accounting Matrices (SAM) contained within the GTAP 10 database (Aguiar et al., 2019[4]). This database describes bilateral trade patterns, production, consumption and intermediate use of commodities and services, including capital, labour, tax revenues and use. The base year of the SAM and of the model is 2014. Therefore, to obtain estimates for 2019, the ENV-Linkages model was run to 2019 (Box A A.1 for an overview of the functioning of the model). The short-term changes to the economy from 2014 to 2019 reflect short-term economic changes captured in international databases: the OECD Economics Department (OECD, 2020[5]) and the International Monetary Fund (2020[6]).

For the development of this Outlook and the Global Plastics Outlook Database, ENV-Linkages has been enhanced to include data on plastics use, waste and waste treatment. In ENV-Linkages, plastics estimates follow economic estimates, and, more precisely, the evolution of the production and consumption of goods in different sectors and regions. Section 2 of this annex describes the implementation of plastics use in ENV-Linkages, while Section 3 of this appendix describes the modelling of waste generation and waste end-of-life fates. A summary of the data sources is available in Chapter 2.

Box A A.1. The ENV-Linkages model

Production in ENV Linkages is assumed to operate under cost minimisation with perfect markets and constant returns-to-scale technology. The production technology is specified as nested Constant Elasticity of Substitution (CES) production functions in a branching hierarchy. This structure is replicated for each output, while the parameterisation of the CES functions may differ across sectors. The model adopts a putty/semi-putty technology specification, where substitution possibilities among factors are assumed to be higher with new vintage capital than with old vintage capital. In the short run this ensures inertia in the economic system, with limited possibilities to substitute away from more expensive inputs, but in the longer run this implies a relatively smooth adjustment of quantities to price changes. Capital accumulation is modelled as in the traditional Solow/Swan neoclassical growth model, where economic growth is assumed to stem from the combination of labour, capital accumulation and technological progress.

Household consumption is the result of within-period maximisation behaviour which is formally implemented as an "Extended Linear Expenditure System". A representative consumer in each region - who takes prices as given - optimally allocates disposable income among the full set of consumption commodities and savings. Saving is considered as a standard good in the utility function and does not rely on forward looking behaviour by the consumer. The government in each region collects various kinds of taxes in order to finance government expenditures. Assuming fixed public savings (or deficits), the government budget is balanced through the adjustment of the tax on consumer income. In each period, investment net-of-economic depreciation is equal to the sum of government savings, consumer savings and net capital inflows from abroad.

International trade is based on a set of regional bilateral flows. The model adopts the Armington specification, assuming that domestic and imported products are not perfectly substitutable. Moreover, total imports are also imperfectly substitutable between regions of origin. Allocation of trade between partners then responds to relative prices at the equilibrium.

Market goods equilibria imply that, on the one side, the total production of any good or service is equal to the demand addressed to domestic producers plus exports; and, on the other side, the total demand is allocated between the demands (both final and intermediary) by domestic producers and the import demand.

ENV Linkages is fully homogeneous in prices and only relative prices matter. All prices are expressed relative to the numéraire of the price system that is arbitrarily chosen as the index of OECD manufacturing exports prices. Each region runs a current account balance, which is fixed in terms of the numéraire.

As ENV-Linkages is recursive-dynamic and does not incorporate forward-looking behaviour, price-induced changes in innovation patterns are not represented in the model. The model does, however, entail technological progress through an annual adjustment of the various productivity parameters, including e.g. autonomous energy efficiency and labour productivity improvements. Furthermore, as production with new capital has a relatively large degree of flexibility in choice of inputs, existing technologies can diffuse to other firms. Thus, within the CGE framework, firms choose the least-cost combination of inputs, given the existing state of technology. The capital vintage structure also ensures that such flexibilities are larger in the long run than in the short run.

Source: Chateau, Dellink and Lanzi, (2014[1]).

The sectoral aggregation of the model adopted in this report is given in Table A A.1, while the regional aggregation is presented in Table A A.2.

Table A A.1. Sectoral aggregation of ENV-Linkages

Agriculture, fisheries and forestry	Manufacturing
Paddy rice	Food products
Wheat and meslin	Textiles
Other grains	Wood products
Vegetables and fruits	Chemicals
Oil seeds	Basic pharmaceuticals
Sugar cane and sugar beet	Primary rubber and plastic products
Fibres plant	Secondary plastic products
Other crops	Pulp, paper and publishing products
Cattle and raw milk	Non-metallic minerals
Other animal products	Fabricated metal products
Fisheries	Electronics
Forestry	Electrical equipment
Non-manufacturing Industries	Motor vehicles
Coal extraction	Other transport equipment
Crude oil extraction	Other machinery and equipment
Natural gas extraction	Other manufacturing including recycling
Other mining	Iron and steel
Petroleum and coal products	Non-ferrous metals
Gas distribution	**Services**
Water collection and distribution	Land transport
Construction	Air transport
Electricity transmission and distribution	Water transport
Electricity generation (8 technologies): *Nuclear electricity; hydro (and geothermal); solar; wind; coal-powered electricity; gas-powered electricity; oil-powered electricity; other (combustible renewable, waste, etc.).*	Insurance Trade services Business services n.e.s. Real estate activities Accommodation and food service activities
	Public administration and defence
	Education
	Human health and social work

Source: OECD ENV-Linkages model.

Table A A.2. Regional aggregation of ENV-Linkages

Macro regions		ENV-Linkages countries and regions	Most important comprising countries and territories
OECD	OECD America	Canada	Canada
		USA	United States of America
		Other OECD America	Chile, Colombia, Costa Rica, Mexico
	OECD Europe	OECD EU 22	Austria, Belgium, Czech Republic, Denmark, Estonia, Finland, France, Germany Greece, Hungary, Ireland, Italy, Latvia, Lithuania, Luxembourg, Netherlands, Poland, Portugal, Slovak Republic, Slovenia, Spain, Sweden
		Other OECD Europe	Iceland, Israel,[1] Norway, Switzerland, Turkey, United Kingdom
	OECD Pacific	OECD Asia[BRE1]	Japan, Korea
		OECD Oceania	Australia, New Zealand
Non-OECD	Other America	Other Latin America	Non-OECD Latin American and Caribbean countries
	Eurasia	Other EU	Bulgaria, Croatia, Cyprus,[2] Malta, Romania
		Other Europe and Caspian	Non-OECD European and Caspian countries, incl. Russian Federation
	Middle East and Africa	Middle East and North Africa	Algeria, Bahrain, Egypt, Iraq, Islamic Rep. of Iran, Kuwait, Lebanon, Libya, Morocco, Oman, Qatar, Saudi Arabia, Tunisia, United Arab Emirates, Syrian Arab Rep., Western Sahara, Yemen
		Other Africa	Sub-Saharan Africa
	Other Asia	China	People's Republic of China, Hong Kong (China)
		India	India
		Other non-OECD Asia	Other non-OECD Asian and Pacific countries

Notes: 1. The statistical data for Israel are supplied by and under the responsibility of the relevant Israeli authorities. The use of such data by the OECD is without prejudice to the status of the Golan Heights, East Jerusalem and Israeli settlements in the West Bank under the terms of international law. 2. Note by Turkey: The information in this document with reference to "Cyprus" relates to the southern part of the Island. There is no single authority representing both Turkish and Greek Cypriot people on the Island. Turkey recognises the Turkish Republic of Northern Cyprus (TRNC). Until a lasting and equitable solution is found within the context of the United Nations, Turkey shall preserve its position concerning the "Cyprus issue". Note by all the European Union Member States of the OECD and the European Union: The Republic of Cyprus is recognised by all members of the United Nations with the exception of Turkey. The information in this document relates to the area under the effective control of the Government of the Republic of Cyprus.
Source: OECD ENV-Linkages model.

1.2. Modelling plastics use in ENV-Linkages

1.2.1. Volumes

The ENV-Linkages model has been extended to include plastics volumes, for both primary and secondary (recycled) plastics use. The data on plastics volumes is presented in million metric tonnes (Mt) and plastics use is split by region, polymer and application.

Volumes of primary plastics on data from Ryberg at al. (2019[7]), that updates and expands on the seminal work in Geyer, Jambeck and Law (2017[8]), providing a database for 2015. Since the estimates from Ryberg et al. (2019[7]) were provided on the one hand by region and application, and on the other hand by application and polymers, an assumption of homogeneity of polymers by application was taken to estimate the primary plastics use by region, polymer and application.

Secondary plastics volumes for 2015 were estimated following a methodology deriving secondary plastics through waste collected for recycling and recycling losses. Loss rates including sorting losses and reprocessing losses were estimated using a methodology developed by the University of Leeds based on a review of the literature (see Section 1.3.3 in this Annex).

The estimates of plastics use for 2019 are based on the 2015 year, using the link between plastics volumes in Mt and plastic inputs to sectors in USD, which are estimated relying on the OECD ENV-Linkages model. In addition, the OECD Global Plastics Outlook Database is complemented with plastics use for the past between 1950 and 2014, for two reasons. The first reason is to be able to accurately compute waste flows in the future, since plastic lifetimes can span up to decades. The second reason is to form the basis for the computation of environmental impacts, as for instance plastic leaked in the ocean accumulates over time.

The 1950-2014 historical plastics use is calculated following a step-wise approach. First, global plastics use is taken from the Geyer, Jambeck and Law (2017[8]) study. The regional split of plastics use builds then on weight-based estimates of waste, from a cross country regression of municipal solid waste on gross domestic product (GDP) per capita, using What a Waste 2.0 (Kaza et al., 2018[9]), multiplied by the regional consumption shares in 2015. Finally, for each region, the split by polymer and application is assumed to be constant prior to 2014, based on the estimates from Ryberg et al. (2019[7]). This methodology is constrained by data availability (and thus necessarily imperfect) but provides estimates of plastics use by region, polymer and application.

1.2.2. Economic flows

The ENV-Linkages model has been modified to include primary and secondary plastics production. ENV-Linkages relies on the GTAP 10 database (Aguiar et al., 2019[4]), which provides economic flows by sector and regions for the year 2014. While in the original database primary and secondary plastic production are aggregated in the same sector (Rubber and plastic products [RPP]), the representation of plastic in ENV-Linkages was enhanced to allow the distinction of a technology producing primary plastic and an alternative technology producing secondary plastics.

Similar to coal power plants and gas power plants both providing the same good (electricity), these two technologies produce a similar plastic good, with an elasticity of substitution of 2. The production of plastic goods was thus split with two data sources. First, the total shares in production for primary and secondary plastics were taken from the volumes in tonnes described above (Ryberg et al. (2019[7]) for primary and own estimates for secondary plastics). Table A A.3 describes the calculated share for the secondary plastic production technology. Furthermore, the Exiobase 3 database (Stadler et al., 2018[10]) was used to adapt the cost structures. The main difference stems from the material inputs: the primary technology uses fossil fuels, while the secondary technology uses inputs from the chemical sector.

Table A A.3. Share of the secondary production technology

	Region	Share of secondary technology in 2015 (in tonnes)
OECD America	USA	3.9%
	Canada	4.6%
	Other OECD America	6.8%
OECD Europe	OECD EU countries	9.0%
	OECD Non-EU countries	5.9%
OECD Pacific	OECD Asia	6.3%
	OECD Oceania	2.4%
Other America	Latin America	7.5%
Eurasia	Other EU	4.9%
	Other Eurasia	3.5%
Middle East and Africa	Middle East & North Africa	3.5%
	Other Africa	4.5%
Other Asia	China	7.3%
	India	6.5%
	Other non-OECD Asia	4.8%

Source: OECD ENV-Linkages model. Primary plastics are based on Ryberg et al. (2019[7]). For the calibration of secondary plastics, recycling rate sources are detailed in Table A A.4 and loss rates for the recycling process are from Cottom et al. (2020[11]).

1.2.3. Link between volumes and economic flows

To model plastics use in ENV-Linkages, data on plastics volumes by application and polymer have been linked to the detailed sectoral production structure of the model and the GTAP 10 database that underlies the model and modified to include both primary and secondary plastics. Two main sources of data (volumes and economic flows described above) were used and put in coherence: 1) plastics production and consumption by economic sector by GTAP 10 adapted with a primary and secondary production technology in monetary values; and 2) regional flows of a range of plastic polymers and application-specific flows of plastics in tonnes. Table A A.4 summarises the mapping of the economic sectors and plastics applications. The initial values for this mapping are calibrated using data from Ryberg et al. (2019[7]), combining polymer distribution by application at the global level with distribution of total plastics use by region and application. The polymer distribution was taken from the global averages and applied for each region taking into account the specific economic structures of the various regions.

Table A A.4. Mapping plastics use by application to economic sectors

Input sectors	Applications	Output sectors	Polymers*
Plastic products	Building & construction	Construction	ABS, ASA, SAN; bioplastics; HDPE; LDPE, LLDPE; PP; PS; PUR; PVC; other
	Consumer & institutional products	Accommodation and food service activities; air transport; education; health; insurance; lumber; non-metallic minerals; Business services; other manufacturing; public services; land transport; pulp, paper and publishing; real estate; textile; water transport	ABS, ASA, SAN; bioplastics; HDPE; LDPE, LLDPE; PP; PS; PUR; PVC; other
	Electrical/electronic	Electrical equipment; electronics	ABS, ASA, SAN; bioplastics; HDPE; LDPE, LLDPE; PP; PS; PUR; PVC; other
	Industrial/machinery	Fabricated metal products; iron and steel; nonferrous metal; Machinery and equipment	HDPE; LDPE, LLDPE; PP; PUR
	Packaging	Food products; chemical products	Bioplastics; HDPE; LDPE, LLDPE; PET; PP; PS; PUR; PVC; other
	Personal care products	Chemical products	HDPE; PET
	Transportation - other	Motor vehicles; public services; other transport equipment	ABS, ASA, SAN; bioplastics; Fibres; HDPE; LDPE, LLDPE; PP; PUR; PVC; other
	Other	Other sectors	Other
Chemicals	Marine coatings	Other manufacturing, other transport equipment	Marine coatings
	Road markings	Construction	Road markings
	Textile sector - clothing	Textiles	Bioplastics; fibres
	Textile sector - others	Textiles	Fibres
	Transportation - tyres	Plastic products	Elastomers (tyres)

Note: *See Table 2.2 in Chapter 2 for abbreviations and examples of use for those polymers.
Source: OECD ENV-Linkages model.

Based on the initial GTAP database, which presents data for 2014, primary plastics use is projected following the flows of "plastic products" into the various corresponding demand sectors, from initial values, following the methodology developed for the OECD's Global Material Resources Outlook (OECD, 2019[3]). In particular, the model incorporates a series of plastics chains from initial production to final demand, either partially or in full depending on the particular structure of each regional economy. The basis for the chain includes flows from "oil" or "biomass" to "chemicals", that are then used for the production of "plastic products" which serve as intermediate goods or for sectors such as food product/appliances/motor vehicles/construction, before reaching final demand. The underlying assumption is that the coefficient

(USD/tonne per polymer, per application, per region) that links monetary flows to physical flows (in tonnes), is kept constant. Plastics production then follows these demands, based on trade flows and plastics use.

There are three steps to project plastics use and the split of primary and secondary plastics to fulfil demand (after 2015). First, total demand for plastics use is estimated following the evolution of the demand for the plastic commodity (produced by both the primary and secondary technologies). Second, as collected and sorted materials (further referred to as plastic scrap) are – after correcting for loss rates (see Section 1.3.2 on Losses from sorting and reprocessing in this Annex) - used to produce secondary plastics, the tonnes of secondary plastics follow the growth of the secondary sector in the ENV-Linkages projections. Third, the volumes of primary plastics are calculated as a residual between the two such that total demand for plastics is met.

1.3. Modelling plastic waste and end-of-life fates in ENV-Linkages

1.3.1. Plastic waste

Plastic waste is calculated linking plastics use to the lifespan distribution of different applications (representing a large range of products). Specifically, plastic waste is calculated as a function of plastics use (in volumes), following Geyer, Jambeck and Law (2017[8]), using a methodology based on lifespan distributions,[2] under the assumption of global homogeneity.

Plastic waste of different applications is grouped into three main categories: Municipal Solid Waste (MSW), Other, and Markings & microbeads. MSW includes packaging, consumer & institutional products, electrical/electronic and textiles. 'Other' incorporates waste that is not included in MSW, therefore mostly reflecting waste from industrial applications (including building and construction, industrial and machinery applications, transportation applications). Markings and microbeads is a very small stream that includes marine coatings, road markings and personal care products.

1.3.2. End-of-Life Fates

Plastic waste is divided into different waste management streams (end-of-life fates) by applying end-of-life shares that vary across countries, polymers and waste categories. MSW and Other plastic waste categories can be 1) recycled; 2) incinerated; or 3) discarded. The latter is further disaggregated into waste that is disposed of in sanitary landfills, mismanaged waste and, in the case of MSW, littering. Littering is included as a separate category to reflect the different drivers and geographical distribution compared to mismanaged waste (this occurs mainly in regions that lack basic waste management infrastructure). Littering is set as a constant share of municipal solid waste following the assumption in Jambeck et al. (2015[12]). Markings & Microbeads form a very small stream (by mass) that is assumed not to be managed and to leak directly to the environment.

The sources of end-of-life fate shares for the year 2019 vary across regions. Recycling (defined here as material that has been collected for recycling) shares for plastics are exogenously fixed based on a range of sources, primarily country sources (Table A A.5). To account for unreported informal recycling (which leads to understating plastic recycling rates) or overly optimistic reported recycling rates, all reported recycling rates were sense-tested, adapted and validated leveraging on consultations with experts and modelling carried out by Ed Cook, Josh Cottom and Costas Velis from the University of Leeds.

The recycling shares are further split across polymers by multiplying the recycling shares for plastics by factors that reflect the recyclability and value of individual polymers based on expert consultations and ensuring that the estimated recycled volumes do not exceed the recycling capacities subject to data availability. Overall, PET and HDPE are assumed to have the highest recycling rates, followed by LDPE, PP and PVC (for construction). PUR, fibres, elastomers, bioplastics, marine coatings and road markings are not recycled, while only a very small proportion of PS, ABS, ASA, SAN and other polymers are recycled.

Table A A.5. Data sources for plastic recycling rates in base year

Region	Recycling Rate Source and Assumptions
USA	United States Envrionmental Protection Agency (EPA) (2020[13]; 2020[14])
Canada	Environment and Climate Change Canada (2019[15])
Other OECD America	Based on SEMARNAT (2020[16]) and FCH (2021[17])
OECD EU countries	Polymer-specific recycling rates have been determined based on expert opinion and applied to the volumes of polymers collected for recycling by ENV-Linkages.*
Other EU	
OECD Non-EU countries	Based on EU adjusted by the proportion of region's MSW recycling rate to EU MSW recycling rate from What a Waste 2.0 (Kaza et al., 2018[9])
OECD Pacific	Plastic Waste Management Institute (2019[18]) and expert judgement to account for plastic recycling rates in Korea
OECD Oceania	Australian Government (2020[19])**
Latin America	Based on Other OECD America adjusted to account for a larger informal sector
Other Eurasia	What a Waste 2.0 (Kaza et al., 2018[9])
Middle East & North Africa	What a Waste 2.0 (Kaza et al., 2018[9])
Other Africa	What a Waste 2.0 (Kaza et al., 2018[9])
China	China Recycling Industry Development Report (2013-18) by the Ministry of Commerce (2019[20])
India	Central Pollution Control Board (2019[21]) and UNIDO (2020[22])
Other non-OECD Asia	What a Waste 2.0 (Kaza et al., 2018[9])

Note: *For the EU, the calculated recycling rate for total plastics has been benchmarked with the numbers presented by Plastics Europe (2020[23]). In the OECD Global Plastics Outlook Database, the amount of plastics taken into account for the calculation of the recycling rate is substantially higher (the denominator: total plastics in OECD Global Plastics Outlook Database includes fibres and other rarely recycled plastics). So the total recycling rate of plastics that is included in the OECD Global Plastics Outlook Database is lower than Plastics Europe (2020[23]).
** An updated report is available: Government of Australia (2021[24]).

The use of incineration as a waste treatment type is country-specific and related to historic elements and local population densities. The share of plastic waste that is incinerated is strongly correlated with the share of total solid waste that is incinerated. Therefore, the incineration shares are set so that the ratio of the incineration share to the non-recycled share is equal to the corresponding ratio for total MSW from the What a waste 2.0 database (Kaza et al., 2018[9]). Moreover, the same incineration shares apply for non-MSW plastic waste, namely the 'Other' waste category.

Regarding discarded waste, its share is equal to the residual, under the assumption that 2% of MSW is littered at all times (Jambeck et al., 2015[12]). The discarded share is further split into sanitary landfilled and mismanaged waste. In this analysis, mismanaged waste includes open dumping and unaccounted waste treatments for all income levels apart from lower and lower middle income countries, for which also unspecified landfilling, waterway treatment and other categories are included based on country level data for MSW (Kaza et al., 2018[9]) and building on assumptions for the previous version of the database in Jambeck et al. (2015[12]). In general, mismanaged plastic waste, as a share of total plastic waste, is expected to decrease with income level. Following this assumption and using MSW data from Kaza et al. (2018[9]), the share of mismanaged plastic waste was estimated by regressing the ratio of mismanaged waste to discarded waste on GDP per capita, accounting for regulatory differences between OECD and non-OECD countries using an OECD dummy. Specifically, the following regression was estimated for 156 countries for which complete data was available:

$$MIS_i/(MIS_i + LAN_i) = \alpha + \beta * ln(gdp\_pc_i) + OECD_i$$

where MIS_i = mismanaged waste/MSW, LAN_i = Landfilled waste/MSW, gdp_pc_i = GDP per capita and $OECD_i$ = dummy for OECD countries, i = country.

Finally, the share for landfilled waste is equal to the residual.

Historical data for recycling, incineration and discarded shares of plastic waste are taken from Geyer, Jambeck and Law (2017[8]) for the period 1980-90 for four regions – United States, European Union, China and Rest of the World. Following, using granular data for MSW recycling and incineration rates from Kaza et al. (2018[9]), the historical shares for 1990 were mapped to the 15 regions within ENV-Linkages, and were linearly interpolated for the period 1990-2018 in line with the methodology previously applied in Geyer Jambeck and Law (2017[8]). Historical data for mismanaged waste and landfilling followed the same methodology as in the base year.

1.3.3. Losses from sorting and reprocessing (University of Leeds)

Plastic waste that has been collected for recycling almost always includes some non-plastic materials and articles. Moreover, collected plastic waste typically includes a multitude of plastics with varying chemical and physical composition. The degree to which these items, objects and fragments are useful to a plastics reprocessor depends on a wide range of factors that influence the value of the material. In general, high income countries implement recyclate collection schemes (programmes) that are designed to yield high material mass through an accessible and simplified system that is easy for people to understand. Conversely, in low- and middle-income countries, plastic waste collection for recycling is carried out by informal workers (IRS) who selectively collect (cherry pick) items and objects that are most valuable, focusing on quality and concentration rather than high yield. Even with diligent, selective collection, plastic articles contain a multitude of intentionally and non-intentionally appended, entrapped, adhered and entrained materials and objects that must be removed from the dominant plastic before it can be comminuted and re-melted under pressure in an extruder. A list of characteristics of waste plastics and their influence on the value of materials and hence their recyclability is reported by Cottom et al. (2020[11]).

Robust and generalisable loss rates during sorting and reprocessing of plastic waste that has been collected for recycling are not commonly reported. Hestin, Faninger and Milios (2015[25]) proffered 18% and 30% for sorting and reprocessing respectively, based on surveys of European reprocessors. However, the nature of the survey was not reported and it is possible that plastic and non-plastic materials and objects have been reported alongside plastic losses. The ENV-Linkages model is only concerned with plastics so data for non-plastic materials were excluded from this component of the model.

The University of Leeds developed a theoretical model for plastic waste collected for recycling in high-income countries and low- and middle-income countries, based on material value. Acknowledging that collection and sorting systems vary enormously worldwide, these two generalised groups were chosen because high income countries largely operate, either single stream collection of dry recyclate or co-collection of mixed plastic waste alongside metal packaging. Conversely in low-income and middle-income countries, collection of plastic waste for recycling is largely carried out by the informal recycling sector whose participants selectively collect materials and have much lower loss rates.

Recycling losses for packaging waste collected for recycling in high income countries, are estimated based on a dataset (Chruszcz and Reeve, 2018[26]) that reports a weighted average for all collection scheme types across the United Kingdom. For LDPE, an approximation was made based on data reported by Lau et al. (2020[27]) (P_2O model), because LDPE is predominantly used as a as a flexible foil in packaging. Although LDPE is commonly collected for recycling, it is almost never reprocessed in high income countries when coming from post-consumer household sources due to the challenges associated with surface contamination and selectivity detailed in Table A A.6. On the other hand, post-consumer LDPE from commercial sources is commonly recycled in high-income countries as it is easily collectable and separately and can be extruded dry, often without undergoing substantial cleaning. The result is a low loss rate. The assumptions from Lau et al. (2020[27]) were used to determine the proportion of material that was from commercial/institutional sources compared to household sources.

A probability of plastic waste items being selected at the sorting stage based on material value was applied to each of the packaging and plastic types. Cottom et al. (2020[11]) calculate these probabilities for Consummer and Institutional products, Electrical and Electronic products, Packaging, and Textiles. Probabilities for other products have been calculated for this report and are reported in

Table A A.7. The probabilities were estimated using cost data summarised by SystemiQ and the Pew Charitable Trust (2020[28]), recyclability imperatives detailed by Recoup (2019[29]) and data on material actually recycled reported by Antonopoulos, Faraca and Tonini (2021[30]) and Plastics Recyclers Europe (2020[31]). In general HDPE, PET and LDPE were considered to have a 100% chance of being selected for reprocessing at the Materials Recovery Facilities (MRF) and PVC and PS were considered to have 0% chance of being selected for reprocessing at the MRF. Although the evidence for PVC for packaging is more clear cut, Antonopoulos, Faraca and Tonini (2021[30]) reported some post-consumer PS selection taking place in Europe. However, these quantities are reported by Plastics Recyclers Europe (2020) to be small and unusual, there is a likelihood that they do not refer to post-consumer material. The probability was set to zero for packaging but an overall probability of 98.5% was set to allow for some small occurrences of non-packaging material.

The loss rates at the reprocessor stage were approximated using data on plastic content reported by Roosen et al. (2020[32]).Non plastic content was excluded and the relative masses were normalised.

High income countries were assumed to have formal collection and the plastic packaging reported there was subject to loss rates at both sorting and reprocessing. Low and middle income countries were assumed to have informal collection and the loss rates were therefore assumed to occur only at the reprocessing stage as informal actors selectively collect.

The assumptions for non-packaging applications were based largely on estimates from the project expert team, as there are no published data to support them. Consumer and institutional products were assumed to be the same as packaging except for PVC for which evidence from VinylPlus (2019[33]) indicates some recycling takes place. For the textiles (fibres), an estimate of 20% from financial modelling by Thompson et al. (2012[34]) was used in the absence of any other robust data. Readers should note that this loss rate is approximated on the basis that post-consumer textiles have been recycled into shoddy fibres and/or flocking (stuffing) rather than items that have been 'reused' and are out of scope of this study.

Table A A.6. Assumptions used to determine loss rates for plastic packaging waste that has been collected for recycling

Plastic item[1]	Plastic type by dominant polymer[1]	Weighted composition[1]	High-income countries			Low- & middle-income countries		
			Probability of being rejected before reprocessing[2]	Loss rate at reprocessor adjusted for wastage[3]	Net losses after sorting & reprocessing[4]	Probability of being rejected before reprocessing[2]	Loss rate at reprocessor adjusted for wastage[3]	Net losses after sorting & reprocessing[4]
Film LA recycling sacks	LDPE	2.9	100	0.00	2.90	25	1.00	0.75
FILM Other film	LDPE	11.2	100	0.00	11.20	25	1.00	2.88
FILM Carrier bags	LDPE	1.5	100	0.00	1.50	25	1.00	0.39
B PET NATURAL	PET	26.4	0	13.45	3.55	0	13.45	3.55
B PET JAZZ	PET	3.1	0	13.45	0.42	0	13.45	0.42
B HDPE Milk Bottles	HDPE	13.2	0	15.93	2.10	0	15.93	2.10
B HDPE All non-milk bottles	HDPE	7.7	0	15.93	1.23	0	15.93	1.23
B PVC ALL	PVC	0	100	0.00	0.00	100	0.00	0.00
B PP ALL	PP	0.4	50	21.31	0.24	0	21.31	0.09
Pack PET NATURAL	PET	10.3	0	14.63	1.51	0	14.63	1.51
Pack PET JAZZ	PET	0.5	0	14.63	0.07	0	14.63	0.07
Pack HDPE NATURAL	HDPE	0.1	100	0.00	0.10	0	14.63	0.01
Pack HDPE JAZZ	HDPE	0.6	100	0.00	0.60	0	14.63	0.09
Pack PVC ALL	PVC	0.1	100	0.00	0.10	100	0	0.10
Pack PP NATURAL	PP	4.4	100	0.00	4.40	0	2.08	0.09
Pack PP JAZZ	PP	5.3	100	0.00	5.30	0	2.08	0.11
Pack PS ALL	PS	1.5	100	0.00	1.50	100	0	1.50
Pack EPS ALL	EPS	0.4	100	0.00	0.40	100	0	0.40
Black PET	PET	1.9	100	0.00	1.90	100	0	1.90
Black PP	PP	0.6	100	0.00	0.60	100	0	0.60
Black Other	Mixture	1.1	100	0.00	1.10	100	0	1.10
Other	Mixture	0.2	100	0.00	0.20	100	0	0.20
Unidentified	Mixture	1.9	100	0.00	1.90	100	0	1.90
Plastic non-packaging	Mixture	4.4	100	0.00	4.40	100	0	4.40

Source: 1. Chruszcz and Reeve (2018[26]). 2. Assumptions based on polymer value by SYSTEMIQ & The Pew Charitable Trust (2020[28]), recyclability reported by Recoup (2019[29]), and material reported to have been recycled by Antonopoulos, Faraca and Tonini (2021[30]) and Plastics Recyclers Europe (2020[31]). 3. Roosen et al (2020[32]).

Table A A.7. Average loss rates by plastic type and application for high income countries and low- middle income countries (Non-MSW)

Plastic type by dominant polymer	Building and Construction			Industrial/Machinery			Other			Transportation - Other			Total ($t\ y^{-1}$)
	Mass ($t\ y^{-1}$)	Loss rate HIC (%)	Loss rate LMIC (%)	Mass ($t\ y^{-1}$)	Loss rate HIC (%)	Loss rate LMIC (%)	Mass ($t\ y^{-1}$)	Loss rate HIC (%)	Loss rate LMIC (%)	Mass ($t\ y^{-1}$)	Loss rate HIC (%)	Loss rate LMIC (%)	
Fibres							0.1	100.0	100.0	0.0	100.0	100.0	0.1
HDPE	1.0	20.0	5.0	0.1	20.0	5.0	1.1	20.0	5.0	0.6	98.0	90.0	2.9
LDPE, LLDPE	0.1	2.0	2.0	0.1	2.0	2.0	0.7	2.0	2.0	0.1	98.0	90.0	1.0
Other	0.0	100.0	100.0				0.2	100.0	100.0	0.1	100.0	100.0	0.4
PP	0.2	20.0	5.0	0.1	20.0	5.0				1.2	100.0	100.0	1.5
PS	0.1	100.0	100.0				0.1	100.0	100.0				0.2
PUR	0.1	40.0	10.0	0.0	40.0	10.0	0.4	40.0	10.0	0.2	100.0	100.0	0.6
PVC	0.6	18.7[3]	18.7[3]				0.4	40.0	18.7[3]	0.1	100.0[3]	100.0[3]	1.1

Source: Calculations by Leeds University. 1. Calculated from Chruszcz and Reeve (2018[26]) and Roosen et al. (2020[32]). 2. Calculated from Lau et al. (2020[27]). 3. Approximated from data reported by VinylPlus (2019[33]). 4. Thompson Willis and Morley (2012[34]).

For simplicity, The European Union, the USA, and Canada were considered to have formal collection and all other regions were considered to have predominantly informal collection for recycling. The exception was China which has been undergoing a partial transition from informal to formal collection for recycling. Due to the lack of robust data on the informal recycling sector, this component of the model assumed a 70:30 ratio for informal/formal collection for recycling.

Table A A.8 puts forward the outcome of the technical calculations. The calculations initially suggested loss rates of 100% for PS and of 98.1% for "Other", but these loss rates have both been set to the loss rate from LDPE, to represent that these polymers are sometimes recycled, but only in small quantities. Furthermore, to reflect that a large share of recycling of PET is rather a downcycling transformation of PET into fibres, the modelling assumes 35% of recycled PET is transformed into fibres.

Table A A.8. Average loss rates by plastic type and region for MSW and non-MSW combined

Loss rates as percentages of collected plastics for recycling, 2016

		ABS, ASA, SAN	Fibers	HDPE	LDPE, LLDPE	Other	PET	PP	PS	PUR	PVC	Average
OECD America	USA	100%	54%	27%	60%	44%	18%	94%	49%	57%	43%	50%
	Canada	100%	55%	26%	60%	43%	18%	95%	49%	57%	43%	49%
	Other OECD America	100%	64%	17%	59%	29%	18%	24%	50%	28%	47%	30%
OECD Europe	OECD EU countries	100%	59%	24%	57%	38%	18%	90%	42%	53%	35%	44%
	OECD Non-EU countries	100%	60%	24%	60%	36%	18%	92%	45%	53%	37%	46%
OECD Pacific	OECD Asia	100%	48%	22%	62%	30%	18%	92%	46%	50%	35%	44%
	OECD Oceania	100%	30%	26%	67%	64%	18%	50%	45%	56%	41%	40%
Other America	Latin America	100%	64%	16%	60%	26%	18%	22%	54%	27%	54%	29%
Eurasia	Other EU	100%	56%	26%	63%	58%	18%	52%	44%	53%	44%	41%
	Other Eurasia	100%	55%	26%	65%	58%	18%	50%	49%	55%	49%	41%
Middle East and Africa	Middle East & North Africa	100%	54%	19%	64%	38%	18%	31%	49%	36%	45%	33%
	Other Africa	100%	71%	16%	61%	22%	18%	21%	53%	24%	56%	30%
Other Asia	China	100%	54%	20%	62%	34%	18%	48%	54%	39%	54%	36%
	India	100%	34%	19%	67%	39%	18%	27%	59%	38%	60%	32%
	Other non-OECD Asia	100%	47%	23%	64%	49%	18%	41%	55%	47%	56%	37%
Global average		100%	53%	22%	61%	38%	18%	63%	49%	46%	43%	40%

Source: OECD ENV-Linkages model, based on Cottom et al. (2020[11]).

1.3.4. Modelling international trade in plastic waste

The ENV-Linkages model has been extended to include international trade in plastic waste per application and polymer type. Volumes of plastic waste exports and imports are calculated based on data from UN Comtrade (United Nations Statistics Division, 2020[35]) following two steps. First, total exports of plastic waste per country and polymer are estimated using the share of plastics exports (Comtrade) to plastic waste (output of ENV-Linkages). Second, exports are split into partner countries and polymers using the projected country and polymer weights for 2019, and historical data for the years before. Bilateral export and import weights per country (row weights) were calculated based on the bilateral data of export and import values for the period 2010-19 (most recent and complete year) and for the four subcategories of plastic waste reported in the UN Comtrade database. The latter were mapped to the polymer types included in ENV-Linkages (Table A A.9), to ensure that global trade balances total imports and exports, bilateral plastic waste imports per reporter-partner pair correspond to the bilateral export of the corresponding partner-reporter pair.

The end-of-life fates of plastic waste that is traded, differ from the domestically treated waste to reflect that a high proportion of traded plastic waste tends to be recyclable. In particular, 50% of traded plastic waste is expected to be recycled, with the remaining being distributed across the other waste streams following the same proportions of end-of-life fates as domestically treated waste excluding littering.

Table A A.9. UN Comtrade plastic waste series mapping to polymers in ENV-Linkages

UN Comtrade code	Series Description	Polymers types in ENVLinkages
3915	Waste, parings and scrap, of plastics	
391510	… of polymers of ethylene	HDPE,LDPE, LLDPE, PET, PP,PUR, Elastomers (tyres)
391530	… of polymers of styrene	PS
391530	… of polymers of vinyl chloride	PVC
391590	… of other	Fibres, Marine coatings, Road marking coatings, ABS, ASA, SAN, Other

Source: United Nations Statistics Division (2020[35]) and OECD ENV-Linkages model.

1.4. Modelling plastic leakage to the environment (Technical University of Denmark)

Estimations on the plastic leakage are based on an interaction of the ENV-Linkages Model with other dedicated models. Each of the dedicated models builds on earlier work that has passed peer review with respect to estimations for current plastic leakage. The sources for leakage to the environment are varied. Consequently, the modelling techniques to make projections on these flows differ. This section explains the methodology and parameters employed by Teddy Serrano, Alexis Laurent, and Morten Ryberg from the section for Quantitative Sustainability Assessment at the Technical University of Denmark (DTU) to estimate leakage of macro and micro plastics into the environment, as well as wastewater pathway and losses via sludge application to land.

1.4.1. Leakage of macroplastics

For losses of macroplastics, four main categories have been considered: mismanaged municipal solid waste, mismanaged non-municipal solid waste, littering, and losses from marine activities. Plastic waste generation is calculated by the ENV-Linkages model as explained in the previous sections. The details on the calculations of the four categories are as follows:

- **Mismanaged MSW** was retrieved from the ENV-Linkages model. In line with Lau (2020[27]), it was assumed that 32% of mismanaged MSW is lost to the environment.
- **Mismanaged non-MSW** was also retrieved from the ENV-Linkages model. Due to a lack of data on the fate of mismanaged non-MSW, the share of mismanaged non-MSW lost to the environment is assumed to be equal to the share of mismanaged MSW lost to the environment (32%).
- Losses occurring via **littering** were calculated as a fraction of generated MSW in two steps. First, in line with Jambeck et al. (2015[12]) and studies carried out for the United Kingdom and Belgium (OVAM, 2018[36]; Resource Futures, 2019[37]), it was assumed that 2% of MSW is littered. Second, a substantial fraction of this littered waste happens in an urban environment and is cleaned up before it makes it to the environment. It is assumed that between 15% and 35% of littered waste is not captured by street sweeping, storm drain catchments and pump stations (Jambeck et al., 2015[12]). The estimated share of litter that is lost to the environment in each region, was established

according to the income level (as GNI/cap, US dollars), with lower shares for the high-income regions, as illustrated in (Table A A.10.).

- In the ENV-Linkages model, the non-collected share of litter is considered lost to the environment. The collected share of litter is reallocated and added to incineration, landfilling, open-pit burning and dumping in line with the respective waste treatment shares per region (see 1.3.2 in this Annex).
- **Losses from marine activities** (fishing gear and non-netting waste) were calculated based on the following information: production data of fishing gear in Europe (PRODCOM, 2016) (Eunomia, 2018[38]; Eurostat, n.d.[39]) upscaled to the rest of the world based on the projected growth of fishing activity (from the ENV-Linkages model), the assumption that 28% of plastic waste in the fishing and aquaculture sector comes from netting (Viool et al., 2018[40]), and the assumption that 15% of fishing gear material is lost every year during use (Viool et al., 2018[40]).

Table A A.10. The share of litter lost to the environment in function of the regional income levels

Category	Low and lower-middle income	Upper-middle income	High income
Income level as GNI/cap [USD]	< 4045	4045-12535	> 12535
Share of litter lost to the environment	35%	25%	15%

Note: The World Bank country classifications by income level: 2020-21 were used to allocate regions into low and lower-middle income, upper-middle income, or high income categories.
Source: World Bank (2020[41]).

1.4.2. Leakage of microplastics

For losses of microplastics, ten categories have been considered: microbeads, primary pellets, textile wash, tyre abrasion, road markings, brake dust, artificial turf, marine coatings, microplastics dust and wastewater sludge. This section presents the methodology employed to calculate emissions of microplastics from the sources considered. Some microplastics directly leak into the environment, but others end up in the sewage system. The fate of the different microplastics ending up in municipal wastewater networks, is discussed in the next section.

The category "**microbeads**" includes losses of microplastics intentionally added to rinse-off personal care and cosmetic products, detergents and maintenance products that are discharged into municipal wastewaters during use. Estimates of microbead consumption in personal care and cosmetic products (PCCPs) are derived from the output of the ENV-Linkages model. All microbeads are assumed to end up in the sewage system in the year that they are consumed.

The category "**primary pellets**" includes losses of primary plastic pellets occurring during production, transportation, and handling. Eunomia (2018[38]) estimated the losses of plastic pellets in 2015 in the European Union, as originating from pellet production from raw materials, intermediary handling processes, processing and conversion, off-site waste management, and transportation and shipping. Assuming that leakage is proportional to the quantity of plastics produced, losses for the European Union were scaled up to the entire world based on the European production share of plastics in 2015 (Plastics Europe, 2017[42]), and then allocated to geographical regions based on production shares. Losses from producers, recyclers, processors and offsite waste management were assumed to enter the sewage network as part of wastewater. Losses from Intermediary facilities and Shipping were assumed to be directly lost to the environment.

The category "**textile wash**" includes losses of synthetic microfibres lost during the washing of textile and apparel products. Estimates are computed based on the total volume (tonnes) of plastics used in the category 'Wearing apparel' (following the textiles sector in ENV-Linkages) in a given year, and the assumption that during the lifespan of a textile product 0.4% of material is lost during washing. The share of material lost during the lifespan of a textile and apparel product was calculated based on an assessment of existing studies accounting for the share of synthetic material lost due to washings over several wash cycles (De Falco et al., 2019[43]; Pirc et al., 2016[44]). It was assumed that all microfibres released during washing enter the sewage system.

Three sources of microplastics emissions from road transport were taken into account:

- The category "**tyre abrasion**" includes losses of elastomers originating from the abrasion of tyre treads of cars, trucks, and motorcycles. Emission estimates are derived from traffic data on the yearly activity in vehicle-km for passenger cars and in tonne-km for trucks from 2016 to 2019 in each region (retrieved from the ENV-Linkages model). Wear rates (i.e. average mass of tyre tread lost per vehicle-km, by vehicle type) employed are those reported by Eunomia (2018[38]). For trucks, an average freight tonnage of 16 t/vehicle was estimated, based on data from Eurostat (2018[45]). It was assumed that 46% of tyre treads is of elastomer content (Sommer et al., 2018[46]), and that the fate of the particles is as follows: 45% are retained in the asphalt pavement or remain close to the road, 45% is transported by road runoff and 10% is airborne (OECD, 2021[47]). The share of particles lost into the environment is dependent on the rural/urban population share of each region (as also used in the ENV-Growth and therefore ENV-Linkages model). In rural regions, road runoff and airborne emissions are considered as lost to the environment, whereas the particles trapped in the asphalt/road sides are not. In urban regions, airborne emissions are considered as lost to the environment, particles trapped in the asphalt/road sides are not, and particles as part of road runoff are assumed to go to a sewer system and treated as in wastewater the region where the loss occurs.
- The category "**road markings**" includes losses from markings applied to road surfaces. Estimates of plastics use for road markings are generated by the ENV-Linkages model, and the fate of road marking particles has been assumed to be similar to that of tyre abrasion particles due to a lack of data.
- The category "**brake wear**" includes losses of synthetic polymers originating from the wear of brake pads and other components. From the average composition of brake pads described by Hallal et al. (2013[48]), the polymer content of brake pads was assumed to be 23%. Similarly to the methodology used for tyre abrasion, loss estimations were based on annual traffic data and abrasion rates based on calculations by Eunomia (2018[38]).The fate of the microplastics in brake dust was assumed to be similar to that of tyre abrasion particles.

The category "**artificial turf**" includes losses of plastics from the infill of sport turfs. Estimates in the literature find losses of 300-730 kg / year per field in Denmark and 550 kg/year in Sweden (Løkkegaard, Malmgren-Hansen and Nilsson, 2018[49]; Swedish EPA, 2019[50]). According to ECHA (2020[51]), the number of artificial sport pitches will reach 39 000 by 2020 and average infill use is between 40 and 120 tonnes of material. Assuming that annual infill consumption is 1-4% of the total volume (ECHA, 2020[51]; Eunomia, 2018[38]), average yearly infill is 101 400 tonnes. Estimates for Europe were upscaled to other regions based on artificial turf market size figures (ResearchNester, 2021[52]) and GDP growth estimates (from the ENV-Linkages model). Based on the composition of rubber granulate used as infill, it was assumed that 96% of all infill is microplastics.[3] In terms of losses and environmental fate, in line with Løkkegaard, Malmgren-Hansen and Nilsson (2018[49]), it was assumed that:

- 10% of rubber granulate particles are lost to the surrounding soil (and therefore considered as lost to the environment).
- 10% are discharged with water. Based on the rural share of the population in each region provided by the ENV-Linkages model from 2016 to 2019, it was assumed those 10% are considered as directly lost to the environment in rural areas. In urban areas, they are considered to enter the wastewater network. For those reaching a treatment system (primary, secondary, tertiary), all

particles are assumed to be removed and therefore end up in sewage sludge, since the relatively large size of turf crumbles allows them to be usually well removed in treatment plants.

The category "**marine coatings**" includes losses of paint and coatings worn off from ships and marine structures. It is expected that 10% of plastics employed in the production of marine coatings is lost over the lifespan of the product, directly into the environment (Boucher and Friot, 2017[53]).

The category "**microplastics dust**" is used to refer to unintentional losses of microplastics occurring during the use phase of a number of products. Specifically, in the model five sources were taken into account: microplastics in household textile dust, the wear off of paint from interior surfaces, the wear off of paint from exterior surfaces, losses from construction and demolition activities, and shoe sole abrasion. These categories do not embody an exhaustive list of all remaining microplastics losses, but only put forward those categories for which sufficient literature has been found to quantify the resulting leakage.

For each source, with the exception of household textile dust, estimates are based on reported losses at the scale of a country or the European Union, which have been scaled down to calculate per capita emissions or per USD of GDP at constant Purchasing Power Parity (PPP) created, and finally scaled up to calculate the emissions for the entire world for each year, using data provided by the ENV-Linkages model. For interior and exterior paints, as well as exterior construction and demolition sources of dust, GDP was used as a scaling proxy under the assumption that the use of these materials is correlated to wealth.

For shoe sole abrasion, population data was considered a more relevant proxy. Because a person can only wear one pair of shoes at a time, the wear of shoes is assumed to be dependent on the activity of the person and not on wealth. In lack of better data, trends in the use of shoes are assumed to follow population trends.

The losses estimations of household textile dust are based on a recent study, according to which airborne-emitted synthetic fibres from textile and apparel products could represent a third of the particles lost to water during washings (De Falco et al., 2020[54]). Therefore, the emissions of textile fibres previously calculated during textile wash were used to calculate the losses of household textile dust.

A summary of the references used to calculate the losses from can be found in Table A A.11. It was assumed that 15% of household textile dust (Kawecki and Nowack, 2020[55]) and 100% of microplastics from interior paints end up in wastewater. For other sources, particles emitted in urban areas were also assumed to enter wastewater systems, whereas they were considered lost to the environment for rural areas.

Table A A.11. Sources for losses from microplastics dust

Microplastics dust sources	Reference (Country or region)	Scaling method
Household textile dust	ENV-Linkages model's textile projections	-
Interior paints	Eunomia (2018[38])(EU)	GDP (USD, PPP)
Exterior paints	Eunomia (2018[38]) (EU)	
Exterior construction and demolition	Kawecki and Nowack (2020[55]) (Switzerland)	
Shoe sole abrasion	Lassen et al. (2016[56]) (Denmark)	Population

The category "**wastewater sludge**" includes losses of microplastics occurring via the application of wastewater sludge to land, as detailed in the next section.

1.4.3. The wastewater pathway and losses via sludge application to land

A large share of the emitted microplastics end up in wastewater or stormwater runoff (OECD, 2021[47]). To estimate the quantities of microplastics that reach the environment, a stylised flow of relevant end-of-pipe treatment systems has been developed as illustrated in Figure A A.2. The model considers a number of possible fates for microplastics, in line with Ryberg et al. (2019[7]). Ultimately, microplastics can either be retained by wastewater treatment or be lost to the environment.

Figure A A.2. Fate of microplastics in wastewaters

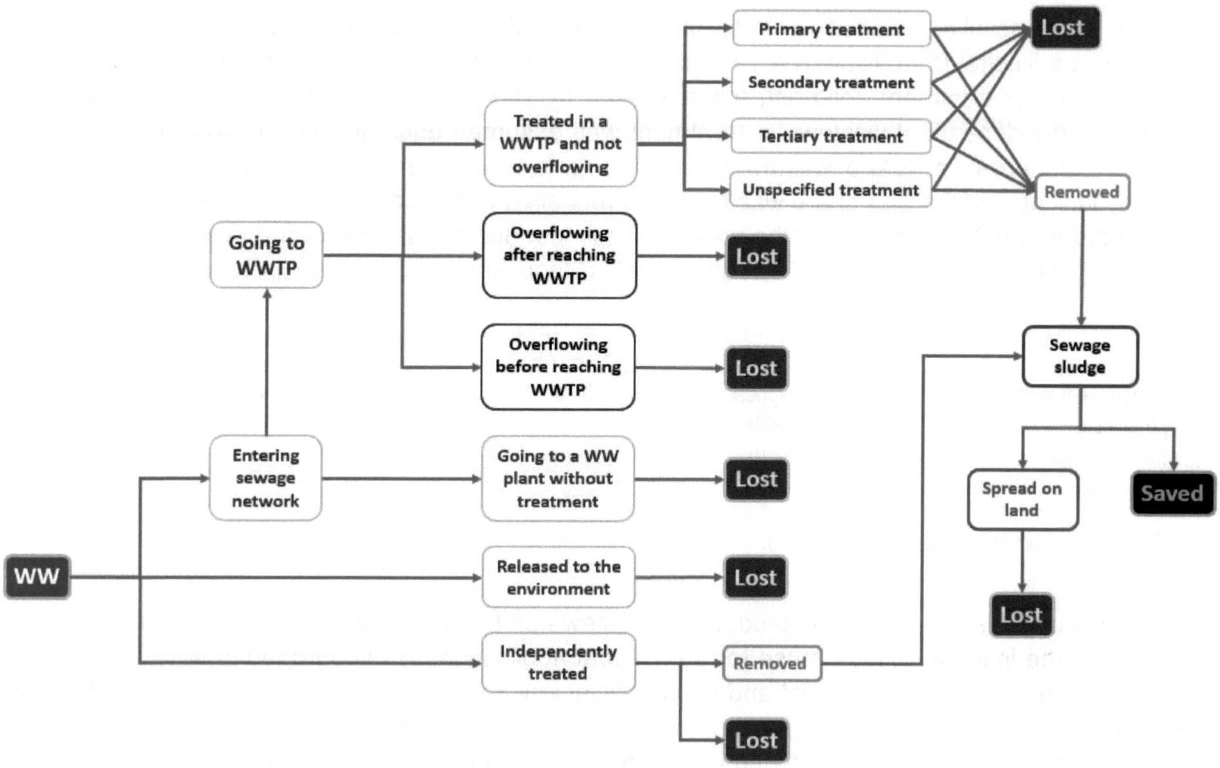

Source: Methodology adapted from Ryberg et al. (2019[7]).

The share of microplastics emissions ending up in different pathways depends on the state of wastewater infrastructure coverage in different countries. Allocation shares for each fate were estimated on a regional level. For each region, most allocation shares leading to treatments (represented by yellow boxes in Figure A A.2) were calculated using allocation shares averages of the countries composing the region, weighted by the population of each country. An assessment of data for 187 countries showed high variability in data availability and quality across countries. For most OECD countries, as well as Brazil, Colombia, and South Africa, the latest available data from the OECD Environment Database (2017[57]) was used and considered representative for wastewater treatment in 2016. For China and India, allocation shares were based on Kalbar, Muñoz and Birkved (2017[58]).

For other countries, the reference data comes from the WHO/UNICEF Joint Monitoring Programme for Water Supply, Sanitation and Hygiene (JMP, 2020[59]). This data is used for monitoring development in SDG 6.3.1 "Proportion of safely treated domestic wastewater flows (%)". In the dataset, the following classification is used:

- Safely managed: use of improved facilities which are not shared with other households and where excreta are safely disposed *in situ* or transported and treated off-site.
- Basic: use of improved facilities which are not shared with other households.
- Limited: use of improved facilities shared between two or more households.
- Unimproved: use of pit latrines without a slab or platform, hanging latrines or bucket latrines.

- Open defecation: disposal of human faeces in fields, forests, bushes, open bodies of water, beaches and other open spaces or with solid waste (JMP 2020).

The "safely managed" share of the wastewater was assumed to at least undergo primary treatment. The remaining share of the wastewater is modelled as being directly released to the environment. Although this is a conservative assumption, it was not possible to retrieve more detailed data on the treatment levels for certain regions.

A microplastics removal rate was assigned to different levels of wastewater treatment (primary, secondary, and tertiary), as illustrated in Table A A.12 and employed to calculate the fate of microplastics passing through wastewater treatment, following the approach by Ryberg et al. (2019[7]). The removal rate of unspecified and independent wastewater treatment was assumed equal to the removal rate for primary treatment. Regional data on loss of wastewater due to overflow (represented by blue boxes in Figure A A.2) is generally lacking and the loss share was therefore modelled using the same loss shares for all regions. It is estimated that 0.6% and 2.4% of the wastewater is lost due to overflow of the sewer system and of the waste water treatment plant (WWTP), respectively (Magnusson et al., 2016[60]; Ryberg et al., 2019[7]).

Table A A.12. Microplastics removal rate for different levels of wastewater treatment

Treatment technology	Microbeads	Fibres	Other microplastics
Primary treatment	86%	87%	69%
Secondary treatment	92%	92%	96%
Tertiary treatment	99%	96%	99%

Source: Calculations from Michielssen et al. (2016[61]).

Wastewater sludge is the waste by-product of wastewater treatment containing the water pollutants removed from the influent. Sludge reuse for agricultural applications is encouraged in several countries, mainly due to the high nutrient content and its beneficial effects on crops, as well as to reduce the need for landfilling or incineration. However, recent evidence suggests that this practice leads to the transfer of a share of the microplastics retained during wastewater treatment to agricultural land (Nizzetto, Futter and Langaas, 2016[62]).

Losses into the environment via agricultural land were calculated based on the share of sludge generated in a given year that is applied on agricultural land. Due to data scarcity on the fate of microplastics during sludge treatment, it was assumed that there is no further removal of microplastics before sludge is applied to land (Ryberg et al. 2019). For Canada, China and the United States, the share of sludge applied to agricultural land follows the fractions reported by Rolsky et al. (2020[63]) (i.e. 43%, 45% and 55% for Canada, China and the United States, respectively). Due to a lack of data, the share of wastewater sludge applied on agricultural fields in all other countries was assumed to be equal to the European average (i.e. 46%) (Eurostat, 2020[64]).

1.5. Modelling plastic leakage to aquatic environments (Laurent Lebreton)

This section explains the methodology and parameters employed by Laurent Lebreton to estimate the amount of leaked plastics ending up in aquatic environments and assesses their mobility as well as degradation in rivers and oceans.

With a wide variety of polymer types, object shapes and sizes, and the dynamic nature of aquatic environments, quantifying sources and the fate of plastics in rivers, lakes, and the ocean is not trivial. Some studies have recently attempted to quantify the amount of mismanaged plastic waste generated by countries worldwide, which likely reach an aquatic environment (Borrelle et al., 2020[65]) and subsequently the ocean (Meijer et al., 2021[66]). These studies utilise spatial models describing the generation of mismanaged plastic waste in relation to topography and other environmental parameters. This section raised country-scale emission results to the modelled global regions represented in the ENV-Linkages model. The transport of emitted plastics was estimated considering geographical variations. Then the fate of plastics for the different regions was modelled as a function of polymer types predicted by projections of waste generation from various sectors of the economy (from ENV-Linkages). Finally, the mass of plastics accumulated in different aquatic environments for each region is reported.

To calculate inputs of plastics by region into aquatic environments, the analysis starts from the leakage to environment calculated by the ENV-Linkages model. The model then computes the probability for leaked plastics to reach an aquatic environment (rivers, lakes, and oceans) as a function of distance and terrain slope direction. The analysis uses the national probability of emissions of plastics into aquatic environments, adapted from Borelle et al. (2020[65]). The probability is independent of the total amount of leaked plastic waste but may differ around the world as a function of population location and topography of countries. In this study, the probability of emissions by region was computed by weighing country scale emission probability by population size and formulating a regional average including confidence intervals (Figure A A.3). The likelihood of plastic waste emissions varies by region. Island nations with predominantly coastal populations have the highest chance that plastics leaked to the environment end up in aquatic environments.

Figure A A.3. Weighted probability of leaked plastics entering aquatic environments

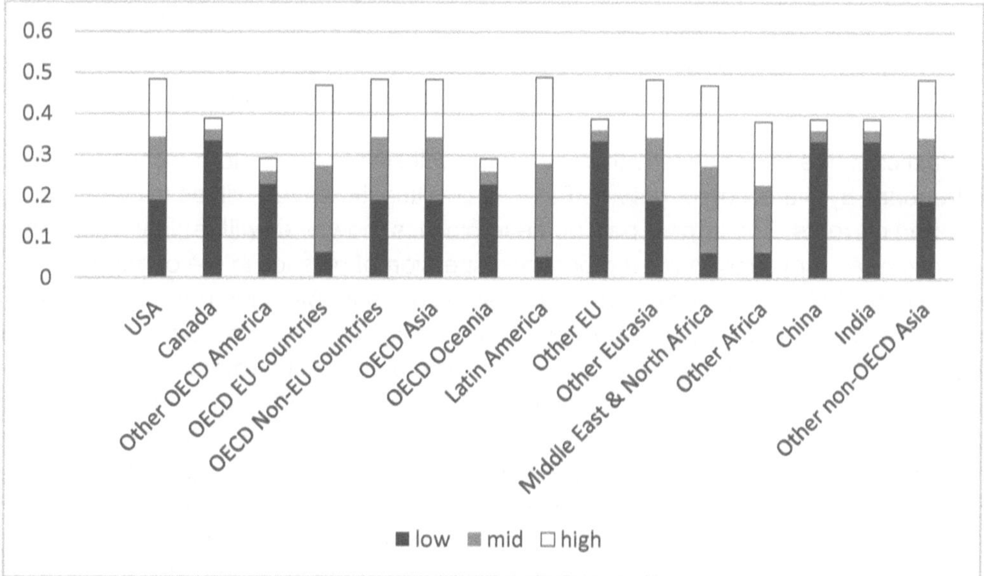

Note: The probability was calculated as the average of the country-scale fraction of emissions weighted by the population size of countries.
Source: Calculations based on Borrelle et al. (2020[65]).

In freshwater, floating plastics may be transported downstream while sinking plastics (plastics with a larger density than freshwater, e.g. PET, PVC or PS) will inevitably reach bottom sediments. Floating plastics may also be retained in freshwater environments in vegetation bordering the river, sediments in the river banks, artificial barriers (e.g. dams), or lakes. Some floating plastics may also be colonised by organisms and sink due to loss of buoyancy. A recent study estimating direct global inputs of plastics into the ocean via waterways reported that only 1% to 2% of plastics leaked annually have a chance to reach the sea globally within a year (Meijer et al., 2021[66]). The study utilised the same probability framework derived from location and quantities of lost plastics to the nearest river network. Still, it computed additional transport probabilities to river mouth from distance to the river mouth, river discharge, and river network order. The results show around one order of magnitude less discarded plastics reaching the ocean than the whole aquatic environment globally, including freshwater ecosystems (Table A A.13). This suggests that a large fraction of emitted plastic waste is likely still retained inland.

Table A A.13. Fractions of leaked macroplastics that enter aquatic environments and that reach the ocean

Macro region	Region	Fraction of leaked macroplastics entering aquatic environments	Fraction of aquatic plastics reaching the ocean
OECD America	USA	32%	3%
	Canada	36%	3%
	Other OECD America	21%	5%
OECD Europe	OECD EU countries	34%	3%
	OECD Non-EU countries	34%	4%
OECD Asia	OECD Pacific	43%	11%
	OECD Oceania	44%	2%
Other America	Latin America	28%	5%
Eurasia	Other EU	27%	1%
	Other Eurasia	32%	1%
Middle East and Africa	Middle East & North Africa	27%	4%
	Other Africa	23%	4%
Other Asia	China	28%	2%
	India	26%	4%
	Other non-OECD Asia	34%	14%

Source: Fraction of mismanaged and littered plastic waste entering aquatic environments (adapted from Borrelle et al. (2020[65])) and fraction of waste in aquatic environment entering the ocean environment (adapted from Meijer et al. (2021[66])) by region.

In the ocean, plastics with a larger density than seawater will sink to the bottom, accumulating in deep-sea canyons and trenches by the action of gravity. Floating plastics, however, will be transported by the action of waves, wind and currents. The largest part of these plastics, however, will rapidly reencounter land and beach on a coastline. A study presenting a model of dispersion of plastics in the ocean from global coastal sources reported that within a year, around 97% of released model particles had resided near a coastline for more than two consecutive days (Lebreton and Andrady, 2019[67]), suggesting a significant fraction had likely beached in that time. Rich coastal ecosystems will also facilitate the retention of floating plastics near the coastline as, similarly to freshwater environments, organisms in the marine environment will colonise floating plastics. Objects with smaller volume to surface ratios, such as plastic films or small microplastics, will likely sink near the coastline. Fragments and objects with a sufficiently large volume to maintain their buoyancy can escape the coastal environments. Over time debris tend to accumulate offshore in subtropical latitudes. Five accumulation zones have been widely reported in the literature from field observations and numerical models. The largest one is located in the North Pacific Ocean between Hawaii and California (Lebreton et al., 2018[68]).

Environmental conditions will also dictate the fate of plastics during their journey in freshwater and marine environments. Particularly under the action of sunlight, plastics degrade by photo-oxidation. As such, it is expected that plastics near the surface in rivers, lakes, or in the ocean are more likely to degrade into smaller particles, commonly referred to as microplastics with varying definitions (usually, particles below 1-5 mm and larger than one micron). Due to the large complexity of mechanisms and under varying conditions, data on the degradation of plastics in natural environments is scarce. Still, results are starting to appear with long-term experiments on the degradation of plastics in controlled environments. Fragmentation rates expressed in the percentage of weight loss per year did not exceed 5% in a laboratory seawater microcosm for various conventional thermoplastics (Gerritse et al., 2020[69]). This is in good agreement with modelled whole-ocean plastic degradation rates expected by numerical models (i.e. 3% of total ocean plastic mass degraded per year from macro- to microplastics, (Lebreton and Andrady, 2019[67]).

For the purpose of this work, the whole-ocean plastic mass budget model presented in Lebreton et al. (2019[70]) was expanded to a simplified representation of the global aquatic environment. The model now differentiates between annual inputs in freshwater and the ocean, allowing floating plastic waste to circulate from one compartment to the other over time. The model was also enhanced by differentiating inputs by polymer types using the OECD waste projections (presented in Chapter 2). The likely fate of emitted plastics was determined depending on their density. Additionally, the degradation rates varied between polymers based on laboratory results (Gerritse et al., 2020[69]). The general model framework is presented in Figure A A.4. To differentiate between freshwater and marine environment inputs, the model uses the results from Meijer et al. (2021[66]), which provides country-scale probabilities of emissions to the ocean. These results were upscaled to the modelled region by following the same weighted method as for inputs into aquatic environments (see the previous section). Thus was estimated the fraction of waste emitted in freshwater and the fraction emitted directly into the ocean for every region and per year. Starting the model in 1951, plastics were emitted into the modelled aquatic environment from every region. Polymers with a density higher than water were assumed to sink on the riverbed, lakebed, or seabed. Floating polymers circulating at the surface could directly reach the coastal ocean surface within the first year or remained in the freshwater system, likely stranded on river and lakeshores. The model also remobilised accumulated waste in river and lakeshores, adding onto inputs from the following year. Floating polymers in the coastal ocean surface followed the same dynamics as in the model presented in Lebreton et al. (2019[70]), with recirculation between the shoreline and the sea surface and transfer from coastal to offshore waters. Floating plastics accumulated in river and lake shore or on the ocean surface and shoreline were considered in contact with sunlight, and a fraction of their mass was degraded yearly to a sink term representing the mass of microplastics accumulated in freshwater and marine environments. For this report, the cycle was repeated for every year until 2019.

Figure A A.4. Mass balance budget model for plastic in global aquatic environments

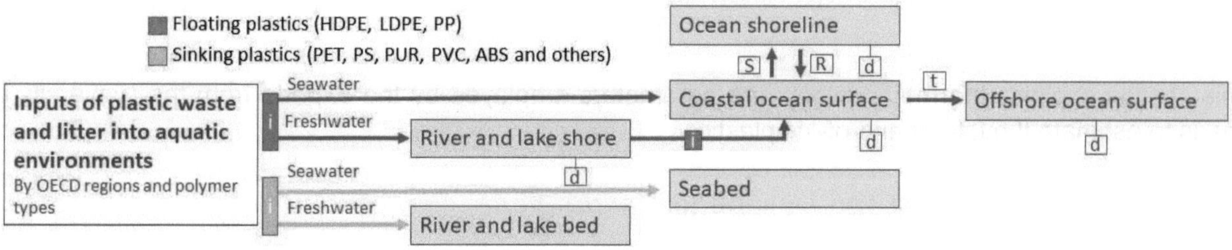

Note: Mass inputs by modelled region, characterised by polymer types, are accumulated from 1951 to 2019 into the plastic fate model. Plastics with a density higher than water sink and accumulate in riverbed, lakebed and seabed. Floating plastics (density lower than water) are transported between different aquatic compartments and are allowed to degrade into microplastics over time from contact with sunlight. The region-specific parameter 'i' is the ratio between plastics remaining in freshwater and the plastics entering the marine environment (Table A A.13). The parameters 's' and 'r' represent the fraction of stranding and release from the global shoreline. The parameter 't' is the fraction of floating plastic circulating from the coastal to the offshore ocean. (s = 97%, r = 3%, t = 33%, (Lebreton, Egger and Slat, 2019[70])). Finally, 'd' is the mass fraction degrading into microplastics annually and varies with polymer types (Table A A.14).
Source: adapted from Lebreton, Egger and Slat (2019[70]) methodology.

Table A A.14. Parameters for fate of plastic in aquatic environments by polymer type

Polymer type	Micro	Floats	Degradation rate in % of mass per year
HDPE	No	Yes	0.6
LDPE, LLDPE	No	Yes	0.8
PP	No	Yes	0.0
PET	No	No	4.9
PS	No	No	0.1
PUR	No	No	3.0
PVC	No	No	-
ABS, ASA, SAN	No	No	-

Bioplastics	No	No	-
Elastomers (tyres)	No	No	-
Fibres	No	No	-
Road marking coatings	Yes	No	-
Marine coatings	Yes	No	-
Other	No	No	-

Source: Degradation rates are sourced from laboratory experiments (Gerritse et al., 2020[69]).

For this report, the model produced time series from 1951 to 2019, for each of the global regions, of inputs and accumulation of plastic waste into rivers, lakes, and the ocean. The model allows us to produce first-order of magnitude estimates of mass distribution in different compartments of the global aquatic environment.

This simplified model has some limitations, and care should be given in the interpretation of the results. The fate of plastics will vary significantly depending on the situation. These estimates should be seen as a whole, describing the regional quantity of plastic leakage from mismanaged and littered waste expressed by orders of magnitude of mass. Some assumptions were made in the design of the model, which does not always reflect reality. For instance, polymers such as PET, PVC or PUR were considered as sinking plastics, but by design, objects made with these polymers can float for a variable period of time (e.g. empty PET bottles with cap on, PVC buoys, or extended PUR foam). On the contrary, some floating plastics such as HDPE or LDPE may also sink rapidly (e.g. biobased plastic bags) in rivers while still considered movable in the model.

1.6. Modelling plastic leakage to terrestrial and aquatic environments (University of Leeds)

This section explains the methodology and parameters employed by the experts from the University of Leeds to estimate the fate of end-of-life plastics.

1.6.1. Waste management and leakage to environment

The end-of life fate, including leakage to the environment from the waste management system, were quantified using the Spatiotemporal Quantification of Plastic Pollution Origins and Transportation (SPOT) model (Cottom, Cook and Velis, 2020[11]). The SPOT model predominantly estimates material flows at Level 2 and 3 administrative boundary resolution, and therefore it had to be adapted to provide outputs at national (Level 0) which were aggregated to OECD regional level. Material flow analysis following Brunner and Rechberger (2016[71]) was the general methodological approach underpinning the distribution of plastic waste generation estimates provided by the ENV-Linkages model and used to describe its flow through the waste system as illustrated in the conceptual diagram (Figure A A.3). This hybrid model is described hereafter as the 'ENVLinkages-SPOT plugin'.

Figure A A.5. ENV linkages-SPOT plugin model structure

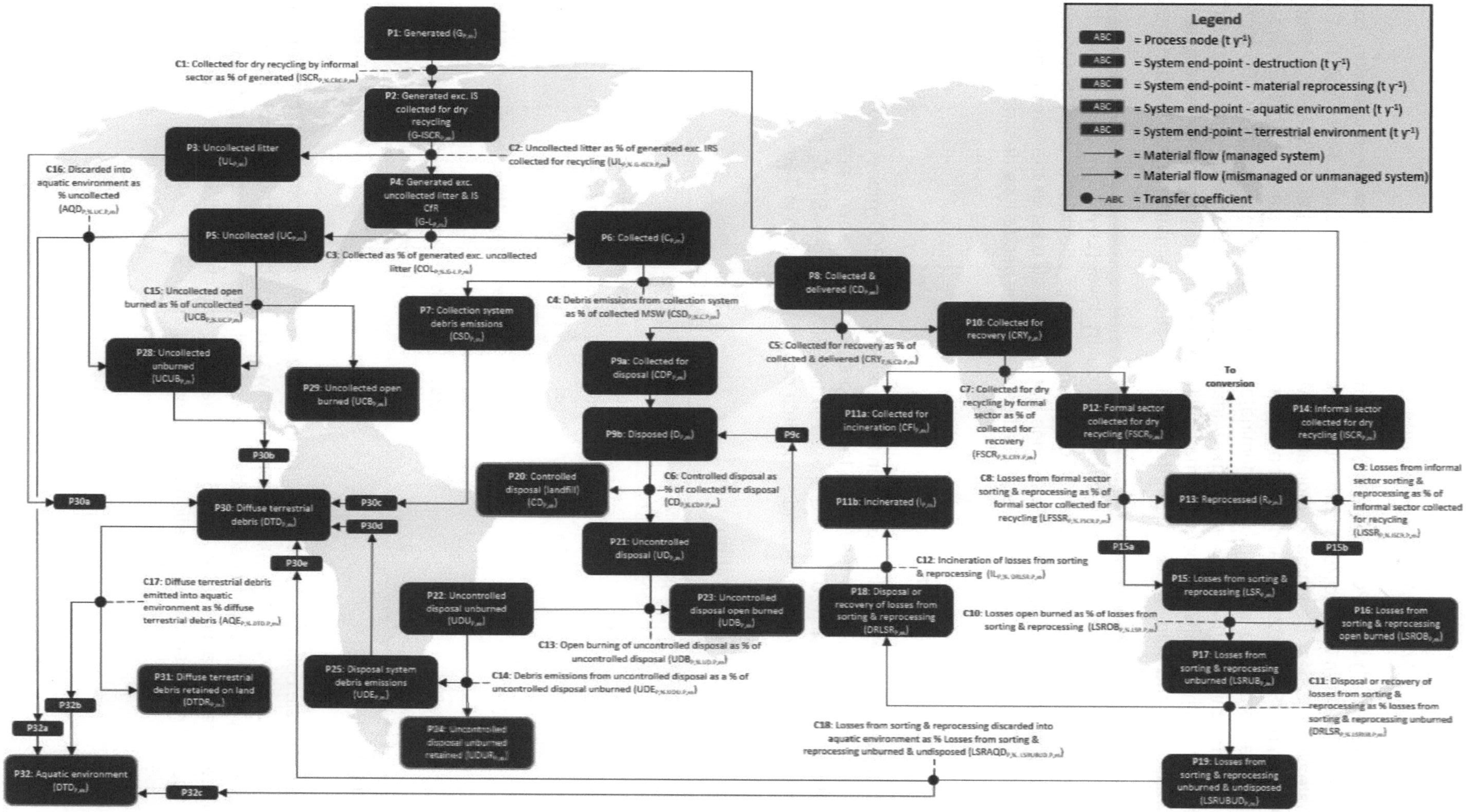

Source: Cottom, Cook and Velis (2020[11]).

1.6.2. Model structure and basic assumptions

Data were processed using the SPOT model in three stages: 1) Municipal waste generation, composition and management data from 2007 to 2021 from four sources, Waste Wise Cities Tool (WaCT) (UN Habitat, n.d.[72]); Wasteaware Cities Benchmark Indicators (WABI) (Wilson et al., 2012[73]); United Nations Statistical Division (UNSD) (2021[74]); and What a Waste 2.0 (WAW2) (Kaza et al., 2018[9]), were cleaned and normalised according to a common denominator, resulting in approximately 500 data records; 2) Random forest machine learning used predictive variables to model data for the remaining 85 088 global municipalities that had no data; 3) Probabilistic material flow analysis used the interpolated data to allocate the flow of waste from the point of generation through managed, mismanaged and unmanaged process nodes.

The ENVLinkages-SPOT plugin uses the aggregated country level (Level 0) mass of rigid and flexible plastic waste estimated by the SPOT model, to determine transfer coefficients used to allocate material between process nodes. However, the SPOT does not present all data in the format required for the ENVLinkages-SPOT plugin to function, so some adjustments are needed as described in the following paragraphs.

1.6.3. Managed waste - baseline

Incineration data were not specifically reported in this version of the SPOT model due to the lack of spatial granularity in the source data which resulted in their aggregation with other types of recovery. Therefore, data obtained from Kaza et al. (2018[9]) were used in the ENVLinkages-SPOT plugin alongside further research which was used to verify or amend some data points as detailed in Table A A.15.

Table A A.15. Validation of incineration data

Country	Mass of MSW incinerated (t y^{-1})	Proportion of MSW incinerated (%)	Verification / addition	Source
Liechtenstein	8 268	25.4	add	Liechtenstein Institute for Strategic Development (2020[75])
Azerbaijan	400 000	9.6	add	(Islamic Development Bank, 2020[76])
Vietnam	1 602 764	5.4	add	(Tun et al., 2020[77])
Thailand	1 389 627	5.0	Verified	(Tun et al., 2020[77])
Ethiopia	350 000	2.5	add	(Cleere, 2020[78]; Mubeen and Buekens, 2019[79])
Lao PDR	32 637	2.0	add	(Tun et al., 2020[77])
India	1 916 250	0.7	add	(Central Pollution Control Board, 2021[80])
Myanmar	21 900	0.2	add	(JFE Engineering Corporation, 2017[81])

Source: Kaza et al. (2018[9]).

The proportion of waste collected for recycling by the informal sector was estimated by adapting the P2O model presented by Lau et al. (2020[27]). Additional data was reported by Cottom, Cook and Velis (2020[11]) for average productivity per waste picker, number of waste pickers per head of urban population, proportion of waste collected that is plastic (Table A A.16). It as was also assumed that workers operate for 235 days on average accounting for sickness, vacation and other downtime.

Table A A.16. Data used to model the activities of the informal recycling sector

Income group (World Bank)	Proportion of urban population that is an informal waste worker (%)	Productivity per waste picker (kg d^{-1})	Proportion of waste collected by informal recycling sector that is plastic (%)
High income	0.01	37.0	5
Upper middle-income	0.26	37.0	28
Lower middle income	0.19	37.0	35
Low income	0.14	37.0	35

Source: Cottom, Cook and Velis (2020[11]).

1.6.4. Dumping mismanaged waste in water

Data to quantify the deliberate dumping of waste into water by waste generators are scarce. Here we present, for the first time, a review of census data that indicate the mass deposited directly into water by householders in the absence of formal waste collection services (Table A A.17). Acknowledging the uncertainty in the data and the high variability in time and across countries, we have taken a conservative approach and approximated the issue by using the mean of the country level median proportion treated in this way: 4.8% of uncollected waste.

Table A A.17. Deliberate dumping into water

Country	Proportion of population engaged in behaviour (median % of uncollected waste)	Source
Malawi	1.0	National Statistical Office (2020[82])
Guatemala	1.8	Guatemala, Instituto Nacional de Estadística (2018[83])
Indonesia	7.6	Sub Direktorat Statistik Lingkungan Hidup (2014[84])
Fiji	0.5	Fiji Bureau of Statistics (2018[85])
Brazil	0.4	Instituto Brasileiro de Geografia e Estatística (2010[86])
Bolivia	15.6	Instituto Nacional de Estadistica (2012[87])
Samoa	0.4	Samoa Bureau of statistics (2019[88])
Ethiopia	10.9	Population Census Commission (2007[89])

1.6.5. Plastic debris emissions to aquatic environments

The leakage transfer from terrestrial to aquatic environments was estimated using transfer ratios suggested by Lau et al. (2020[27]) and detailed in Table A A.18.The GWPv4 (2015) (United Nations, 2019[90]) UNAdj population density map (CIESIN, 2018[91]) was used to estimate the proportion of rural and urban inhabitants in line with Dijkstra and Poelman (2014[92]) using grid cells >300 population and >5 000 inhabitants in contiguous cells. The urban and rural attribution was mapped onto the HydroSHEDS 30 arc river and coastline dataset. Population data for countries above 60°N latitude were approximated using ratios for the nearest similar countries which were below 60°N.

Waste transfer from the terrestrial to aquatic environment was estimated using transfer ratios suggested by Lau et al. (2020[27]) and detailed in Table A A.18. The GWPv4 (2015) (United Nations, 2019[90]) UNAdj population density map (CIESIN, 2018[91]) was used to estimate the proportion of rural and urban inhabitants using definition from was estimated using Dijkstra and Poelman (2014[92])); that a grid cell has >300 population and >5 000 inhabitants in contiguous cells. The urban and rural attribution was mapped onto the HydroSHEDS 30 arc river and coastline dataset. Population data for countries above 60°N latitude were approximated using ratios for nearest similar countries which were below 60°N.

Table A A.18. Plastic waste transfer rate from terrestrial to aquatic environment (% wt. y^{-1})

Flexibility	Distance population to aquatic environment	Proportion of plastic waste in terrestrial environment that transfers to the aquatic environment (% wt.)
Rigid	< 1 km	10
	>1 km	3
Flexible	<1 km	35
	>1 km	8

Source: Lau et al. (2020[27]).

1.7. Plastic leakage to terrestrial and aquatic environments (OECD Global Plastics Outlook Database)

The OECD Global Plastics Outlook Database includes three estimates for leakage to the environment (sum of terrestrial and aquatic environments) and three estimates for leakage to aquatic environments: central, high and low estimates. They are calculated by combining the estimates based on the different methodologies outlined in the previous sections, namely estimates provided by: the DTU, the University of Leeds and Laurent Lebreton.

More specifically, the central estimate of the leakage to the environment corresponds to the average of the leakages to the environment reported by DTU and the University of Leeds. The high and low estimates refer to the maximum and minimum of these values correspondingly.

The leakage to aquatic environments, is calculated by using the central estimate for the leakage to the environment as input in the model of Laurent Lebreton. The central and high estimates for leakage to water come from Laurent Lebreton. The low estimate represents the number reported by the University of Leeds.

The mobility of plastics in aquatic environments uses the central estimate for the leakage to aquatic environments as input for the methodology described earlier (Annex 'Modelling plastic leakage to aquatic environments – Laurent Lebreton').

1.8. Modelling particulate matter emissions to air from tyre and brake wear (Norwegian Institute for Air Research)

This section explains the methodology and parameters employed by Nicolaos Evangeliou from the Norwegian Institute for Air Research (NILU) to estimate the emission of airborne road-traffic-related microplastics and their contribution to particulate matter pollution.

1.8.1. Calculation of emissions from tyre and brake wear

Tyre and brake wear particles (TWPs and BWPs) are calculated using the GAINS (Greenhouse gas – Air pollution Interactions and Synergies) model (Amann et al., 2011[93]). GAINS is an integrated assessment model where emissions of air pollutants and greenhouse gases are estimated for nearly two hundred regions globally considering key economic activities, environmental regulation policies and region-specific emission factors. For emissions of particulate matter (PM), GAINS provides PM distinguishing PM_1, $PM_{2.5}$, PM_{10}, total PM, as well as carbonaceous particles (BC, OC) that derive from combustion processes, as described in Klimont et al. (2017[94]).

Emissions of non-exhaust PM in GAINS include TWPs, BWPs, as well as road abrasion. The calculation of these emissions is based on region-specific data and estimates of distance driven (km/vehicle-type/year) and vehicle-type specific emission rates (mg/km). The types of vehicles considered include motorcycles, cars, light-duty vehicles, buses, and heavy-duty vehicles. The estimates of distance driven for 2015 are derived using data on fuel use in road transport from the International Energy Agency's Word Energy Outlook (IEA, 2011[95]), supported by national data on vehicle numbers and assumptions of per-vehicle mileage travelled. Considering vehicle-type specific emission rates and use, allows for better reflection of significant regional differences in fleet structure, e.g. large number of motorcycles in South and South-East Asia and lower car ownership numbers in parts of the developing world. GAINS emissions are estimated globally at the grid level (0.5°×0.5°) using road network data, assumptions about road-type vehicle density, and population data.

The vehicle-type specific TWP and BWP emission factors used in GAINS draw on a review of several measurement papers (Klimont et al., 2002[96]) that were recently updated (Klimont et al., 2017[94]) using primarily van der Gon et al. (2013[97]), EEA (2013[98]) and Harrison et al. (2012[99]). There are large uncertainties in emission factors including concerning the PM size distribution. GAINS provides total suspended particulates (TSP), and then assumes that PM_{10} from TWPs represent about 10% of TSP, and $PM_{2.5}$ about 1% of total TWPs, whereas PM_{10} from BWPs is about 80% of TSP and $PM_{2.5}$ is 40–50% of total BWPs (Klimont et al., 2002[96]).

1.8.2. Atmospheric transport modelling

Emissions of PM_{10} calculated with the GAINS model are used as input in the FLEXPART (FLEXible PARTicle) atmospheric transport model version 10.4 (Pisso et al., 2019[100]). Atmospheric dispersion of particulate matter, including both transport and deposition of particles, were simulated for the reference year 2014. The FLEXPART model was run in forward mode from 2014. Atmospheric processes affecting particle transport in clouds (e.g. boundary layer turbulent mixing and convection processes) are parameterised in the model (Forster, Stohl and Seibert, 2007[101]). The model was driven by 3-hourly 1°×1° operational analyses from the European Centre for Medium Range Weather Forecast (ECMWF), the spatial output resolution of concentration and deposition fields was set to 0.5°×0.5° in a global domain with a daily temporal resolution. In FLEXPART the dispersion of road microplastics is modelled assuming a spherical shape of particles (Pisso et al., 2019[100]).

The simulations also accounted for below-cloud scavenging and dry deposition, assuming a particle density for TWPs of 1 234 kg/m^3, which is in the middle of the densities of 945 kg/m^3 for natural rubber and 1 522 kg/m^3 for synthetic rubber (Walker, 2019[102]; Federal Highway Administration Research and Technology, 2019[103]). This density is within the reported range for microplastics (940-2 400 kg/m^3) (Unice et al., 2019[104]). For BWPs a higher density was assumed (2 000 kg/m^3) considering that BWP may also contain metals (Grigoratos and Martini, 2014[105]). Plastics are generally hydrophobic and should therefore be rather inefficient cloud condensation nuclei (CCN) (Di Mundo, Petrella and Notarnicola, 2008[106]; Ganguly and Ariya, 2019[107]). However, coatings may make the particles more hydrophilic with time in the atmosphere (Bond et al., 2013[108]). The efficiency of aerosols to serve as ice nuclei (IN) is also not well known. Based on Evangeliou et al. (2020[109]), it is more realistic to use intermediate scavenging coefficients for CCN/IN in the model.

The emissions of TWPs and BWPs were extrapolated from 2014 to 2019, using the road passenger data from the IEA's World Energy Outlook (IEA, 2018[110]) for the 15 geographical regions of the OECD ENV-Linkages model. Year 2014 was taken as base year and the ratio to year 2014 was calculated for each year between 2015 and 2019 and for each of the 15 regions (from now on referred as "regional scaling factor"). This regional scaling factor could be negative, if the road passenger data decreased as compared to 2015, or positive, if an increase is shown.

The FLEXPART model was run with the 2014 emissions for the 15 ENV-Linkages regions; thus creating 15 different model simulations, each representing the dispersion from the respective region. Then, the regional scaling factor was used to scale modelled dispersion that results from each individual regional emission for each year between 2015 and 2019. Finally, the 15 regional annually-scaled modelled dispersions were used to calculate global TWP and BWP estimates.

1.9. Modelling greenhouse gas emissions from primary plastics in ENV-Linkages

This section explains the methodology and parameters employed to estimate the contribution of the lifecycle of plastics to GHG emissions at the global level, based on the OECD ENV-Linkages model.

In the GTAP database (Aguiar et al., 2019[4]), plastics production occurs in two sectors: Chemicals and Rubber and plastics products, along with other products. In ENV-Linkages, the plastic products sectors has been split into primary and secondary plastics production (see Section 1.2 in this Annex). The difficulty in estimating plastic-related greenhouse gas emissions is that in ENV-Linkages there is no direct link between emissions and emissions attributable to plastics. The plastics producing sectors use inputs from the electricity generation sector, fossil fuel extraction sectors and other sectors of the economy. However, these plastics producing sectors also produce other goods, so that not all emissions can be attributed to plastics. Furthermore, emissions outside these sectors can also be attributed to plastics. Furthermore, emissions from the extraction of raw materials and from plastic waste management, are also mixed with emissions not attributable to plastics.

Therefore, to approximate the global lifecycle emissions from plastics, an emission factor-based approach is retained:

$$Emi_{g,t}^{plastics} = \sum_{p} \left(\lambda_{g,p,t}^{prod} + \lambda_{g,p,t}^{conv}\right) C_{p,t} + \sum_{f} \lambda_{g,f,t}^{eol} W_{f,t}$$

where $Emi_{g,t}^{plastics}$ are emissions of greenhouse gas g (comprising CO_2, CH_4 and N_2O, measured in CO_2-equivalents)[4] from the plastics lifecycle at time t, $\lambda_{g,p,t}^{prod}$ and $\lambda_{g,p,t}^{conv}$ are respectively the emission factors per tonne of plastic product for production and conversion of plastic for polymer p that are applied to the level of primary plastics consumption $C_{p,t}$ estimated by the model (by convention, emissions from the production of secondary plastics are allocated to waste management emissions). Finally, $\lambda_{g,f,t}^{eol}$ is the emission factor for a specific end-of-life fate f (incineration, sanitary landfilling and recycling only are considered, due to data availability), applied to the amount of plastic waste generated $W_{j,t}$.

The literature provides estimates of emission factors for year 2015 (Zheng and Suh, 2019[111])[5] that are used to calibrate the emissions for 2015. These emission factors comprise emissions from the whole value-chain of plastics production, and have no reason to be constant over time due to structural changes in the production process. As a consequence, the GHG intensity of plastics production and conversion is updated to 2019 based on the structural change observed in the model. An index based on the global average scope 2 emissions (direct emissions plus emissions from electricity demand) of the sectors related to plastics production and conversion (chemicals, primary rubber and plastics products, oil extraction, gas extraction and petroleum and coal products) represents the evolution over time of production and conversion emissions. Another index based on scope 2 emissions of the secondary plastics sector represents the evolution over time of recycling emission intensity, while emissions factors are constant for incineration and landfilling (Figure A A.6).

Figure A A.6. Greenhouse gas emission factors for plastics lifecycle in ENV-Linkages in 2015

Panel A. Production and conversion emissions by polymer type (t CO_2e per tonne of plastic product)

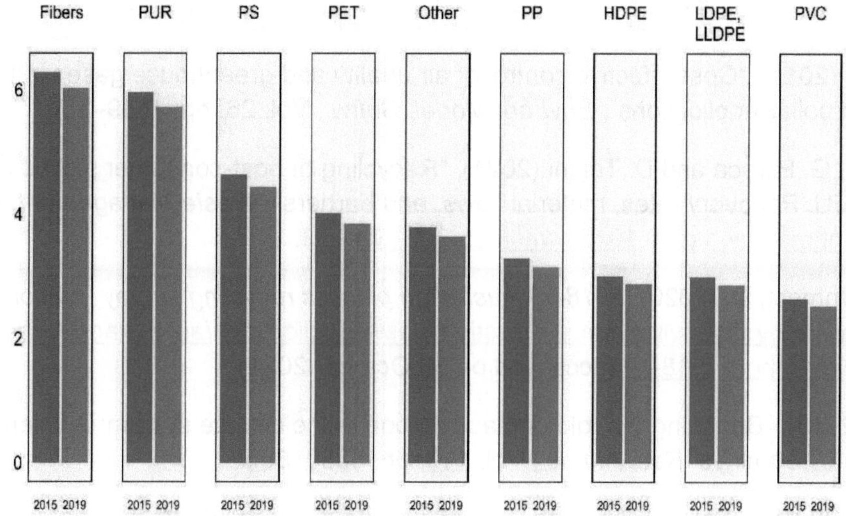

Panel B. End-of-life emissions by end-of-life fate (t CO_2e per t of plastic waste)

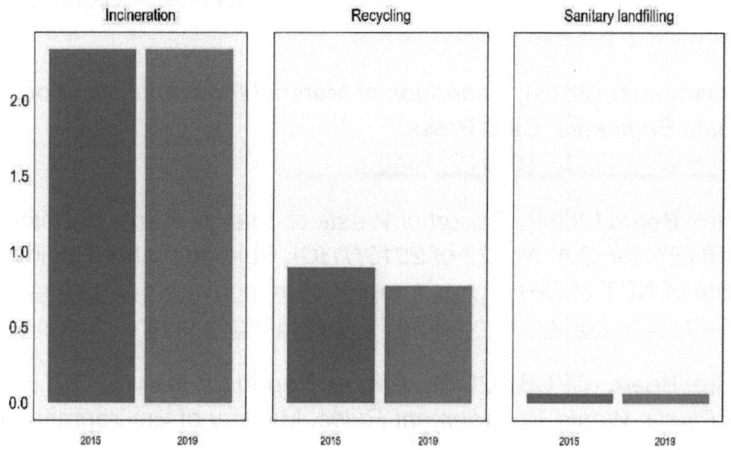

Note: Emissions from recycling and incineration are direct emissions from their respective industrial processes. Avoided emissions (emissions from electricity generation that are replaced by waste incineration and emissions from primary plastics production that are replaced by secondary plastics) are not included in the emission factors depicted here, because they are included directly in the ENV-Linkages model (changes in the input structure of the electricity generation sector and changes in the balance between primary and secondary plastics, both being driven by the change in the relative prices of products, are endogenously determined by the model).
Source: Adapted from Zheng and Suh (2019[111]).

References

Aguiar, A. et al. (2019), "The GTAP Data Base: Version 10", *Journal of Global Economic Analysis*, Vol. 4/1, pp. 1-27, http://dx.doi.org/10.21642/jgea.040101af. [4]

Amann, M. et al. (2011), "Cost-effective control of air quality and greenhouse gases in Europe: Modeling and policy applications", *Environ. Model. Softw.*, Vol. 26, pp. 1489–1501. [93]

Antonopoulos, I., G. Faraca and D. Tonini (2021), "Recycling of post-consumer plastic packaging waste in the EU: Recovery rates, material flows, and barriers", *Waste Management*, Vol. 126, pp. 694-705, https://doi.org/10.1016/j.wasman.2021.04.002. [30]

Australian Government, D. (2020), *2018-19 Australian plastics recycling survey - national report*, https://www.awe.gov.au/environment/protection/waste/publications/australian-plastics-recycling-survey-report-2018-19 (accessed on 28 October 2021). [19]

Bond, T. et al. (2013), "Bounding the role of black carbon in the climate system: A scientific assessment", *J. Geophys. Res. Atmos.*, Vol. 118, pp. 5380–5552. [108]

Borrelle, S. et al. (2020), "Predicted growth in plastic waste exceeds efforts to mitigate plastic pollution", *Science*, Vol. 369/6510, pp. 1515-1518, http://dx.doi.org/10.1126/science.aba3656. [65]

Boucher, F. and D. Friot (2017), *Primary Microplastics in the Oceans: A Global Evaluation of Sources.*. [53]

Brunner, P. and H. Rechberger (2016), *Handbook of Material Flow Analysis: For Environmental, Resource, and Waste Engineers*, CRC Press, http://dx.doi.org/doi.org/10.1201/9781315313450. [71]

Central Pollution Control Board (2021), *Report of Waste to Energy Plants in Delhi by CPCB in OA No. 640 of 2018 (Earlier O.A. No. 22 of 2013(THC)*, Sukhdev Vihar Residents Welfare Association Vs State of NCT of Delhi, https://greentribunal.gov.in/report-waste-energy-plants-delhi-cpcb-oa-no-640-2018-earlier-oa-no-22-2013thc-sukhdev-vihar. [80]

Central Pollution Control Board (CPCB) (2019), *Annual Report for the year 2018-2019 on Implementation of Plastic Waste Management Rules*, Ministry of Environment, Forest and Climate Change, Govt of India. [21]

Chateau, J., R. Dellink and E. Lanzi (2014), "An Overview of the OECD ENV-Linkages Model: Version 3", *OECD Environment Working Papers*, No. 65, OECD Publishing, Paris, http://dx.doi.org/10.1787/5jz2qck2b2vd-en. [1]

Chateau, J., C. Rebolledo and R. Dellink (2011), "An Economic Projection to 2050: The OECD "ENV-Linkages" Model Baseline", *OECD Environment Working Papers*, No. 41, OECD Publishing, Paris, http://dx.doi.org/10.1787/5kg0ndkjvfhf-en. [2]

Chruszcz, A. and S. Reeve (2018), *Composition of plastic waste: Results of a waste compositional analysis of plastics at MRFs and PRFs*, WRAP. [26]

CIESIN (2018), *Gridded population of the world, version 4 (GPWv4): population count adjusted to Match 2015 revision of UN WPP country totals, revision 11.*, Center for International Earth Science Information Network - Columbia University, https://sedac.ciesin.columbia.edu/data/set/gpw-v4-population-count-adjusted-to-2015-unwpp-country-totals-rev11. [91]

Cleere, R. (2020), “The New Reppie Incinerator at Koshe Landfill in Addis Ababa, Ethiopia.”, *[Online data set] Environmental Justice Atlas*, https://ejatlas.org/conflict/the-new-reppie-incinerator-at-koshe-landfill-in-addis-ababa-ethiopia-leaves-the-wastepickers-without-livelihood. [78]

Cottom, J., E. Cook and C. Velis (2020), “Spatio-temporal quantification of plastic pollution origins and transportation (SPOT)”, *University of Leeds, UK*, https://plasticpollution.leeds.ac.uk/toolkits/spot/. [11]

De Falco, F. et al. (2020), “Microfiber Release to Water, Via Laundering, and to Air, via Everyday Use: A Comparison between Polyester Clothing with Differing Textile Parameters”, *Environmental Science & Technology*, doi: 10.1021/acs.est.9b06892, pp. 3288-3296, http://dx.doi.org/10.1021/acs.est.9b06892. [54]

De Falco, F. et al. (2019), “The contribution of washing processes of synthetic clothes to microplastic pollution”, *Scientific Reports*, Vol. 9, p. 6633, https://doi.org/10.1038/s41598-019-43023-x. [43]

Di Mundo, R., A. Petrella and M. Notarnicola (2008), “Surface and bulk hydrophobic cement composites by tyre rubber addition”, *Constr. Build. Mater.*, Vol. 172, pp. 176–184. [106]

Dijkstra, L. and H. Poelman (2014), *A harmonised definition of cities and rural areas: the new degree of urbanisation*, https://ec.europa.eu/regional_policy/sources/docgener/work/2014_01_new_urban.pdf. [92]

ECHA (2020), *Committee for Risk Assessment (RAC) Committee for Socio-economic Analysis (SEAC). Opinion on an Annex XV dossier proposing restrictions on intentionally added microplastics.* [51]

EMEP/EEA (2013), *Air pollutant emission inventory guidebook 2013: Technical guidance to prepare national emission inventories*, http://dx.doi.org/10.2800/92722. [98]

Environment and Climate Change Canada (2019), *Economic Study of the Canadian plastic industry, markets and waste*, Environment and Climate Change Canada. [15]

Eunomia (2018), “Investigating options for reducing releases in the aquatic environment of microplastics emitted by (but not intentionally added in) products”, *Report for DG Env EC*, Vol. Vol. 62, N/February, pp. 1596-1605, http://dx.doi.org/10.1002/lsm.22016. [38]

Eurostat (2020), *Statistics | Sewage sludge production and disposal.*, https://ec.europa.eu/eurostat/databrowser/view/ENV_WW_SPD/default/table. (accessed on 28 January 2021). [64]

Eurostat (2018), *Average loads for total road freight transport, 2018 (tonnes)*, https://ec.europa.eu/eurostat/statistics-explained/index.php?title=File:Average_loads_for_total_RFT,_2018_(tonnes).png. (accessed on 21 May 2021). [45]

Eurostat (n.d.), *Sold production, exports and imports by PRODCOM list (NACE Rev. 2) - annual data*, https://ec.europa.eu/eurostat/web/prodcom/data/database. [39]

Evangeliou, N. et al. (2020), “Atmospheric transport is a major pathway of microplastics to remote regions”, *Nat Commun*, Vol. 11, p. 3381, https://doi.org/10.1038/s41467-020-17201-9. [109]

FCH (2021), “NEW PLASTICS ECONOMY”, https://fch.cl/en/initiative/new-plastics-economy. [17]

Federal Highway Administration Research and Technology (2019), *User Guidelines for Waste and Byproduct Materials in Pavement Construction*. [103]

Fiji Bureau of Statistics (2018), *2017 Fiji population and housing census.*, https://www.statsfiji.gov.fj/component/advlisting/?view=download&format=raw&fileId=5970. [85]

Forster, C., A. Stohl and P. Seibert (2007), “Parameterization of convective transport in a Lagrangian particle dispersion model and its evaluation”, *J. Appl. Meteorol. Climatol.*, Vol. 46, pp. 403–422. [101]

Ganguly, M. and P. Ariya (2019), “Ice Nucleation of Model Nanoplastics and Microplastics: A Novel Synthetic Protocol and the Influence of Particle Capping at Diverse Atmospheric Environments”, *ACS Earth Sp. Chem*, Vol. 3, pp. 1729–1739. [107]

Gerritse, J. et al. (2020), “Fragmentation of plastic objects in a laboratory seawater microcosm”, *Scientific Reports*, Vol. 10/1, p. 10945, http://dx.doi.org/10.1038/s41598-020-67927-1. [69]

Geyer, R., J. Jambeck and K. Law (2017), “Production, use, and fate of all plastics ever made”, *Science Advances*, Vol. 3/7, p. e1700782, http://dx.doi.org/10.1126/sciadv.1700782. [8]

Government of Australia (2021), *Australian plastics flows and fates 2019-2020.* [24]

Grigoratos, T. and G. Martini (2014), *Non-exhaust traffic related emissions. Brake and tyre wear PM*, http://dx.doi.org/10.2790/21481. [105]

Guatemala, Instituto Nacional de Estadística (2018), *Características generales del hogar. Censo 2018: Cuadro B6.1 - Hogares por forma principal de eliminación de la basura, según departamento. [Online data set]*, https://www.censopoblacion.gt/explorador. [83]

Hallal, A. et al. (2013), “Overview of Composite Materials and their Automotive Applications”, in *Advanced Composite Materials for Automotive Applications*, John Wiley & Sons, Ltd, https://doi.org/10.1002/9781118535288.ch1. [48]

Harrison, R. et al. (2012), “Estimation of the contributions of brake dust, tire wear, and resuspension to nonexhaust traffic particles derived from atmospheric measurements”, *Environ. Sci. Technol.*, Vol. 46, pp. 6523–6529. [99]

Hestin, M., T. Faninger and L. Milios (2015), *Increased EU Plastics Recycling Targets: Environment, Economic and Social Impact Assessment*, https://743c8380-22c6-4457-9895-11872f2a708a.filesusr.com/ugd/0af79c_d3c616e926e24896a8b82b833332242e.pdf. [25]

IEA (2018), *World Energy Outlook.* [110]

IEA (2011), *World Energy Outlook.* [95]

IMF (2020), *World Economic Outlook, October 2020: A Long and Difficult Ascent*, International Monetary Fund, Washington, D.C., https://www.imf.org/en/Publications/WEO/Issues/2020/09/30/world-economic-outlook-october-2020 (accessed on 22 January 2021). [6]

Instituto Brasileiro de Geografia e Estatística (2010), *Demographic Census: Table 1395 - Permanent private households, by household situation and existence of bathroom or toilet and number of toilets for the exclusive use of the household, according to the type of household, the form of water supply, the desti*, https://sidra.ibge.gov.br/tabela/1395. [86]

Instituto Nacional de Estadistica (2012), *Disposal of garbage in the house, according to province and municipality, 2012 census [Online data set]*, https://www.ine.gob.bo/index.php/estadisticas-sociales/vivienda-y-servicios-basicos/censos-vivienda/. [87]

IPCC (1995), *Climate Change 1995: A report of the Intergovernmental Panel on Climate Change - IPCC Second Assessment*. [112]

Islamic Development Bank (2020), *Waste to Energy: Averting environnmental damage in Azerbaijan.*, https://www.isdb.org/sites/default/files/media/documents/2020-06/Success_Lflt_Azerbaijan_EN.pdf. [76]

Jambeck, J. et al. (2015), "Plastic waste inputs from land into the ocean", *Science*, Vol. 347/6223, pp. 768-771, http://dx.doi.org/10.1126/science.1260352. [12]

JFE Engineering Corporation (2017), *Opening Ceremony for Myanmar's First Waste to Energy Plant*, https://www.jfe-eng.co.jp/en/news/2017/20170410.html. [81]

JMP (2020), *Wash Data*, https://washdata.org/data/household#!/table?geo0=region&geo1=sdg. (accessed on 29 January 2021). [59]

Kalbar, P., I. Muñoz and M. Birkved (2017), "WW LCI v2: A second-generation life cycle inventory model for chemicals discharged to wastewater systems.", *Sci Total Environ.*, http://dx.doi.org/10.1016/j.scitotenv.2017.10.051. [58]

Kawecki, D. and B. Nowack (2020), "A proxy-based approach to predict spatially resolved emissions of macro- and microplastic to the environment", *Science of The Total Environment*, Vol. 748, p. 141137, https://doi.org/10.1016/j.scitotenv.2020.141137. [55]

Kaza, S. et al. (2018), *What a Waste 2.0: A Global Snapshot of Solid Waste Management to 2050*, The World Bank, http://dx.doi.org/10.1596/978-1-4648-1329-0. [9]

Klimont, Z. et al. (2002), *Modelling Particulate Emissions in Europe. A Framework to Estimate Reduction Potential and Control Costs*. [96]

Klimont, Z. et al. (2017), "Global anthropogenic emissions of particulate matter including black carbon", *Atmos. Chem. Phys.*, Vol. 17, pp. 8681–8723. [94]

Lassen, C. et al. (2016), *Microplastics Occurrence, effects and sources of releases to the environment in Denmark*, Danish Environmental Protection Agency, Copenhagen. [56]

Lau, W. et al. (2020), "Evaluating scenarios toward zero plastic pollution", *Science*, Vol. 369/6510, pp. 1455-1461, http://dx.doi.org/10.1126/science.aba9475. [27]

Lebreton, L. and A. Andrady (2019), "Future scenarios of global plastic waste generation and disposal", *Palgrave Communications*, Vol. 5/1, p. 6, http://dx.doi.org/10.1057/s41599-018-0212-7. [67]

Lebreton, L., M. Egger and B. Slat (2019), "A global mass budget for positively buoyant macroplastic debris in the ocean", *Scientific Reports*, Vol. 9/1, p. 12922, http://dx.doi.org/10.1038/s41598-019-49413-5. [70]

Lebreton, L. et al. (2018), "Evidence that the Great Pacific Garbage Patch is rapidly accumulating plastic", *Scientific Reports*, Vol. 8/1, http://dx.doi.org/10.1038/s41598-018-22939-w. [68]

Liechtenstein Institute for Strategic Development (2020), *Circular economy strategy for Liechtenstein.*, https://www.alpine-space.org/projects/greencycle/deliverables/t2/lisd---circular-economy-strategy-for-liechtenstein-vol1-10-03-2020-1.pdf. [75]

Løkkegaard, H., B. Malmgren-Hansen and N. Nilsson (2018), *Mass balance of rubber granulate lost from artificial turf fields, focusing on discharge to the aquatic environment*. [49]

Magnusson, K. et al. (2016), *Swedish Sources and Pathways for Microplastics to the Marine Environment.*. [60]

Meijer, L. et al. (2021), "More than 1000 rivers account for 80% of global riverine plastic emissions into the ocean", *Science Advances*, Vol. 7/18, http://dx.doi.org/10.1126/sciadv.aaz5803. [66]

Michielssen, M. et al. (2016), "Fate of microplastics and other small anthropogenic litter (SAL) in wastewater treatment plants depends on unit processes employed", *Environmental Science: Water Research and Technology*, Vol. 2/6, pp. 1064-1073, http://dx.doi.org/10.1039/c6ew00207b. [61]

Ministry of Commerce (2019), *The China Recycling Industry Development Report (2013-2018)*. [20]

Mubeen, I. and A. Buekens (2019), "Chapter 14 - Energy From Waste: Future Prospects Toward Sustainable Development", in Kumar, S., R. Kumar and A. Pandey (eds.), *Current Developments in Biotechnology and Bioengineering*, Elsevier, https://doi.org/10.1016/B978-0-444-64083-3.00014-2. [79]

National Statistical Office (2020), *2018 Malawi population and housing census: water and sanitation report Zomba*, http://www.nsomalawi.mw/images/stories/data_on_line/demography/census_2018/Thematic_Reports/Water%20and%20Sanitation%20Report.pdf. [82]

Nizzetto, L., M. Futter and S. Langaas (2016), *Are Agricultural Soils Dumps for Microplastics of Urban Origin?*, American Chemical Society, http://dx.doi.org/10.1021/acs.est.6b04140. [62]

OECD (2021), *Policies to Reduce Microplastics Pollution in Water: Focus on Textiles and Tyres*, OECD Publishing, Paris, https://dx.doi.org/10.1787/7ec7e5ef-en. [47]

OECD (2020), *OECD Economic Outlook, Volume 2020 Issue 2*, OECD Publishing, Paris, https://dx.doi.org/10.1787/39a88ab1-en. [5]

OECD (2019), *Global Material Resources Outlook to 2060: Economic Drivers and Environmental Consequences*, https://doi.org/10.1787/9789264307452-en. [3]

OECD (2017), *Environment Database - Wastewater treatment (% population connected) (dataset)*, http://stats.oecd.org/index.aspx?DatasetCode=WATER_TREAT. (accessed on 29 January 2021). [57]

OVAM (2018), *Huishoudelijk afval en gelikkaardig bedrijfsafval.*, https://www.ovam.be/inventarisatie-huishoudelijke-afvalstoffen. [36]

Pirc, U. et al. (2016), "Emissions of microplastic fibers from microfiber fleece during domestic washing", *Environ Sci Pollut Res*, Vol. 23, pp. 22206–22211, https://doi.org/10.1007/s11356-016-7703-0. [44]

Pisso, I. et al. (2019), "The Lagrangian particle dispersion model FLEXPART version 10.4", *Geosci. Model Dev.*, Vol. 12, pp. 4955–4997. [100]

Plastic Waste Management Institute (2019), *An Introduction to Plastic Recycling*. [18]

Plastics Europe (2020), "Plastics – the Facts 2020". [23]

Plastics Europe (2017), *Plastics: the Facts (2017) An analysis of European plastics production, demand and waste data*, Plastics Europe. [42]

Plastics Recyclers Europe (2020), *Report on Plastics Recycling Statistics*, http://743c8380-22c6-4457-9895-11872f2a708a.filesusr.com/ugd/dda42a_2544b63cfb5847e39034fadafbac71bf.pdf. [31]

Population Census Commission (2007), *2007 Population and Housing Census of Ethiopia.*, https://microdata.worldbank.org/index.php/catalog/2747/download/39216. [89]

Recoup (2019), *Recyclability by Design*, https://www.bpf.co.uk/design/recyclability-by-design. [29]

ResearchNester (2021), *Artificial Turf: Market Insights, Demand & Growth Forecast 2027.*, https://www.researchnester.com/reports/artificial-turf-market/995. (accessed on 28 January 2021). [52]

Resource Futures (2019), *Composition analysis of litter waste in Wales*. [37]

Rolsky, C. et al. (2020), "Municipal sewage sludge as a source of microplastics in the environment.", *Curr. Opin. Environ. Sci. Heal.*. [63]

Roosen, M. et al. (2020), "Detailed Analysis of the Composition of Selected Plastic Packaging Waste Products and Its Implications for Mechanical and Thermochemical Recycling", *Environmental Science & Technology*, doi: 10.1021/acs.est.0c03371, pp. 13282-13293, http://dx.doi.org/10.1021/acs.est.0c03371. [32]

Ryberg, M. et al. (2019), "Global environmental losses of plastics across their value chains", *Resources, Conservation and Recycling*, Vol. 151, p. 104459, http://dx.doi.org/10.1016/j.resconrec.2019.104459. [7]

Samoa Bureau of statistics (2019), *Samoa's Experimental Solid Waste Accounts FY2013-14 to FY2015-16*, https://www.sbs.gov.ws/digi/Samoa's%20Experimental%20Solid%20Waste%20Arrounts_2013-2014%20to%202015-2016.pdf. [88]

SEMARNAT (2020), *Diagnostico basico para la gestion integral de los residuos*. [16]

Sommer, F. et al. (2018), "Tire Abrasion as a Major Source of Microplastics in the Environment", *Aerosol and Air Quality Research*, Vol. 18/8, pp. 2014-2028, http://dx.doi.org/10.4209/aaqr.2018.03.0099. [46]

Stadler, K. et al. (2018), "EXIOBASE 3: Developing a Time Series of Detailed Environmentally Extended Multi-Regional Input-Output Tables", *Journal of Industrial Ecology*, Vol. 22/3, pp. 502-515, http://dx.doi.org/10.1111/jiec.12715. [10]

Sub Direktorat Statistik Lingkungan Hidup (2014), *Indikator Perilaku Peduli Lingkungan Hidup (2014 Environmental Care Behavior Indicators*, https://www.bps.go.id/publication/2015/12/23/2cdc2ef08c706d6f205c69fc/indikator-perilaku-peduli-lingkungan-hidup-2014.html. [84]

Swedish EPA (2019), *Microplastics in the Environment 2019*, http://www.naturvardsverket.se/Om-Naturvardsverket/Publikationer/ISBN/6900/978-91-620-6957-5/. [50]

SystemIQ and the Pew Charitable Trust (2020), *Breaking the Plastic Wave: A Comprehensive Assessment of Pathways Towards Stopping Ocean Plastic Pollution*, https://www.systemiq.earth/breakingtheplasticwave/. [28]

Thompson, P., P. Willis and N. Morley (2012), *A review of commercial textile fibre recycling technologies*, Waste and Resources Action Programme (WRAP), UK, https://refashion.fr/eco-design/sites/default/files/fichiers/A%20review%20of%20commercial%20textile%20fibre%20recycling%20technologies.pdf. [34]

Tun, M. et al. (2020), "Renewable Waste-to-Energy in Southeast Asia: Status, Challenges, Opportunities, and Selection of Waste-to-Energy Technologies", *Applied Science*, Vol. 10/20, p. 7312, http://dx.doi.org/10.3390/app10207312. [77]

UN Habitat (n.d.), *Cities' Waste Data*, https://unhabitat.org/waste-wise-cities-waste-data (accessed on 20 September 2021). [72]

Unice, K. et al. (2019), "Characterizing export of land-based microplastics to the estuary - Part I: Application of integrated geospatial microplastic transport models to assess tire and road wear particles in the Seine watershed", *Sci. Total Environ.*, Vol. 646, pp. 1639–1649. [104]

UNIDO (2020), *Recycling of plastics in Indian perspective*, UNIDO Office, VIC, Vienna, https://www.unido.org/sites/default/files/files/2018-11/Plenary%202%20-%20Plastics%20-%20Mohanty.pdf. [22]

United Nations (2019), *World urbanization prospects: The 2018 revision.*, https://population.un.org/wup/Publications/Files/WUP2018-Report.pdf. [90]

United Nations Statistics Division (2020), *UN Comtrade*, https://comtrade.un.org (accessed on 21 September 2020). [35]

United States Envrionmental Protection Agency (EPA) (2020), "Advancing Sustainable Materials Management: 2018 Tables and Figures", https://www.epa.gov/sites/default/files/2021-01/documents/2018_tables_and_figures_dec_2020_fnl_508.pdf. [13]

United States Envrionmental Protection Agency (EPA) (2020), *Plastics: Material-Specific Data*, https://www.epa.gov/facts-and-figures-about-materials-waste-and-recycling/plastics-material-specific-data. [14]

UNSD (2021), *UNSD Environmental Indicators: Waste In Environment Statistics*, https://unstats.un.org/unsd/envstats/qindicators.cshtml. [74]

van der Gon, H. et al. (2013), "The policy relevance of wear emissions from road transport, now and in the future--an international workshop report and consensus statement", *Air Waste Manag Assoc.*, Vol. 63/2, pp. 136-49, http://dx.doi.org/10.1080/10962247.2012.741055. [97]

VinylPlus (2019), *PVC Recycling in Action*, https://vinylplus.eu/uploads/images/Leaflets/Recovinyl_21x21_04-05_web.pdf. [33]

Viool, V. et al. (2018), *Study to support impact assessment for options to reduce the level of ALDFG*. [40]

Walker, R. (2019), *The mass of 300 different 'dry' materials*. [102]

Wilson, D. et al. (2012), "Comparative analysis of solid waste management in 20 cities", *Waste Management & Research*, doi: 10.1177/0734242X12437569, pp. 237-254, http://dx.doi.org/10.1177/0734242X12437569. [73]

World Bank (2020), *New World Bank country classifications by income level: 2020-2021.*, https://blogs.worldbank.org/opendata/new-world-bank-country-classifications-income-level-2020-2021 (accessed on 28 January 2021). [41]

Zheng, J. and S. Suh (2019), "Strategies to reduce the global carbon footprint of plastics", *Nature Climate Change*, Vol. 9/5, pp. 374-378, http://dx.doi.org/10.1038/s41558-019-0459-z. [111]

Notes

[1] https://doi.org/10.1787/c0821f81-en.

[2] To simulate lifespan distributions for plastic applications from historical years, an exogenous component of waste generated by earlier produced commodities is added in the first years.

[3] In particular, ECHA (2020[51]) reports that the share of end-of-life tyre-derived granules would represent 78% on the infill, whereas EPDM and TPE would account for 18%, and cork 4%, by 2028. As artificial turf is only made up of the rubber part of tyres (EuRIC MTR 2020), 96% of all infill is assumed to be microplastics.

[4] The nominal emissions of CH_4 and N_2O are converted to CO_2-equivalents using the 100-year GWP from 2nd assessment report (IPCC, 1995[112]).

[5] We would like to thank the authors for providing greenhouse-gas specific emission factors that are not available directly in their paper.

Annex B. Modelling the economic effects of the COVID-19 pandemic and government response measures

1.1. Scenario assumptions

The implications of the pandemic and lockdown measures are determined by comparing a counterfactual pre-Covid baseline scenario, i.e. the pre-Covid projection, with a scenario where the Covid-related shocks are included. The impacts of the COVID-19 pandemic and government response measures are based on the following modelling assumptions; see (Dellink et al., 2021[1]) for more details:

- Increases in regional unemployment levels in 2020 are based on the OECD Economic Outlook 108 (OECD, 2020[2]), the updates on GDP forecasts in the Interim Outlook (OECD, 2021[3]) and the IMF Economic Outlook for the countries that are not covered by the OECD forecasts (IMF, 2020[4]). For the few countries missing in both databases, ad-hoc assumptions are made based on effects in similar countries.
- Sectoral demand shocks are implemented for 2020 following Arriola and Van Tongeren (2021 forthcoming[5]). For energy sectors, the shocks are based on (IEA, 2020[6]). No demand shocks are included for the plastics producing sectors.
- Short-term government stimulus packages as provided in 2020 are implemented as a reduction in capital and labour taxes for firms, and as a reduction in income taxes for households. These are based on Arriola et al. (2021 forthcoming[5]).
- Trade shocks are implemented as an increase in the costs of international trade ("iceberg costs"), with a differentiation between services sectors and agriculture and manufacturing. This mimics the trade shocks in Arriola et al. (2021 forthcoming[5]).
- Reductions in regional labour productivity reflect productivity losses during lockdown and is included crudely as a uniform decline in productivity in all sectors and regions, based on Arriola et al. (2021 forthcoming[5]).
- Finally, regional total factor productivity shocks reflecting the combined effects of all elements not captured explicitly above are added based on the macroeconomic decline in GDP OECD (2020[2]). This approach ensures that the immediate effects of the pandemic on the macro economy are scaled to reach the GDP growth rates for 2020 as forecast by OECD (2020[2]) and by the IMF for the countries that are not covered by the OECD forecasts (IMF, 2020[4]).

1.1. Economic impacts

Increased unemployment, reduced labour productivity, a collapse in demand for certain commodities and higher trade costs all depress economic activity. This is only partially compensated by government support to firms and households. The result is a significant contraction of global GDP in 2020, with the annual global GDP growth rate dropping from around +4% in 2019 to -3.5% in 2020 (OECD, 2021[3]). For 2021 and beyond, the projections for global GDP are more optimistic and foresee a gradual recovery; this will be covered in Volume 2 of the Global Plastics Outlook (OECD, forthcoming[7]).

The pandemic is truly global and affects all economies. Moreover, economic integration means that regional economic effects propagate through all economies. Thus, GDP levels in 2020 were well below those of 2019 in all regions except China (Figure A B.1, left panel). However, in a normal year GDP levels would grow, and thus the deviation between realised GDP in 2020 and the level for 2020 that was projected pre-Covid, i.e. the 2019 GDP levels plus the expected growth rate for 2020, is larger. Thus, even though the Chinese economy recovered rapidly from the first shock to the economy, the GDP growth rate was much lower than anticipated.

All other regions had more substantial losses in GDP, with the largest drop compared to 2019 in the European Union and India (cf. OECD (2021[3])), and relatively large losses compared to the pre-Covid projection on most emerging economies as a year of expected high growth was wiped out. Furthermore, global trade collapsed thereby depressing economic activity in emerging economies that rely heavily on exports as a source of growth.

On balance, in 2020 GDP in the OECD countries was 5% below 2019 levels (7% below the pre-Covid projection), while in non-OECD countries the average reduction from 2019 levels was smaller at 2% (6% below the pre-Covid projection).

The structure of the economy plays a key role in how strong the macroeconomic effects of the pandemic are. Parts of the services sectors were severely hit by the pandemic, especially the accommodation and food services sector (Figure A B.1, right panel). The reductions in demand for fossil fuels were quite large, not least through the effects of the lockdown measures on transport. Electricity demand also declined, especially in production, as firms close down temporarily, but less than fuel use. Construction activities and motor vehicle sales are among the most severely affected.

Figure A B.1. The COVID-19 pandemic and lockdown measures have reduced GDP across the world and reduced output in most sectors

Deviation in 2020 from pre-COVID projection

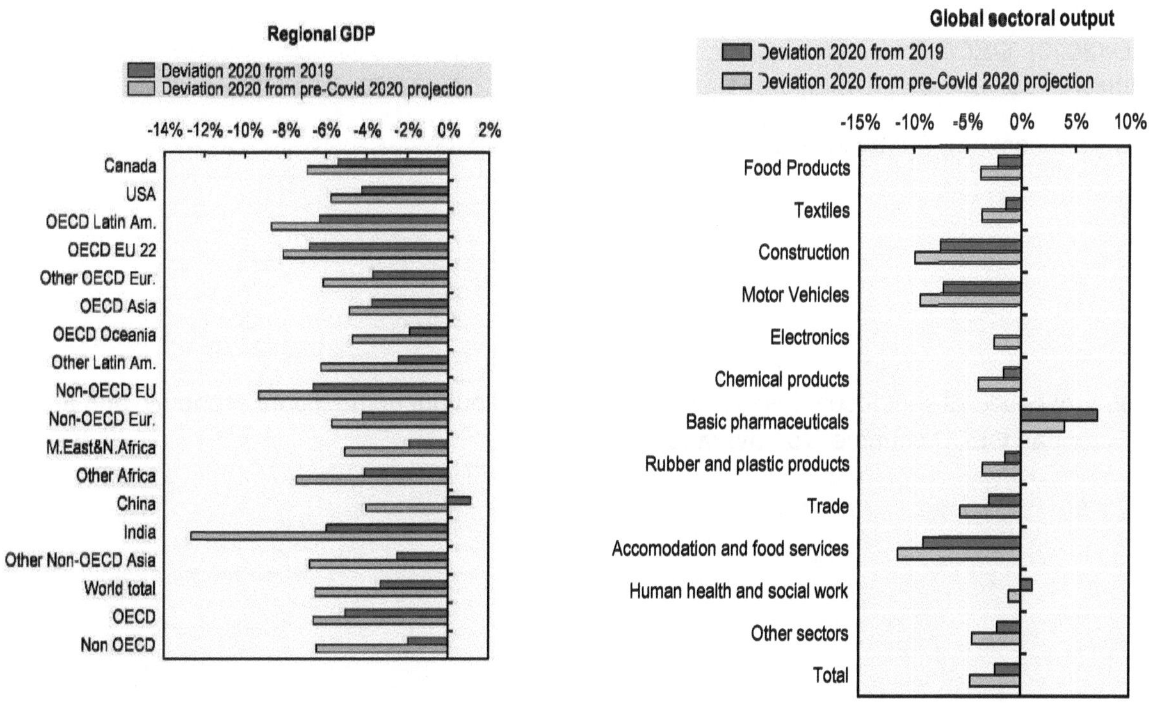

Note: Sector names are associated with the products they produce.
Source: OECD ENV-Linkages model and Dellink et al. (2021[1]).

Other manufacturing sectors are only indirectly affected: while there was – at least in the model simulations – no direct shock to demand for the commodities of these sectors, the slowdown in other sectors, and the reduction in consumption levels dragged these sectors down as well. This includes for instance textiles, electronics and the chemical sector, as well as plastics and rubber production.

The only sector that is estimated to have a short-term increase in output is pharmaceuticals (as well as some subsectors that are aggregated in larger sectors in the modelling, such as e-commerce).[1] When compared to 2019, the health sector also grew somewhat, albeit less than in the pre-Covid projection.

References

Arriola, C., P. Kowalski and F. Van Tongeren (2021 forthcoming), *Assessment of the Covid-19 pandemic: insights from the METRO model*, OECD. [5]

Dellink, R. et al. (2021), "The long-term environmental implications of COVID-19", *OECD Environment Working Papers*, No. 176, OECD Publishing, Paris, http://dx.doi.org/10.1787/123dfd4f-en. [1]

IEA (2020), *World Energy Outlook 2020*, OECD Publishing, Paris, https://dx.doi.org/10.1787/557a761b-en. [6]

IMF (2020), *World Economic Outlook, October 2020: A Long and Difficult Ascent*, International Monetary Fund, Washington, D.C., https://www.imf.org/en/Publications/WEO/Issues/2020/09/30/world-economic-outlook-october-2020 (accessed on 22 January 2021). [4]

OECD (2021), *OECD Economic Outlook, Interim Report March 2021*, OECD Publishing, Paris, https://dx.doi.org/10.1787/34bfd999-en. [3]

OECD (2020), *OECD Economic Outlook, Volume 2020 Issue 2*, OECD Publishing, Paris, https://dx.doi.org/10.1787/39a88ab1-en. [2]

OECD (forthcoming), *Global Plastics Outlook, Volume 2*, OECD. [7]

Notes

[1] The pharmaceuticals sector comprises around 0.7% of total output of the global economy, and above 1% in the European OECD countries (on average).

Glossary

Disclaimer: This glossary presents definitions for key terms employed in the report. Definitions are condensed and may not be complete. They are not to be considered official definitions, rather descriptions of terms as used for the purpose of this report.

Term	Definition used in the Global Plastics Outlook
Biobased plastics	Plastics manufactured from biomass.
Degradation	The partial or complete breakdown of a polymer as a result of e.g. UV radiation, oxygen attack, biological attack. This implies alteration of the properties, such as discolouration, surface cracking, and fragmentation.
Environmentally-relevant plastics technologies	Plastics technologies that are relevant to the environment including technologies for prevention, recycling, conversion or disposal of waste; for leakage removal; and for biobased feedstock.
(Waste) incineration	Incineration in a state-of-the-art industrial facility.
(Sanitary) landfilling	The final disposal of waste in or on land in a controlled way and according to state-of-the-art sanitary, environmental protection and other safety requirements.
(Plastic) leakage	Plastic leakage refers to plastics that enter terrestrial and aquatic environments.
Litter	Waste that results from littering by individuals in the environment and from fly-tipping. Littered waste is distinct from mismanaged waste, because littering behaviour not necessarily correlated to the provision of basic waste collection and disposal infrastructure. Littered waste can either be collected for further disposal or remain uncollected and leak into the environment.
Macroplastics	Recognisable plastic items, such as littered plastic bottles and packaging. In this report, the use of the term encompasses plastics above 5 mm in diameter (i.e. what is often defined as meso and macro plastics elsewhere in the literature).
Microplastics	Solid synthetic polymers smaller than 5 mm in diameter.
Mismanaged waste	Waste that is not captured by any state-of-the-art waste collection or treatment facilities. It includes waste that is burned in open pits, dumped into seas or open waters, or disposed of in unsanitary landfills and dumpsites.
Plastic	Plastic in the singular form is used as an adjective describing a noun. For example, plastic waste.

Plastic pollution	Broadly, all emissions and risks resulting from plastics production, use, waste management and leakage.
Plastics	All plastic polymers studied in the report.
Primary microplastics	Plastics that are smaller than 5 mm in diameter by design, such as cosmetic scrubbing agents and plastic pellets.
Primary or virgin plastics	Plastics manufactured from fossil-based (e.g. crude oil) or biobased (e.g. corn, sugarcane, wheat) feedstock that has never been used or processed before.
Recycling rate	Depending on the context, either the share of waste that is collected for recycling or the share of waste that is available as recycled scrap after reprocessing and after taking into account the disposal of recycling residues.
Secondary (recycled) plastics	Plastic polymers made from recycled material.
Secondary microplastics	Microplastics that are formed from the fragmentation of larger plastics, such as microplastics from tyre abrasion, synthetic microfibres shed from textile products and microplastics stemming from the degradation and fragmentation of macroplastics that have already been lost to the environment.

Printed by Libri Plureos GmbH in Hamburg,
Germany